Deploying Microsoft System Center Configuration Manager

Manage complex and heterogeneous workloads with
ConfigMgr 1706

Jacek Doktor
Pawel Jarosz

BIRMINGHAM - MUMBAI

Deploying Microsoft System Center Configuration Manager

First published: September 2017

Production reference: 1130917

Published by Packt Publishing Ltd.
Livery Place
35 Livery Street
Birmingham
B3 2PB, UK.

ISBN 978-1-78588-101-5

www.packtpub.com

Credits

Authors
Jacek Doktor
Pawel Jarosz

Reviewers
Rafael Delgado
Rafal Kubiciel
Ronni Pedersen

Commissioning Editor
Kartikey Pandey

Acquisition Editor
Heramb Bhavsar

Content Development Editor
Sweeny Dias

Technical Editor
Khushbu Sutar

Copy Editors
Stuti Srivastava
Madhusudan Uchil

Project Coordinator
Virginia Dias

Proofreader
Safis Editing

Indexer
Aishwarya Gangawane

Graphics
Kirk D'Penha

Production Coordinator
Aparna Bhagat

About the Authors

Jacek Doktor is a Microsoft Certified Trainer. From 2008 to 2015, he held the Most Valuable Professional title in Enterprise Client Management granted by Microsoft. Apart from leading training sessions on System Center/Active Directory, he also performs IT system implementations and provides support to clients. His main scope of operation is Configuration Manager and all related technologies. He works for large Polish companies, and participates in projects led by Microsoft Poland. Apart from System Center, Jacek has enormous experience in Windows 10 deployment, migrations to Windows 10, and ConfigMgr report data usage.

Pawel Jarosz is an IT engineer with experience in various IT fields and platforms, including Microsoft Exchange and ConfigMgr. He is a Microsoft Exchange expert with experience in designing and maintaining hybrid infrastructures. Pawel is a cofounder of the Polish PowerShell User Group, and is passionate about automation, building monitoring solutions, and system integration. He runs the paweljarosz blog on Wordpress, where with a good dose of humor he shares his daily IT experiences.
Pawel believes that the most stunning projects comes not from the brain, but directly from the heart.

www.PacktPub.com

For support files and downloads related to your book, please visit www.PacktPub.com. Did you know that Packt offers eBook versions of every book published, with PDF and ePub files available? You can upgrade to the eBook version at www.PacktPub.com, and as a print book customer, you are entitled to a discount on the eBook copy. Get in touch with us at service@packtpub.com for more details.

At www.PacktPub.com, you can also read a collection of free technical articles, sign up for a range of free newsletters and receive exclusive discounts and offers on Packt books and eBooks.

https://www.packtpub.com/mapt

Get the most in-demand software skills with Mapt. Mapt gives you full access to all Packt books and video courses, as well as industry-leading tools to help you plan your personal development and advance your career.

Why subscribe?

- Fully searchable across every book published by Packt
- Copy and paste, print, and bookmark content
- On demand and accessible via a web browser

Customer Feedback

Thanks for purchasing this Packt book. At Packt, quality is at the heart of our editorial process. To help us improve, please leave us an honest review on this book's Amazon page at https://www.amazon.com/dp/1785881019.

If you'd like to join our team of regular reviewers, you can email us at customerreviews@packtpub.com. We award our regular reviewers with free eBooks and videos in exchange for their valuable feedback. Help us be relentless in improving our products!

Table of Contents

Preface

This book might differ from other publications related to System Center Configuration Manager. It is not strictly for administrators and operators as we do not go very deep into the details of the configuration and administration of individual system components. In this book we put the emphasis on understanding what circumstances ConfigMgr can be used in, what kinds of function it may play in the environment, and what goals can be achieved. ConfigMgr is not only a system used to deploy operating systems, updates, and other software, but it is also a system of much wider scope and usage--and this is what we intended to cover.

What this book covers

Chapter 1, *Design Planning*, covers basic topics regarding designing and deploying a single ConfigMgr server as well as environments with more than one server. You'll learn what important factors should be taken into consideration while deploying a ConfigMgr server and its roles.

Chapter 2, *Installing Configuration Manager*, presents the process of preparing the environment for a ConfigMgr server as well as the installation itself.

Chapter 3, *Configure Sites and Boundaries*, covers topics related to boundaries and boundary groups as well as the configuration of roles typically used in deployments.

Chapter 4, *Configuration Manager Agent Installation*, presents the ConfigMgr client installation process, available installation methods, and information about checkouts if installation goes successfully.

Chapter 5, *Creating Client Settings for Servers and Workstations*, covers creating your own custom settings for ConfigMgr clients.

Chapter 6, *Compliance Settings*, discusses how ConfigMgr can be used to verify computers' compliance with company standards.

Chapter 7, *Software Distributions*, covers topics related to software deployment.

Chapter 8, *Software Update Management*, presents the process of scanning, the installation of updates, and the management of this process.

Chapter 9, *Endpoint Protection*, contains topics related to the deployment and management of Endpoint Protection in order to better secure the environment against malware.

Chapter 10, *Operating System Deployment*, covers basic concepts for operating system deployment.

Chapter 11, *Configuration Manager Assets*, presents the process of collecting data from clients, and many possible ways of using this data.

Chapter 12, *Role-Based Administration and Security*, discusses the configuration of access to the ConfigMgr console.

Chapter 13, *Site Server Maintenance Tasks*, covers the topic of protecting the ConfigMgr server against failure and administrative tasks related to daily monitoring.

What you need for this book

In order to practice the scenarios from this book, you need the following software:

Operating system:

- Windows Server 2012 R2
- Windows Server 2016

Software:

- SQL Server 2016 Standard edition
- System Center Configuration Manager 2701
- Windows ADK 10 1607 version
- Active Directory

Who this book is for

If you are a systems engineer and administrator planning to deploy Microsoft System Center 2016 Configuration Manager, then this book is for you. This book will also benefit system administrators who are responsible for designing and deploying one or more System Center 2016 Configuration Manager sites in their new or existing systems. It is also a book for those who would like to know about the ConfigMgr possibilities and what benefits it can bring to the organization.

Conventions

In this book, you will find a number of text styles that distinguish between different kinds of information. Here are some examples of these styles and an explanation of their meaning. Code words in text, database table names, folder names, filenames, file extensions, pathnames, dummy URLs, user input, and Twitter handles are shown as follows: "New items can be created under `Asset and Compliance\Compliance Settings\Configuration Items` on the ConfigMgr console."

New terms and **important words** are shown in bold. Words that you see on the screen, for example, in menus or dialog boxes, appear in the text like this: "The **Remediate noncompliant rules when supported** and **Allow remediation outside the maintenance window** options enable the repair of configuration drift by the server."

Warnings or important notes appear like this.

Tips and tricks appear like this.

Reader feedback

Feedback from our readers is always welcome. Let us know what you think about this book-what you liked or disliked. Reader feedback is important for us as it helps us develop titles that you will really get the most out of. To send us general feedback, simply email `feedback@packtpub.com`, and mention the book's title in the subject of your message. If there is a topic that you have expertise in and you are interested in either writing or contributing to a book, see our author guide at `www.packtpub.com/authors`.

Customer support

Now that you are the proud owner of a Packt book, we have a number of things to help you to get the most from your purchase.

Downloading the color images of this book

We also provide you with a PDF file that has color images of the screenshots/diagrams used in this book. The color images will help you better understand the changes in the output. You can download this file from `https://www.packtpub.com/sites/default/files/downloads/DeployingMicrosoftSystemCenterConfigurationManager_ColorImages.pdf`.

Errata

Although we have taken every care to ensure the accuracy of our content, mistakes do happen. If you find a mistake in one of our books-maybe a mistake in the text or the code-we would be grateful if you could report this to us. By doing so, you can save other readers from frustration and help us improve subsequent versions of this book. If you find any errata, please report them by visiting `http://www.packtpub.com/submit-errata`, selecting your book, clicking on the **Errata Submission Form** link, and entering the details of your errata. Once your errata are verified, your submission will be accepted and the errata will be uploaded to our website or added to any list of existing errata under the Errata section of that title. To view the previously submitted errata, go to `https://www.packtpub.com/books/content/support` and enter the name of the book in the search field. The required information will appear under the **Errata** section.

Piracy

Piracy of copyrighted material on the internet is an ongoing problem across all media. At Packt, we take the protection of our copyright and licenses very seriously. If you come across any illegal copies of our works in any form on the internet, please provide us with the location address or website name immediately so that we can pursue a remedy. Please contact us at `copyright@packtpub.com` with a link to the suspected pirated material. We appreciate your help in protecting our authors and our ability to bring you valuable content.

Questions

If you have a problem with any aspect of this book, you can contact us at `questions@packtpub.com`, and we will do our best to address the problem.

1
Design Planning

Delivering services for an enterprise data center is a focal point of all System Center family applications. The main idea is to ease maintaining the systems in each stage of the life cycle.

To gain as much as possible from each solution, it is crucial to understand that there is no such thing as one supported or preferred configuration. Having a solution properly planned and well tailored to your needs will bring much more value than a generic installation without proper planning and designing, which may later bounce with an infrastructure hiccup.

This is the same as with a house, where a foundation is the most crucial part. When badly planned or, for instance, if a construction project doesn't have enough details and, as a result the house is not diligently enough isolated, the repercussions might be really serious. Sometimes, you even need to cut the house from the foundations in order to repair what has been done wrong during the construction phase.

This chapter covers the fundamental topics related to architecture design on ConfigMgr:

- Why a well-prepared design is the most important part of each deployment
- What the features of the ConfigMgr server are
- Conditions and requirements when planning an upgrade to ConfigMgr 1706
- ConfigMgr hierarchy types
- Conditions that determine which hierarchy should be applied
- Security for the ConfigMgr server
- MS SQL Server roles in ConfigMgr deployments
- What the functions of distribution and management points in ConfigMgr deployments are

System Center Configuration Manager

The history of managing operating systems reaches way back to 1994, when Microsoft released Systems Management Server 1.1 version. Since that time, Microsoft has systematically developed this tool until now. After the first one--SMS 1.1 version, other system versions that showed up were SMS 2.0, SMS 2003, ConfigMgr 2007, and ConfigMgr 2012. Additionally, three service packs were prepared (R2 and the one and only in Microsoft history: R3) and an endless number of cumulative updates and patches.

In the last 20 years, ConfigMgr has changed a lot, and it has been subject to a real upturn. Earlier, it used to be called a **slow message system** because of many limitations, which caused it to be slow and problematic.

Starting from ConfigMgr 2012, the server became really stable and efficient and there were no huge problems as with the legacy versions. A lot of changes were implemented, including the following:

- Console build using .NET: previously it was based on Microsoft Management Console 3.0. The console works faster and more firmly and provides much more data than the previous ones.
- Functional enhancements for many components such as the data synchronization of software update data between the servers.
- Saving data in the SQL database for each type of ConfigMgr server. This has radically improved efficiency and the speed of synchronization between the servers.
- Introducing the application mode to natively support .msi files.
- An endless number of updates for old features and introducing a large scope of new features.
- The possibility to install ConfigMgr clients on macOS, Linux/Unix.
- The possibility of managing mobile systems with Windows, iOS, and Android.
- The ability to install applications on non-Windows systems.

ConfigMgr 2012 R2 and R3 were the next system versions where already existing features underwent development and changes. One of the changes that did not have an impact on functionality was the naming convention change. All versions beyond ConfigMgr 2012 R3 were named after the year and month of the release date. The first version that had this naming convention was ConfigMgr 1511, which signifies that it was released in November 2015.

ConfigMgr 1511, when compared to ConfigMgr 2012 R2, had many important changes.

The most significant changes were as follows:

- Windows 10 servicing
- Side loading app for Windows 10
- Compliance settings for Windows 10
- Preferred management point
- Primary site support up to 150k clients
- Support for SQL Server Always On
- Native support for deploying updates for Office 365
- Task sequences in-place upgrade for Windows 10
- Multiple automatic deployment rules
- Deploy Windows Update for Business

The current, and newest, version is *1706*.

ConfigMgr brings the following significant changes:

- Changes in managing updates
- Improved clean up for old updates
- Introducing Data Warehouse service point role
- OMS connector
- The ability to assign software update points to boundary groups
- New compliance settings for iOS
- Hardware inventory collects UEFI information
- Converting BIOS to UEFI during in-place upgrade
- Deploying Office 365 apps to clients
- Managing express installation files for Windows 10 media
- Support for Android for work

Note that it is always best and safest to use *current branch* versions instead of the technical preview ones. Using the current branch version ensures you get proper support from the vendor as well as from the community--so you can actually get some support not only from your paid MS subscription, but also from other engineers on the forums (and available MSFT engineers who are often on these forums as well) on the internet.

When planning an upgrade

If you plan to upgrade servers ConfigMgr 1607 to 1706, first ensure that all of the site servers the across the hierarchy run the same version of ConfigMgr. The versions supported for upgrade to 1706 are 1602, 1606, and 1610.

Along with 1706 ConfigMgr, version support for a few systems got deprecated:

- SQL Server 2008 R2 for site database servers
- Windows Server 2008 R2 for site system servers and most site system roles
- Windows Server 2008 for site system servers and most site system roles
- Windows XP Embedded as a client operating system

ConfigMgr installer automatically installs .NET 4.5.2 on each machine if it is not installed already:

- Enrollment proxy point
- Enrollment point
- Management point
- Service connection point

 Remember that, after installing .NET 4.5.2 and before the reboot, the server might experience some failures.

Apart from the prerequisites related to the operating system and .NET 4.5.2, other important points are as follows:

- Remember to install all critical and security updates on the machines
- Remember to review the status of your **Software Assurance (SA)** agreement because, if you plan to upgrade to/install ConfigMgr 1706, this needs to be active
- If you plan to deploy workstations, remember to ensure that Windows **Assessment and Deployment Kit (ADK)** for Windows 10 is at least at version 1703
- Check your hierarchy for any ongoing issues and fix them before upgrading to 1706
- Ensure that replication between sites works without issues; to check it, you might use Replication Link Analyzer

When planning an upgrade for a hierarchy containing the central administration site and the primary site, the process needs to be initiated from the top, which means the central administration needs to be upgraded first. Next up are primary sites, and last but not least, are secondary sites.

ConfigMgr hierarchy planning

As mentioned earlier, spending some time on planning and analyzing your business may significantly help you in building a solution that will meet the requirements without being an overkill. It is always good to include some growth in your design plans, but there is a significant difference between planned overhead and overkill in achieving the goal.

With ConfigMgr 2007 still in your environment, the administrator would need to go through an upgrade process to migrate to the 1706 version. For 2012, there is an in-place upgrade possibility. Note that upgrade process topics won't be covered in this book.

When it comes to hierarchy planning, ConfigMgr gives a few possible options. Since ConfigMgr 1511, Microsoft has supported running ConfigMgr on the cloud.

When considering your design, be aware that as of now, there is no support for using VM in Azure as a distribution point for WDS deployments using PXE. In such cases, use the on-premise distribution point.

SMS 2003 servers and ConfigMgr 2007 were supporting hierarchies made of many levels. It was causing a lot more issues related to data synchronization between servers. In ConfigMgr 2012, Microsoft introduced some significant changes. Hierarchy might consist of only three levels, and data synchronization is made directly between SQL Servers, which is a significant factor in improving the functioning of the entire system.

Possible on-premise scenarios

When designing a ConfigMgr deployment, we may choose between a few server types, and we also have the ability to combine these few servers together.

An important thing to keep in mind is that there is, in fact, the possibility of changing the environment after the deployment. The administrator might start with one server, and have a few of them at the end, or the other way--the number of servers might go down.

ConfigMgr is a scalable solution, so it can be changed and might grow together with the organization.

 There is, however, one thing that cannot be changed--if we wish to have two primary site servers, we need to have a central administration site to connect them in one solid structure.

Primary site

Primary site is a fundamental ConfigMgr server type that manages the clients. We start each deployment by installing this server. As you can see, the smallest possible implementation is a single standalone server. This solution is often chosen, not only by small and average sized companies, but also by big firms with a dozen or so branches.

Even when you don't have the best connection between offices, you may use a distribution point that will be a local repository for clients; the idea of distribution points will be described later in this chapter.

In this scenario, all clients report to one single ConfigMgr server. So, simplified administrations here are an undisputed benefit for both administrators and workstations that have one point to report to. Having only one server eliminates the need to replicate the database.

When installing the standalone/primary site server, the complete version of the SQL database server is required. Being a primary site server, the machine participates in database replication:

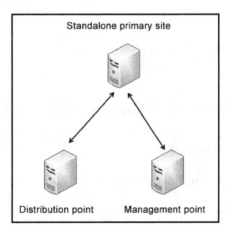

Hierarchy with one sever primary site

Primary site with secondary site

This scenario goes a step further. With a secondary site, we tell the clients in satellite offices/branches to report to the secondary site instead of the primary one. The reason we want a secondary site is that our primary site has very bad **wide area network** (**WAN**) connections with branches; additionally, during the day, we prefer not to fill this link with ConfigMgr traffic.

Imagine a situation where we have New York, which is our primary site, and Philadelphia, where we have an office with approximately 5,000 computers, and we have a really slow WAN link between these two offices (which may be considered any link slower than 10 MB) in addition to some latency issues. Having computers reported to New York might be a real bottleneck, not just for workstation to ConfigMgr communications, but it will surely impact applications that try to send data over this WAN link, so it may have serious repercussions for your business. Secondary sites come into play when one of the following factors is important:

- Traffic compression between sites
- Scheduling time for data exchange between the primary and secondary site

Usually, you won't need a secondary site; as I mentioned, even in global enterprise deployments, people often choose to have one primary site with distribution points in satellite offices:

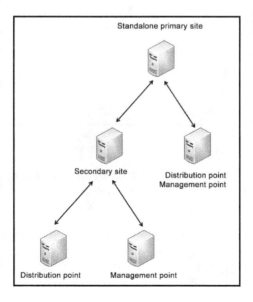

Hierarchy with one primary site and secondary site

Central administration site with primary sites and secondary sites

This is the most complex scenario we can get. A **central administration site** may coexist with one or more primary sites--it is the top-level site in the hierarchy. You may consider using central administration if you have two or more very big sites (where the sum of Windows clients, for instance, might be bigger than 150,000), or you would like to separate clients from each site from each other--the legal factor might come into play in this case:

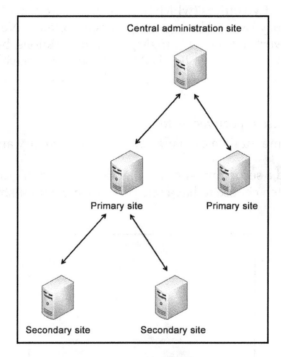

Most complex structure of ConfigMgr

A **central administration site** does not play any role in managing the clients in terms of actually having some clients assigned to it. You are not able to assign any clients here. It does not process any client data; it just saves data about the whole hierarchy.

 Server central administrations might be added to the primary site at any time. There is no need to install the central administration site as the first server in the hierarchy.

With the central administration site and two primary servers connected to it, it is possible--in the case of failure of one of them--to switch endpoints to report to the working one. This feature is the easiest form of high availability provided for endpoints. However, this switch does not happen automatically, and it needs to be triggered from the server console.

> There is always a possibility to add or remove servers from the hierarchy and switch endpoints to report to the other server.

Important servers roles

The most important roles, which need to be considered when designing the environment, are management point and distribution point.

If these roles are properly designed and deployed, the environment will work swiftly, firmly, and in accordance with expectations.

Management point server role

Management point is the most important server role that needs to be deployed in the ConfigMgr environment as it provides communication between the ConfigMgr server and the clients. If the mentioned role is not functioning correctly, clients will be unable to communicate with the server, which results in an immediate break in managing the environment. It makes communication on both sides impossible and clients won't be able to send any data to the ConfigMgr server.

> We might connect more than one management point to each ConfigMgr server. This situation might be desired when one single ConfigMgr server is servicing many clients or when endpoints are located in various geolocations and the administrator wants to provide good communication between the ConfigMgr server and the clients.

Clients choose the management point they will connect to, based on the boundary group, which will be described in more detail in Chapter 3, *Configure Sites and Boundaries*. Incorrectly designed infrastructure, resulting in a badly chosen management point by clients, might cause many unpredictable effects; for instance, clients won't perform installations, won't send data to the ConfigMgr server, or will connect and communicate with the wrong management point.

In versions prior to 2012, it was not possible to tell the workstations which management point should be used. Secondary servers were used as a workaround, as it was possible to assign a workstation to a particular secondary server. Starting from the 2012 version, there has been the option of setting the management point as the preferred one from a certain site.

For better and more efficient usage of the network between the central office and company branches, it is possible to place the primary site server or simply a management point in these branches. In this scenario, all data targeting clients will be sent only once--from the primary site server to the management point from which clients will download the data using the local network.

This happens on the other side as well. When clients are making a hardware inventory, they send all pieces of data to the management point server; it aggregates the data and sends it at once to the ConfigMgr server. In this way, the administrator is able to significantly lower the amount of information sent over the network in the ConfigMgr environment.

Distribution point server role

Let's imagine a situation where we have a standalone server that is used as a distribution point for the main office in New York. We would like to install a few applications on 100 computers in Philadelphia, 200 computers in Washington, and 50 in Pittsburgh. All these workstations will download content from the New York server. To prevent such situations, we should use a distribution point that will act as a local application repository for clients.

With distribution points, we may push binaries to the local servers at the most convenient time of the day/or night--simply the quietest time from the network perspective. Having said that, we may now go to our workstation configuration and tell them to download binaries from the local distribution point server.

 Starting from ConfigMgr 2012, each and every distribution point associated with ConfigMgr might have different settings for data, sending configuration such as the days and hours in which ConfigMgr is allowed to distribute the content to the distribution point.

The ability to configure separate settings for each distribution point is a major ease when configuring the ConfigMgr environment. In this way, the administrator can fully control the time, the way, as well as from where data is being sent between ConfigMgr servers and clients.

If you're combining the aforementioned separated roles with a properly designed structure management point role, the administrator will have a clean view of which clients send data to which distribution points and management points. Each distribution point supports connections from up to 4,000 clients and a combined total of up to 10,000 packages and applications.

MS SQL Server role in ConfigMgr environment

There have been a lot of changes in SQL Server use cases since ConfigMgr 2007. In all versions prior to 2012, SQL Server was only used for primary site needs. Since version 2012, all server types--central administration site, primary site, and secondary site, use SQL Server to store data.

For **central administration site** and **primary site**, we may use MS SQL Standard or Enterprise Edition. Secondary sites support MS SQL in Standard or Express versions:

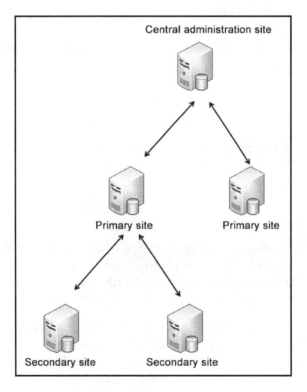

The configuration of SQL Servers for ConfigMgr servers

When installing the **secondary site** server, SQL Express installation is conducted automatically by the ConfigMgr server. If we are more likely to use SQL Standard, we need to install SQL Server before starting the installation of the **secondary site** server.

 Because SQL Server is being used by all ConfigMgr server types, to ease work, it is recommended that you use GPO to open appropriate ports on the Windows firewall, allowing communication between SQL and ConfigMgr servers.

Sizing and scaling of ConfigMgr

ConfigMgr can be scaled to a size that will accommodate any type and size of organization. Keep in mind that we often split ConfigMgr installations and create additional sites/sub-sites, not because we are reaching limits in ConfigMgr, but to:

- Ease administration/maintenance
- Separate administrator access
- Physically separate the data (for example, to meet regulations)
- Put boundary lines between some instances

Site types

There are three types of ConfigMgr servers, and each has already been mentioned in the context of designing the hierarchy. Each of the following presented server types has a different role and way to be configured.

Central administration site

A central administration site is used to manage the whole hierarchy. All connected primary site servers synchronize with it, so all information about what is going on in the environment is available in one place. A central administration site supports up to 25 child primary sites.

A central administration site does not support clients directly, neither does it process client data. All this work is done by primary and secondary site servers that send the data to the central administration site. Because the CAS role does not support communication with clients, it is not possible to install management point or distribution point roles on the server. Additionally, some of the server roles are supposed to be installed only on a CAS server, such as a *service connection point*.

Primary site

A primary site server is a fundamental server type deployed in the ConfigMgr environment. The main difference between this server and central administration is that it directly supports the clients as well as shares and receives data from them. This is a reason why this server type supports installing server roles such as management point and distribution point. It requires MS SQL and being connected to a central administration site; it replicates its own data and data received from the associated secondary site.

Each primary site can support up to:

- 250 secondary sites
- 15 management point
- 250 distribution points

The number of secondary sites per primary site is based on continuously connected and reliable WAN connections. For locations that have fewer than 500 clients, consider a distribution point instead of a secondary site.

Secondary site

A secondary site server should always be considered an optional one. In many cases, one primary site server is able to successfully serve the whole company. However, once a company has many branches, low-quality network links and lots of systems to manage, the secondary site server is what the administrator should consider.

Secondary sites don't support child sites. This is the last level in the ConfigMgr hierarchy.

Each secondary site supports a single management point that must be installed on the secondary site server. However, despite installing a management point, assigning clients to it will not be possible. Clients always need to be assigned to the superior server, in this case, the primary site.

Supported number of clients

When talking about supported clients, we can outline three different types:

- **Client type 1**: Windows Server, Windows Clients, and Windows Embedded, Linux, and Unix
- **Client type 2**: Devices managed by Windows Intune and those enabled for Exchange Server connector
- **Client type 3**: Devices enrolled by ConfigMgr and devices supported by the mobile device legacy client, macOS clients
- **Central administration site**:
    - Up to 700,000 type 1 clients
    - Up to 25,000 type 3 clients
    - Up to 100,000 devices that you manage using on-premises MDM or up to 300,000 cloud-based devices
- **Standalone primary site**: The overall number of devices managed by standalone primary site is 175,000, where subdivisions are:
    - Up to 150,000 type 1 clients
    - Up to 50,000 type 2 clients
    - Up to 25,000 type 3 clients
    - 50,000 devices that you manage using on-premises MDM or up to 150,000 cloud-based devices
- **Secondary site**: Up to 15,000 type 1 clients
- **Management point**: The overall number of devices managed by the management point is 25,000, where subdivisions are:
    - 25,000 type 1 clients
    - Up to 10,000 devices that are managed using on-premises MDM or up to 10,000 type 3 clients

ConfigMgr in Azure

As you may already know, Azure is a public cloud computing platform created by Microsoft. There are three main categories of computers that Microsoft Azure offers, and they are as follows:

- **Infrastructure as a service (IaaS)**
- **Platform as a service (PaaS)**
- **Software as a service (SaaS)**

ConfigMgr in an IaaS model is simply a VM with the ConfigMgr application installed on it.

As for the PaaS model, there is no real scenario for ConfigMgr; however, the SaaS approach has its *use case* for ConfigMgr in the form of cloud-based distribution points.

ConfigMgr as a VM in Azure

As mentioned earlier, starting from the 1511 version, ConfigMgr supports deployment in Azure. Leveraging this option, we get three options:

- ConfigMgr might be placed in Azure and manage cloud-based VMs
- ConfigMgr might be placed in Azure but manage on-premise VMs
- ConfigMgr might be placed in Azure only to some extent, which means only certain roles, such as distribution point, are deployed on the cloud

When it comes to the prerequisites, scaling, and sizing--the same applies to the cloud as the on-premise deployments.

To start using Azure to deploy ConfigMgr VMs, you need a subscription that is charged based on the number of virtual machines and Azure resource usage.

Cloud-based distribution points

A cloud-based distribution point is a slightly different approach. It is not a VM but a service in Azure, which is automatically scaling for the needs. It supports your internal and external (internet) clients. Similar to the preceding solutions, you need an Azure subscription.

Planning for high availability with ConfigMgr

As ConfigMgr does not provide data in real time, short intermittent down times should not usually be considered a problem.

 ConfigMgr does not support any high availability (HA) cluster solution for the application node other than switching clients to a different ConfigMgr server. However, you might use SQL clustering or a feature that started to be supported with ConfigMgr 1602 by Microsoft--Always On availability groups for SQL--to implement HA on the database level.

Always On availability groups continuously synchronize transactions from the primary replica to each of the secondary replicas. This replication can be configured as synchronous or asynchronous to support local high availability or remote disaster recovery.

The preceding mechanism cannot be used for secondary site databases, and secondary site databases cannot be restored from the backup--this applies only to the central administration site and the primary site. The only way to recover the secondary site is to recreate it from its parent--the primary site.

Maintaining the central administration site and more than one primary site allows the redirecting of clients to the other server while the first one is inaccessible. The same is the case with management points and distribution points.

By configuring the sites to publish the data about the site servers, and services in Active Directory and DNS, it becomes available for clients to identify when new site system servers that can provide important services, such as management points, are available.

Reporting

Reporting is an important design factor when you plan to run long time period reports across hundreds of nodes. However, running such a report might be a big overhead for the machine processing the report.

The MS SQL database might be installed on the same server or on a separate machine. The separation of SQL and the ConfigMgr server might significantly improve the efficiency of both systems. It is also possible to move *SQL Server Reporting Services* to another SQL on a different machine. This might additionally improve the efficiency of the SQL Server and SQL Server Reporting Services.

Additionally, ConfigMgr in version 1706 introduced the possibility of using the Data Warehouse service point, which holds all long-term historical data of ConfigMgr deployment. Data is synchronized with the ConfigMgr site database and can hold up to 2 TB of data.

Data Warehouse can be installed only on the top of the hierarchy, so it can be installed on the central administration or the primary site. Keep in mind that, if you wish to expand the standalone primary site, you need to remove the Data Warehouse service point role from that site. After CA is installed, you can install the role on the newly created top site.

Summary

The idea of this chapter was to give you a view of what the important factors are when planning the deployment of ConfigMgr 1706. We went through a few topics such as the following:

- Software prerequisites when planning an upgrade
- Description of available site roles and to what extent we can scale them
- Important factors when planning a hierarchy
- Possible hybrid scenarios with Azure
- What the possibilities are for HA when planning the infrastructure
- New features available for reporting

This chapter gave you a good overview of the available deployment scenarios, so you can go ahead and install ConfigMgr in your environment.

As we've reached the end of this chapter, let's now go straight to the chapter where you install your own instance of ConfigMgr 1706.

The following factors should always be considered when designing an environment:

- The number of endpoints managed by the environment
- The number of locations where these endpoints reside
- Features the environment should support
- Administrative factors, for instance, separating the management of servers and workstations
- Political factors; for instance, each country has separate ConfigMgr server
- Organizational factors; for instance, each AD domains should be managed by separate hierarchy
- Network latency and quality; the poorer the network conditions, the more servers we need in the environment
- Installing MS SQL Server on a separate machine to provide optimal efficiency for the ConfigMgr database

ConfigMgr is a very complex product; consequently, this book focuses mainly on fundamental configuration. It does not contain information about cooperation with systems other than Windows.

2
Installing Configuration Manager

Well-thought hierarchy and properly planned configuration of the server is the foundation of success while deploying ConfigMgr server.

This chapter covers the following topics:

- The process of installing all prerequisites and configuring the environment before installing the ConfigMgr server
- Preparation for the ConfigMgr server installation
- The ConfigMgr installation process in the primary site type

Configuration Manager installation process

This chapter covers topics related to the installation of ConfigMgr in the primary site type. Firstly, it will take you through all the prerequisites that the environment must fulfill for the installation to be successful, and then it will introduce the process of server installation.

The requirements that need to be met are not especially hard to achieve either.

Here are the core steps when installing ConfigMgr:

1. The installation of an operating system.
2. Configuration and updating the operating system.
3. Granting permissions for the creation of the System Management container.
4. Granting permissions for the computer account to save configuration in the Active Directory database.

5. The installation of the Web Server (IIS) role and additional components.
6. The installation of Windows Assessment and Deployment Kit.
7. The installation of the ConfigMgr 1706 server.

Basic knowledge about the installation of Windows Server 2016 or 2012 is desired for the ConfigMgr 1706 installation. Knowledge about creating, configuring, and granting permissions in Active Directory will be also needed.

The environment in this book has been based on Windows Server 2016. However, it doesn't matter if we talk about preinstallation steps, as preparing Windows Server 2016 and Windows Server 2012 are almost alike in order to install ConfigMgr 1706. The only significant differences are in the details; for instance, for Windows Server 2016, .NET 4.5 is installed, whereas on Windows Server 2012, the installed version of .NET is 3.5.

System Center Configuration Manager 1706 requirements

As mentioned earlier, before we attempt to install the ConfigMgr server, certain requirements need to be fulfilled.

The prerequisites for server systems are as follows:

- ConfigMgr cannot and must not be installed on Windows Server 2008 or Windows Server 2008 R2
- ConfigMgr cannot be installed on Windows Server Core
- ConfigMgr cannot be installed on Windows Server 2012 Foundation or Windows Server 2012 R2 Foundation
- Server ConfigMgr 1706 can cooperate with MS SQL Server 2014 or higher
- Server ConfigMgr 1706 cannot be installed on Windows failover cluster
- Only the ConfigMgr database can be installed with high availability using SQL cluster or Always On availability

Prerequisites for a server handling the ConfigMgr server role are as follows:

- Windows Assessment and Deployment Kit in version 1703
- IIS server role
- MS SQL

If we plan to install MS SQL Server and MS **SQL Server Reporting Services** (**SSRS**) on one machine, it is worth checking that option to be installed during MS SQL installation so it will be installed and configured. If you plan to separate a database from SSRS, we need to install (as well as configure) it separately.

Before the installation, we need to make choices for the following settings:

- **Site code**: Three character strings identifying our installed server
- **Site name**: Name of the location identifying our installed server

 It is impossible to change the site code or name after the server has been installed. The only way to change it is to uninstall and install the server again from scratch.

Before starting the installation, we need to prepare AD user accounts and groups that will be used for installation:

- Prepare an administrative Active Directory installation account or accounts for MS SQL Server. All of the accounts should have administrative permissions on a machine where MS SQL will be installed.
- Prepare an administrative Active Directory installation account for ConfigMgr with administrative permissions on a machine where the ConfigMgr server will be installed.

Apart from the preceding permissions, the mentioned accounts are regular Active Directory domain user accounts.

Prerequisites for System Center Configuration Manager 1706

Before installing the server, we need to prepare the environment. To prepare the environment, we need to install all the required prerequisites on the server, as well as configure the environment (such as Active Directory).

The configuration of the environment consists of the following steps:

- Extending the Active Directory schema.
- Granting the computer account permission to the `System` container in Active Directory. These permissions are needed for ConfigMgr to create the `System Management` container as well as save any future configuration.

> Extending the Active Directory schema and integration with Active Directory are not required either for installing ConfigMgr or for its proper work. However, extending the schema eases daily administration of the system, so it is always good to consider whether or not to perform such an operation.

Installing software prerequisites consists of the following:

- **Windows Assessment and Deployment Kit**: An essential tool set for ConfigMgr installation. After the server is installed, these tools are used to manage administrative tasks related to OS deployment.
- **The IIS server role and its components**: This role is responsible for servicing communication between clients and the ConfigMgr server. Configuration of IIS components is done during the IIS role installation, so there is no need to install it manually.
- **MS SQL 2014 or higher**: SQL Server will be handling the ConfigMgr database.

> The order of the mentioned tasks is not important.

Environmental components

The environment described in the book consists of the following components:

- Domain name: `doctor.com`
- AD controller: `DC01`
- ConfigMgr 1706 with MS SQL 2016 Standard: `CM16.doctor.com`

- Domain functional level: Windows Server 2016
- Location code: `PA1`
- Name of the primary site server: `CM16.doctor.com`
- Management point: `CM16.doctor.com`
- Distribution point: `CM16.doctor.com`
- Operating system: Windows Server 2016

Granting permissions to the System container

The ConfigMgr server, after extending the Active Directory schema, is able to save core configuration data in the Active Directory database inside the `System Management` container. Thanks to these pieces of information, clients are able to find the assigned ConfigMgr server and establish connection with it. Any changes made to the management point role are also saved and stored in the Active Directory database.

There are two ways of the `System Management` container creation:

- The container can be created manually and grant permissions to the ConfigMgr computer account
- ConfigMgr creates it by itself thanks to the granted permissions

> The presence of this container is not obligatory to go through the ConfigMgr installation process. The container, as well as permissions, might be created later after the server is installed.

To manually create the `System Management` container using the **Active Directory Users and Computers** console, follow these steps:

1. Run the console, highlight the `System` container, right-click on it, and choose **Properties**:

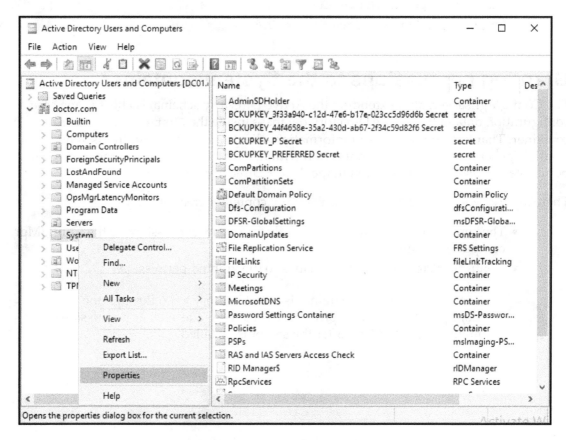

System container in Active Directory Users and Computers console

2. On the **Security** tab, click on **Add...** to add a computer account for the ConfigMgr server:

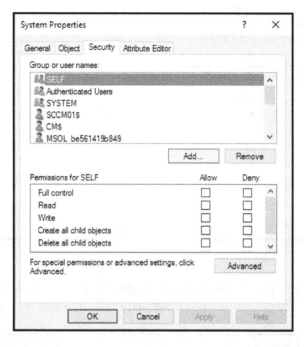

Properties of System container

3. By default, the system does not show computer accounts when adding permissions. To see them, we need to check **Computers** in the **Object Types...** section and click on **OK**:

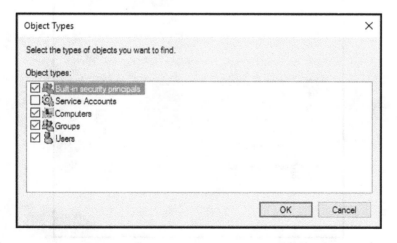

Adding computer accounts to searchable objects in Active Directory

4. We fill in the computer name, and to ensure that we typed it correctly, we click on **Check Names** and then we click on **OK**:

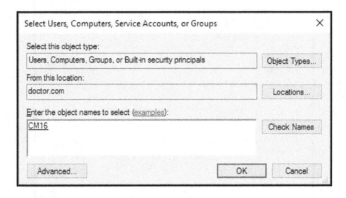

Pointing ConfigMgr computer account

5. The next step is to add permissions to the computer AD account. Highlight the computer account visible on the **Security** tab and click on **Advanced**:

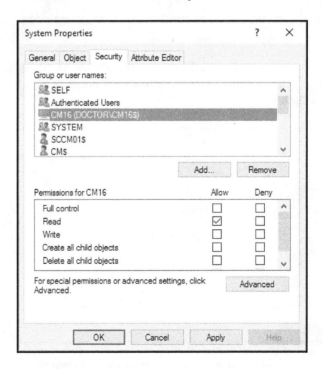

Choosing a computer account for granting permissions

6. Windows **Advanced Security Settings for System** appears. Highlight the
   ConfigMgr computer account and choose **Edit**:

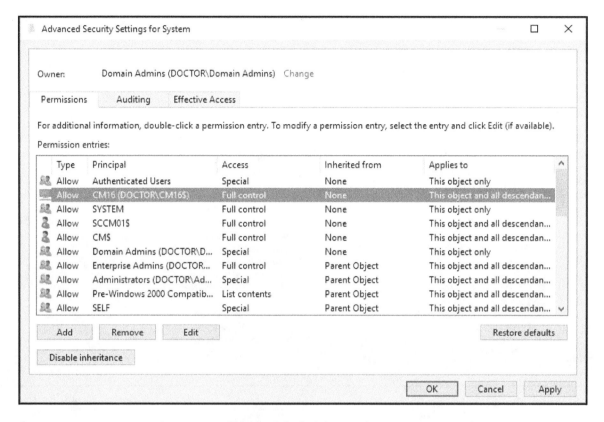

Editing of permissions for the System container

7. On the **Permission Entry for System** tab, check **Full control** and change the **Applies to** section to **This object and all descendant objects**:

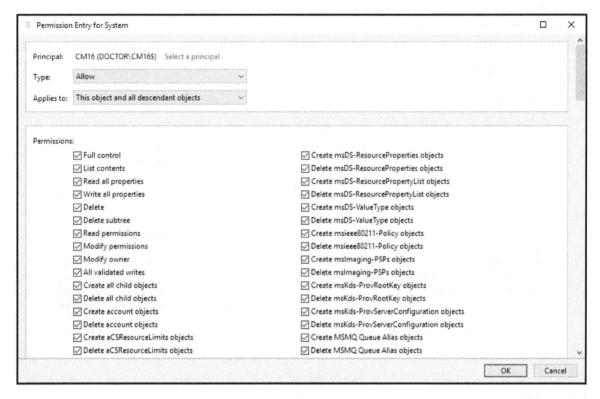

Configuring permissions for a computer account

8. After granting permissions, click on **OK** thrice. At this point, the environment is prepared for ConfigMgr to create the System Management container on its own and save the configuration data in there.

Extending the Active Directory schema

As mentioned earlier, ConfigMgr never has the ability to save its own data in the Active Directory database. It is not essential; however, it significantly eases administration effort.

The following information is being saved in the `System Management` container:

- Information about the available management points
- Information about the configured boundaries and boundary groups
- ConfigMgr servers and location codes

Extending the schema can be performed only with Schema Admins permissions. This can be achieved by adding an account to the Schema Admins AD group. The actual extension of the schema is done using the `extadsch.exe` program from the installation drive, placed in the `SMSSETUP\BIN\X64` folder:

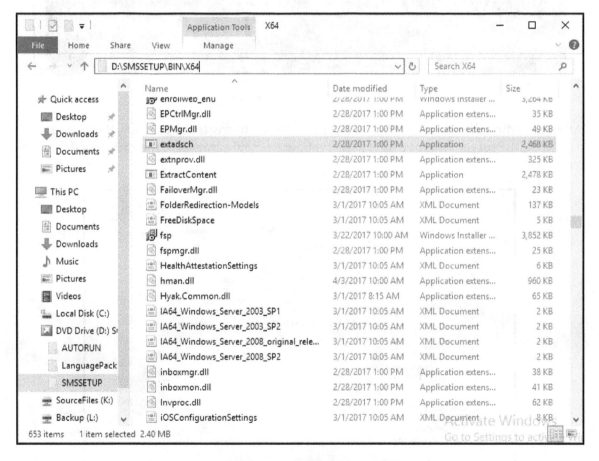

Extadsch.exe--application to extend Active Directory schema

All we need to do is start the application and wait for a while. A successfully finished operation should return a result similar to the following one:

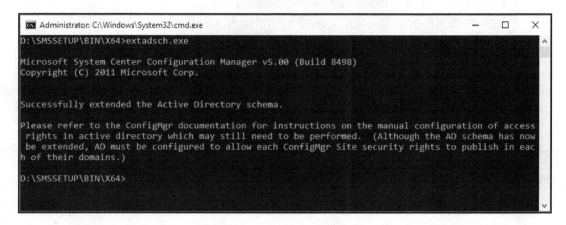

Result of extending the schema with extadsch.exe

After extending the schema and granting permissions to create the `System Management` container, the server will save information about its configuration in the mentioned container:

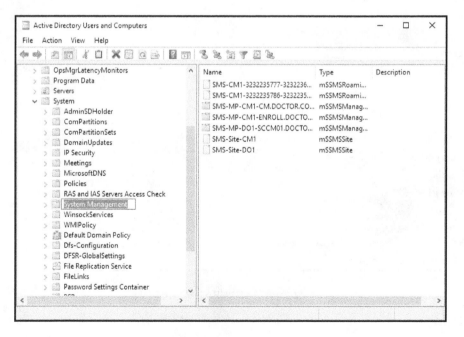

Information saved by ConfigMgr in System Management container

Permissions to the `System Management` container must not be taken away while the ConfigMgr server is working. The operation can be performed after the server is uninstalled. Taking away these permissions while the server is running will lead to a lack of communication between the ConfigMgr server and its clients.

Extension of the Active Directory schema can be done before or after the ConfigMgr server installation.

Installing operating system components

Before performing the installation of the ConfigMgr server, the operating system needs to be properly prepared. Firstly, we need to install the required roles and features for the server:

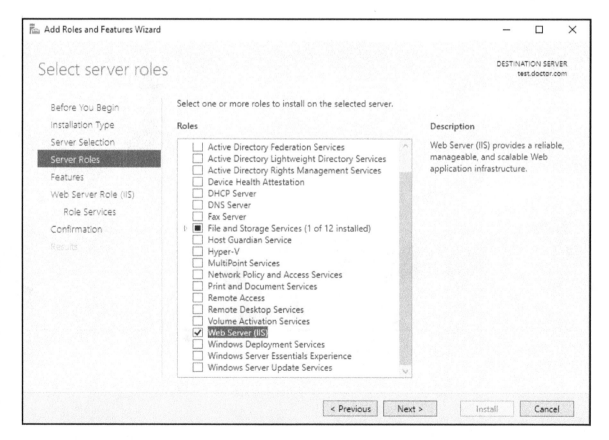

Installing Web Server (IIS) role

When installing IIS role, the following components should be installed:

- **Application Development: ASP.NET 3.5, .NET Extensibility 3.5, .NET Extensibility 4.5, ISAPI Extensions**
- **Security: Windows authentication**
- **IIS 6 Management Compatibility: IIS Management Console, IIS 6 Metabase Compatibility, IIS 6 WMI Compatibility, IIS Management Scripts and Tools**

Apart from server roles, a few additional features also need to be installed:

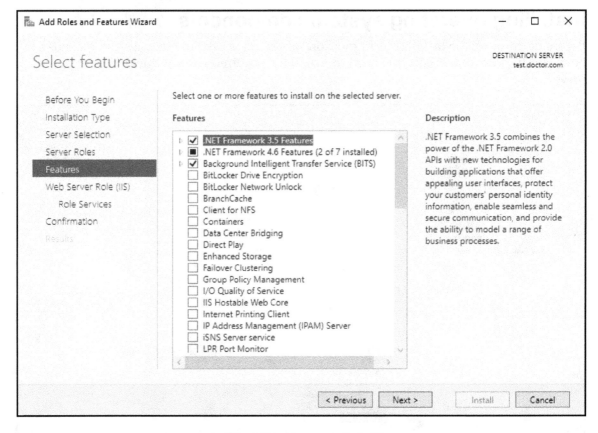

Installation of additional features required by ConfigMgr

This is a list of all the features required by the ConfigMgr server:

- **.NET Framework 3.5** and all sub-features
- **.NET Framework 4.6** and all sub-features
- **Background Intelligent Transfer Service (BITS)** and all sub-features
- **Remote Differential Compression**

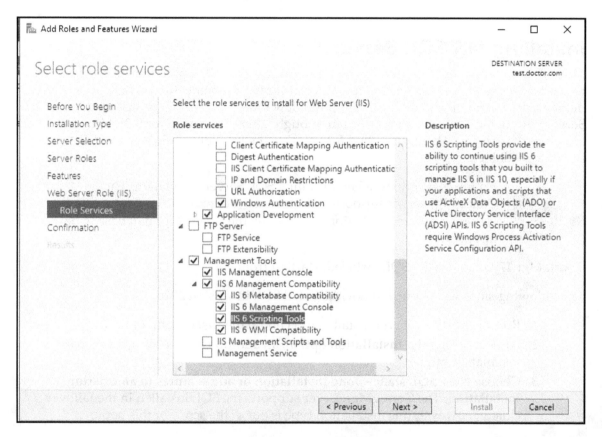

Installation of features required by ConfigMgr server

After installing all the roles and features, bear in mind to run the Microsoft update against the server to get all the required updates.

After having installed all the required updates, we can now go to the next stage--installing MS SQL Server.

Installing MS SQL Server

MS SQL is a component required by the ConfigMgr server. This prerequisite must be met regardless regardless of the server type. ConfigMgr requirements for MS SQL are not that demanding. Even when planning to support a few thousands of clients, installing MS SQL Server with default settings should be fair enough. There is no need for SQL to be placed on a separate disk array. There is no need for splitting the roles of ConfigMgr and SQL on two separate machines.

An important thing when installing SQL Server is collation. The ConfigMgr server supports `SQL_Latin1_General_CP1_CI_AS` collation. Having a different collation won't allow the ConfigMgr database to be installed.

ConfigMgr 1706 can use the SQL installed, starting from version 2014.

The following steps will show you how to install SQL in version 2016:

1. Run the MS SQL Server installer and choose the **Installation** option.
2. After choosing the **Installation** option, an additional window appears with installation modes.
3. Choose **New SQL stand-alone installation or add features to an existing installation**. The ConfigMgr server supports the SQL installed in the failover cluster; however, this installation type is out of the scope of this book:

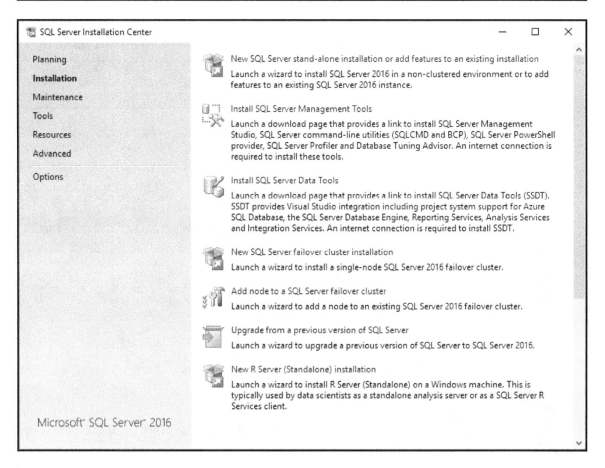

Choosing the SQL installation mode

4. At the beginning of the installation, we need to provide the MS SQL product key.

5. The next step is to accept the ConfigMgr license terms.

The ConfigMgr server contains the license for MS SQL in the Standard version. There is, however, a condition that MS SQL Server can only hold the ConfigMgr database.

6. After accepting the license terms, the installer checks whether there are any updates for the installer itself. When found, it downloads and installs them. In the next steps, it checks whether there are any problems that might prevent MS SQL Server from being installed:

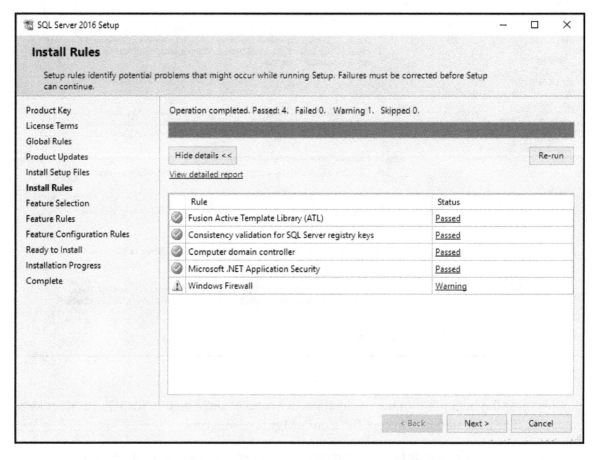

Checkouts of whether there are any problems preventing MS SQL server from being installed

7. If there are no impediments, the installer will go further. In the next step, we decide what MS SQL components should be installed and in which folders; ConfigMgr requires the following components to be installed:
   - **Database Engine Services**
   - **Reporting Services - Native**

8. It is not possible to install MS SQL Server Management Studio along with MS SQL Server. This needs to be downloaded and installed separately:

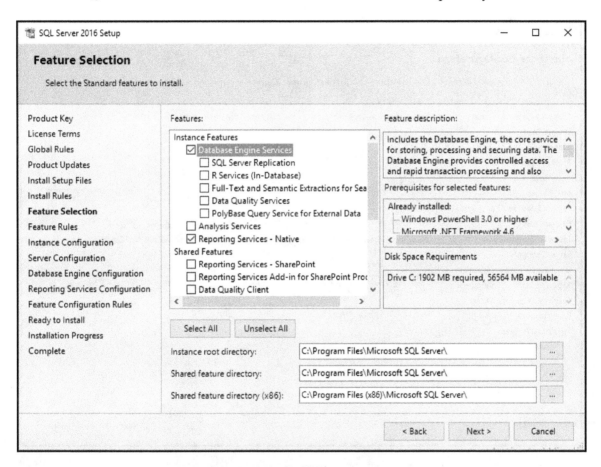

Choosing MS SQL Server components for installation

9. After deciding and choosing the required SQL Server components, we need to decide about the SQL instance name:

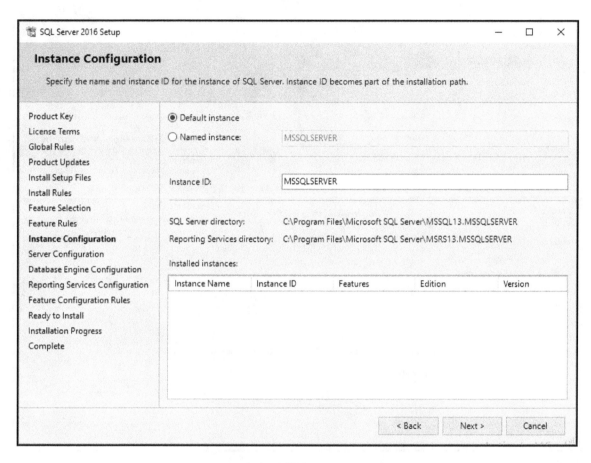

Naming MS SQL Server instance

Leaving the **Default instance** name would be the best choice.

10. In the next step, we define an account that will be used by MS SQL Server. We define it on the **Service Accounts** tab:

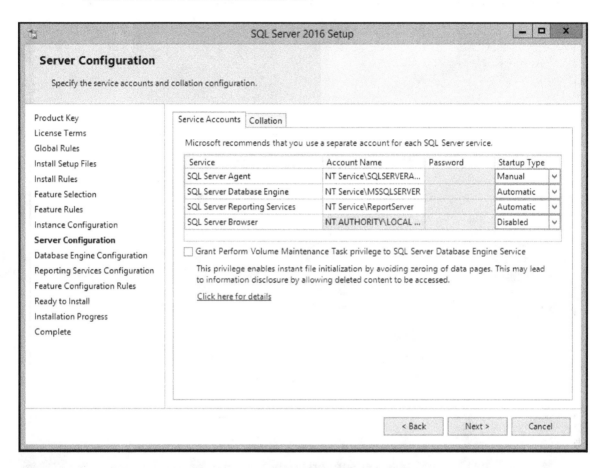

Choosing SQL Service Accounts

ConfigMgr server cannot be installed on an MS SQL Server that uses **NT Service** accounts or **LOCAL SERVICE**. The best way is to have a regular Active Directory account with administrative rights to the SQL Server.

This is the moment when we need to remember about the **Collation** tab:

SQL Server 2016 Setup — □ ×

Server Configuration

Specify the service accounts and collation configuration.

Product Key	Service Accounts	Collation
License Terms	
Global Rules	Database Engine:
Product Updates	SQL_Latin1_General_CP1_CI_AS Customize...
Install Setup Files	Latin1-General, case-insensitive, accent-sensitive, kanatype-insensitive, width-insensitive for Unicode Data, SQL Server Sort Order 52 on Code Page 1252 for non-Unicode Data
Install Rules	
Feature Selection	
Feature Rules	
Instance Configuration	
Server Configuration	
Database Engine Configuration	
Reporting Services Configuration	
Feature Configuration Rules	
Ready to Install	
Installation Progress	
Complete	

< Back   Next >   Cancel

Choosing the right collation for the SQL server

The ConfigMgr server supports only the `SQL_Latin1_general_CP1_CI_AS` collation. If we install SQL Server using a different collation, ConfigMgr will not be able to go through the installation process.

It is possible to change collation on the SQL Server after it is installed. This process, however, does not always end successfully, and hence it is important to choose the right collation while installing the server.

The MS SQL installation automatically sets the collation based on the server regional settings on which it is installed.

11. After choosing the **Service Accounts** and **Collation** on the **Server Configuration** tab, we need to choose the way of authentication that will be used for the SQL Server as well as the accounts we will use for administration:

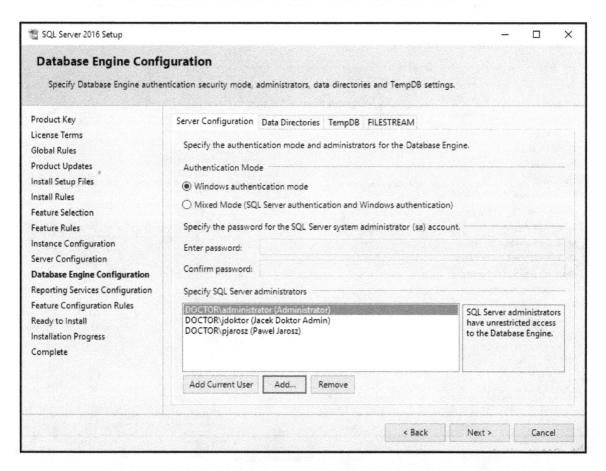

Choosing of administrative accounts or groups for SQL Server from Active Directory

12. On the **Data Directories** tab, choose the folders in which SQL Server will create the database and log files:

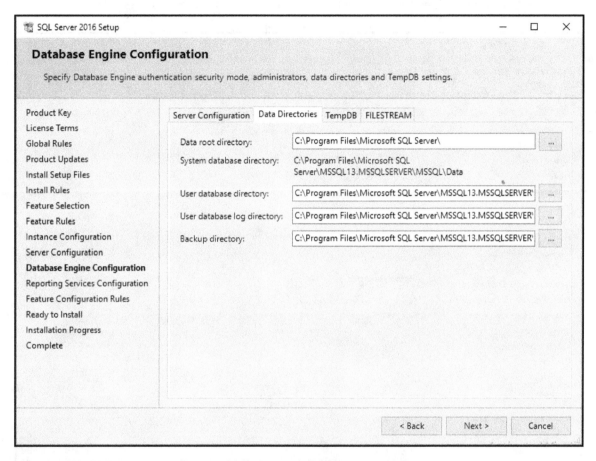

Choosing folders for the database and logs

13. Choose the Reporting Services to be installed. During the installation, we have a choice to either install it or install and configure it automatically during the installation process. Choose **Install and configure**:

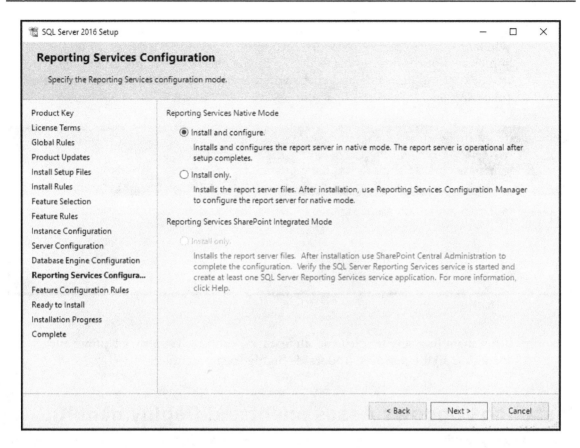

Installing Reporting Services

 Reporting Services might be installed either on the same server where SQL Server resides or on a separate one. If Reporting Services has a negative impact on SQL Server in some way, it is possible to move it later to a separate machine.

14. The last step is a summary of our configuration of SQL Server. After checkouts, if all the settings are as intended to be, we may start the installation process.

15. The installation of SQL Server shouldn't take long. It is important to check whether Reporting Services works properly, as it often happens that it is somehow not configured correctly. To do the checkout, simply enter the URL `http://cm16/reports` and check whether the website looks similar to the following one:

Reporting Services home page

16. After installing server roles and all features, running Windows Update and installing all the pending updates is highly recommended.

Installing Windows Assessment and Deployment Kit

The next step of environment configuration before installing ConfigMgr is the installation of special tool set:

1. The Windows Assessment and Deployment Kit can be downloaded from the internet: `https://developer.microsoft.com/en-us/windows/hardware/windows-assessment-deployment-kit`. The mentioned tool set needs to be installed before starting with the ConfigMgr installation.

> Keep in mind that the version of ADK needs to be compatible with the ConfigMgr server. For ConfigMgr 1706, we need to choose the ADK in version 1703.

2. After downloading the files from the internet, we can start the installation process. The installer will ask whether we would like to anonymously send data about the way we use ADK to Microsoft.

3. The next step is choosing the folder we would like ADK to be installed in:

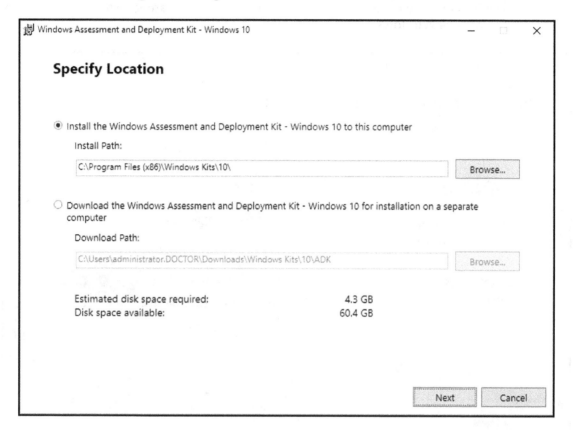

ADK folder location

4. The last step is choosing which individual tools from the tool set shall be installed. ConfigMgr requires the following components:
   - **Deployment Tools**
   - **Windows Preinstallation Environment (Windows PE)**
   - **User State Migration Tool (USMT)**

5. Additionally, **Imaging And Configuration Designer (ICD) and Configuration Designer** can be installed. These are responsible for creating installation packages for various Windows systems:

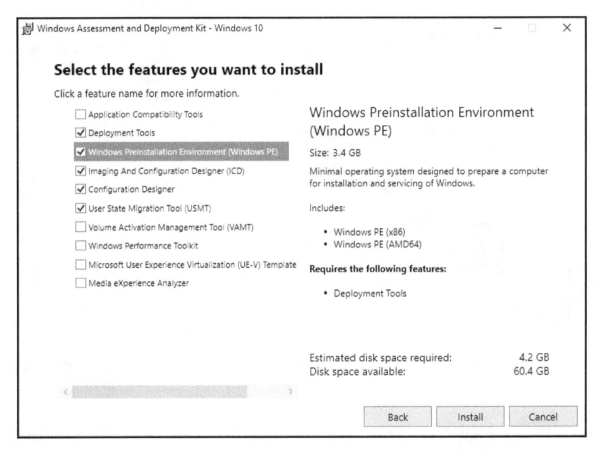

Finalizing ADK installation

After the ADK installation is finished, the next step will be installing the ConfigMgr server.

The Windows ADK is required while installing the ConfigMgr server. Unfortunately, after the server is installed, the ADK package may be uninstalled. The ConfigMgr server will continue to work; however, not all features related to deployments will be working properly.

ConfigMgr server installation

After all prerequisites have been fulfilled, finally, the ConfigMgr server will be installed. Before we start the installation, a couple of matters need to be considered:

- Three-character location code
- The name of the ConfigMgr server

These two are used to identify a server in the hierarchy. Why are these two things so essentially important? That's because these cannot be modified after the server is installed. The only way to change them is to reinstall the ConfigMgr server from scratch:

1. After starting the installer, the type of installation needs to be chosen. Choose the primary site and the **Install a Configuration Manager primary site** option:

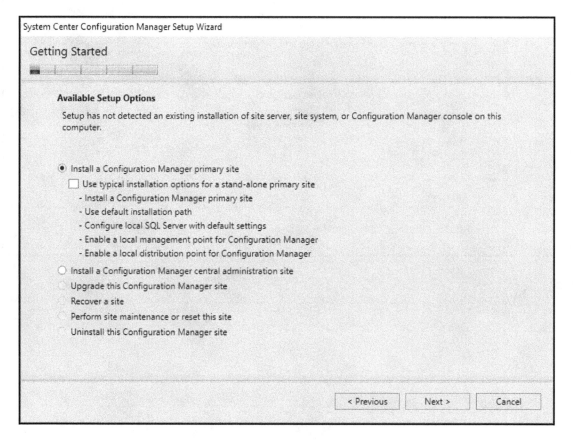

Choosing the installation type

2. The ConfigMgr license comes along with Software Assurance. The installer asks for the license key and the date until which Software Assurance is valid:

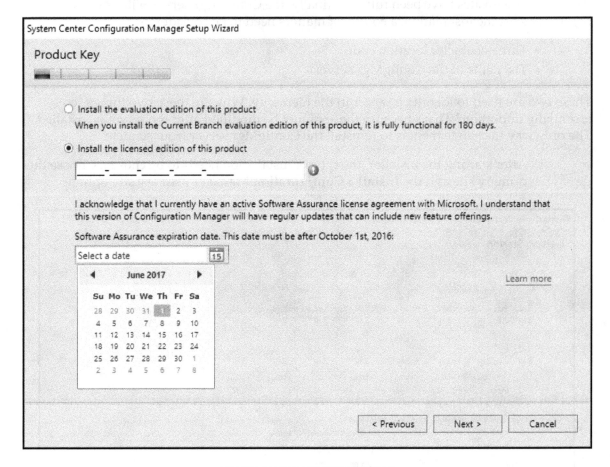

License key and expiration date of Software Assurance

3. The next step is accepting the license terms for the application used by the ConfigMgr server:

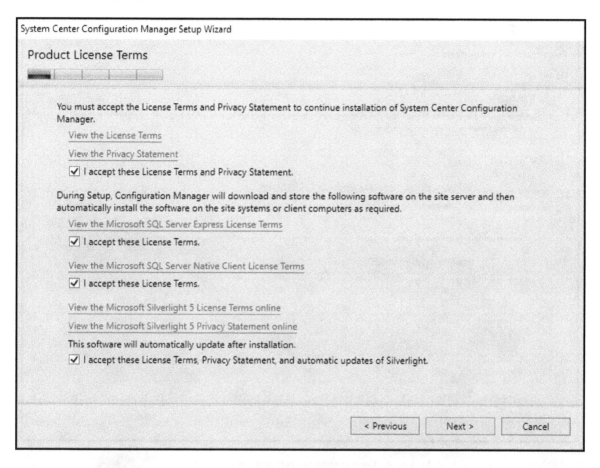

System Center Configuration Manager Setup Wizard

Product License Terms

You must accept the License Terms and Privacy Statement to continue installation of System Center Configuration Manager.

View the License Terms

View the Privacy Statement

☑ I accept these License Terms and Privacy Statement.

During Setup, Configuration Manager will download and store the following software on the site server and then automatically install the software on the site systems or client computers as required.

View the Microsoft SQL Server Express License Terms

☑ I accept these License Terms.

View the Microsoft SQL Server Native Client License Terms

☑ I accept these License Terms.

View the Microsoft Silverlight 5 License Terms online

View the Microsoft Silverlight 5 Privacy Statement online

This software will automatically update after installation.

☑ I accept these License Terms, Privacy Statement, and automatic updates of Silverlight.

| < Previous | Next > | Cancel |

Accepting the license terms

4. The ConfigMgr installer does the checkout of prerequisites--if some prerequisites haven't been met, the installer will try to install the missing components. These files are downloaded from the internet and saved in a location chosen by us--it might be a network share or a local folder on a ConfigMgr server. If we installed ConfigMgr server or client somewhere in the past, we might point the installer to this folder so it can be used, for instance, to install another ConfigMgr server, and there will be no need to download the required binaries again.

5. The mentioned folder also handles the install files of SQL Express, which are used when installing the secondary site:

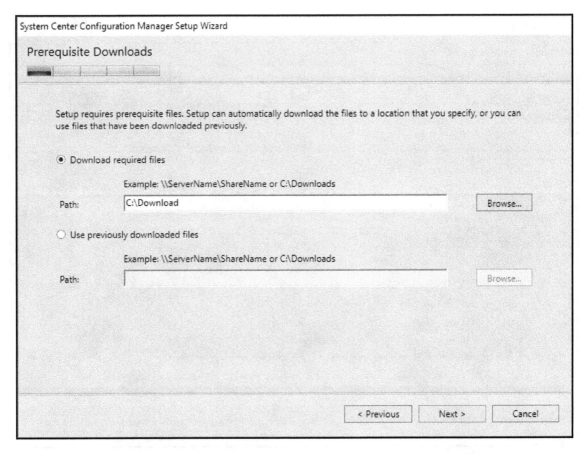

System Center Configuration Manager Setup Wizard

Prerequisite Downloads

Setup requires prerequisite files. Setup can automatically download the files to a location that you specify, or you can use files that have been downloaded previously.

◉ Download required files

Example: \\ServerName\ShareName or C:\Downloads

Path: C:\Download   Browse...

○ Use previously downloaded files

Example: \\ServerName\ShareName or C:\Downloads

Path: Browse...

< Previous   Next >   Cancel

Choosing the folder location for installation files

The mentioned folder needs to be accessible after the ConfigMgr server is installed. If this folder gets deleted, the installation of the clients will not be available, as well as installing the secondary site which leverages SQL Express.

6. The installer downloads files from the internet; if the download operation finishes with success, the installer goes further:

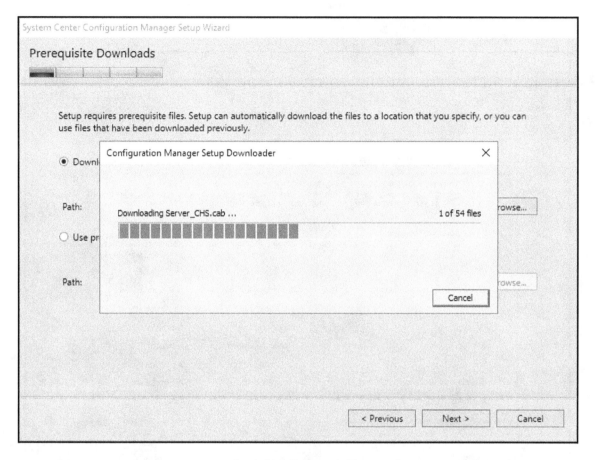

Downloading files by the server installer

7. Working with the server, there is an opportunity to use many different languages for the console as well as for clients. During installation, the installer asks which versions of languages for console and clients should be installed during the installation procedure:

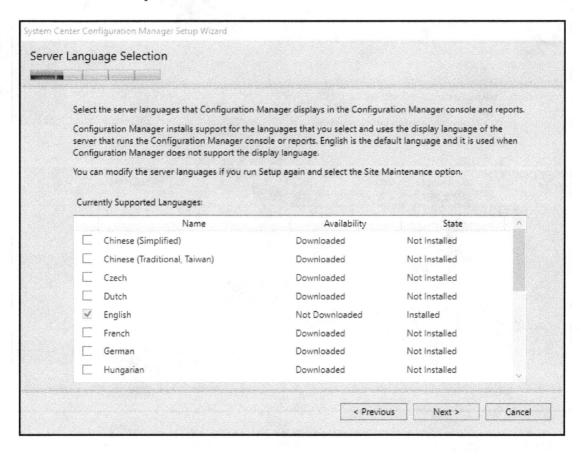

Choosing the language packs

The ConfigMgr server console will adjust the installing language automatically, depending on the operating system language it is being installed on. The same happens with the client. **English** is the default installed language, and unfortunately, this cannot be changed.

8. Next, the language for the clients needs to be chosen:

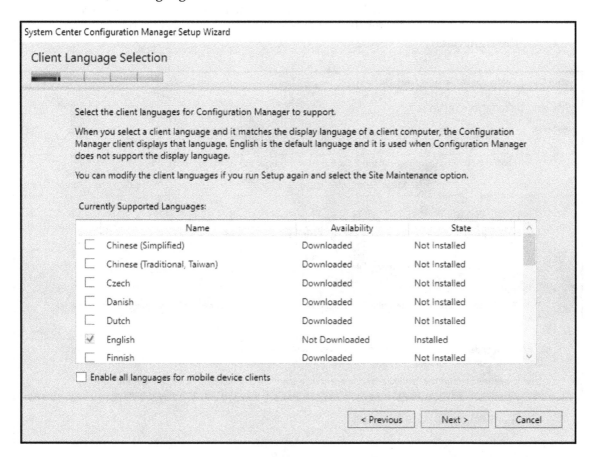

Choosing the language version for clients of ConfigMgr

9. After choosing the language, the installer will ask for the location name, the server name, and the installation folder. As mentioned earlier, these two settings cannot be modified after the server is installed, so we need to be sure we provide the right data:

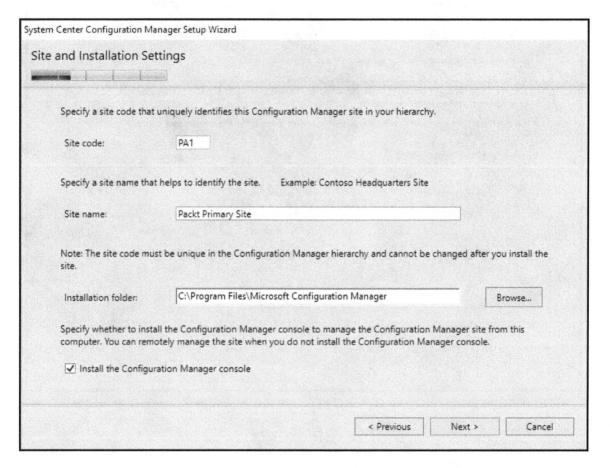

Setting the location and server name

10. ConfigMgr can work as a standalone unit, or it can cooperate with other servers in the hierarchy. The decision about which option to choose is done at this moment by the administrator:

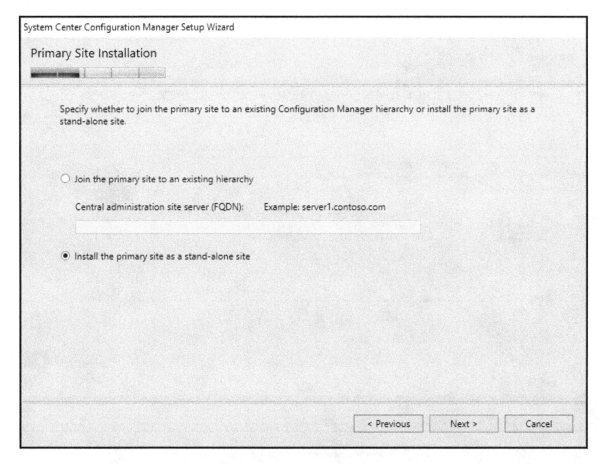

Installing the standalone server connected to the hierarchy

11. After choosing the standalone installation option, the installer shows information that the server might later be connected to the hierarchy:

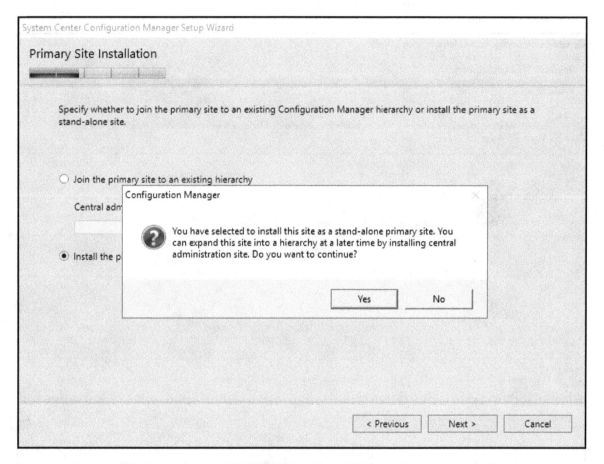

Information about connecting the server to the hierarchy

12. Each ConfigMgr server saves data in the SQL. During deployment, the installer asks for the FQDN of the server and the SQL instance, a person who will be maintaining the ConfigMgr database. The default ConfigMgr database name is CM_{location_code}. If there is a need, the database name might be changed later:

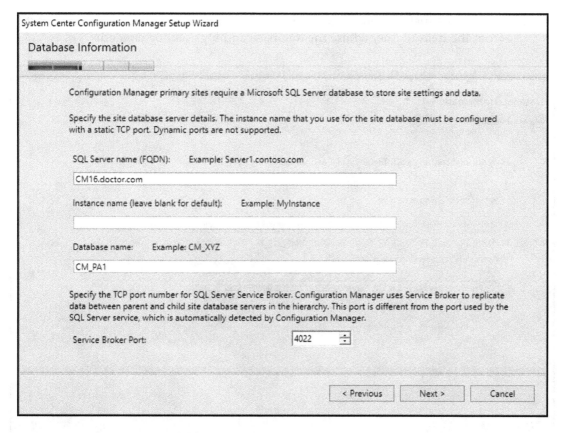

System Center Configuration Manager Setup Wizard

Database Information

Configuration Manager primary sites require a Microsoft SQL Server database to store site settings and data.

Specify the site database server details. The instance name that you use for the site database must be configured with a static TCP port. Dynamic ports are not supported.

SQL Server name (FQDN):   Example: Server1.contoso.com

    CM16.doctor.com

Instance name (leave blank for default):   Example: MyInstance

Database name: Example: CM_XYZ

    CM_PA1

Specify the TCP port number for SQL Server Service Broker. Configuration Manager uses Service Broker to replicate data between parent and child site database servers in the hierarchy. This port is different from the port used by the SQL Server service, which is automatically detected by Configuration Manager.

Service Broker Port: 4022

[< Previous]   [Next >]   [Cancel]

Configuration related to SQL and database

There is a possibility of installing a database in another instance than the default one. However, this is not the recommended state as there might be issues related to the Reporting Service Point role.

Despite a situation where MS SQL and ConfigMgr server are installed on one machine, two firewall ports still need to be opened: 4022 and 1433. Otherwise, the ConfigMgr server will report a configuration problem even if the server is functioning correctly.

13. During the installation, there is a possibility to point to another location apart from the default one, where the database and logs will be created:

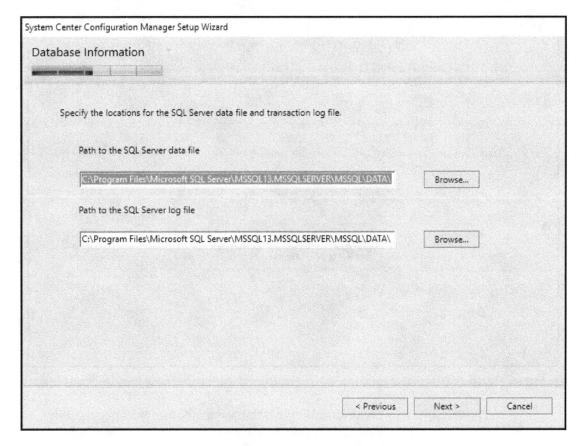

Configuring database and logs location

14. Each administration console instance connects to the ConfigMgr server using **SMS Provider (FQDN)**. The complete FQDN of this server needs to be provided during the server installation. SMS Provider can be installed on one machine only:

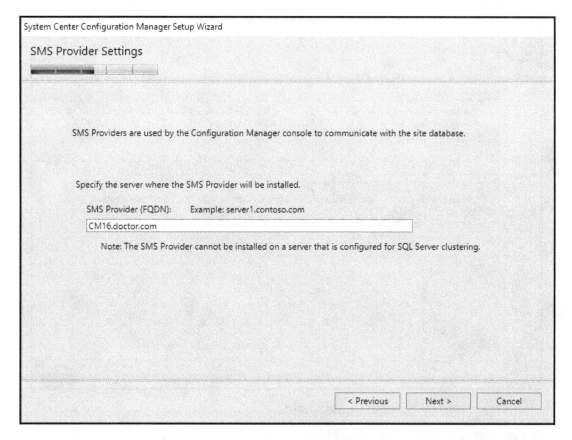

System Center Configuration Manager Setup Wizard

SMS Provider Settings

SMS Providers are used by the Configuration Manager console to communicate with the site database.

Specify the server where the SMS Provider will be installed.

SMS Provider (FQDN):   Example: server1.contoso.com

CM16.doctor.com

Note: The SMS Provider cannot be installed on a server that is configured for SQL Server clustering.

< Previous   Next >   Cancel

Configuring SMS Provider

15. Starting with ConfigMgr 2007, the server might work using the HTTP or HTTPS mode. Depending on the needs, the mode needs to be set up during the configuration:

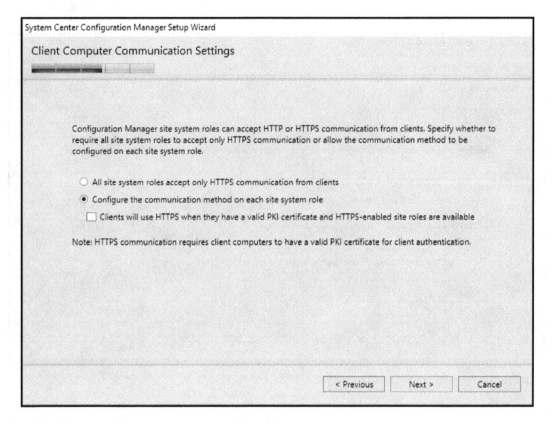

Securing the communication channel between the server and ConfigMgr clients

TIP

Before configuring ConfigMgr to work in HTTPS, the PKI infrastructure needs to be prepared. The ConfigMgr server uses various certificates to secure communication between the server and the clients. There is a possibility to change the mode after the server is installed.

Each ConfigMgr installation has one fundamental tenet that has two roles, management point and distribution point, which need to be deployed. Management point supports communication between the server and the clients, whereas distribution point shares all the binaries needed for configured administrative actions with clients, for instance, application installation:

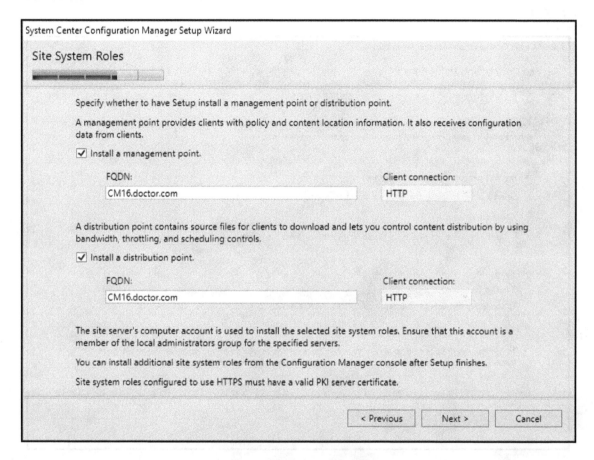

Configuring management point and distribution point

Microsoft, as a part of its continuous improvement process, gathers some usage data from all the ConfigMgr servers. This feature cannot be completely turned off; the only option is to lower the amount of shared data.

Along with ConfigMgr 1511, Microsoft has changed its approach for patching the server and upgrades to new versions. Similarly to Windows Server, ConfigMgr works in the current branch mode, and it searches for new patches and versions and shows information on the console. The server role is responsible for checking whether there are any new patches for the server, called **service connection point**. We may install it or not--there is no requirement:

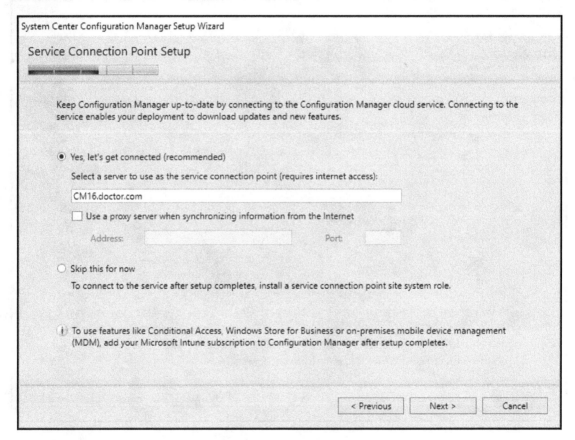

Configuring service connection point

 Some of the features related to managing mobile devices or the Intune service require service connection point to be installed on the ConfigMgr server.

After configuring service connection point, the installer will sum up the settings on screen:

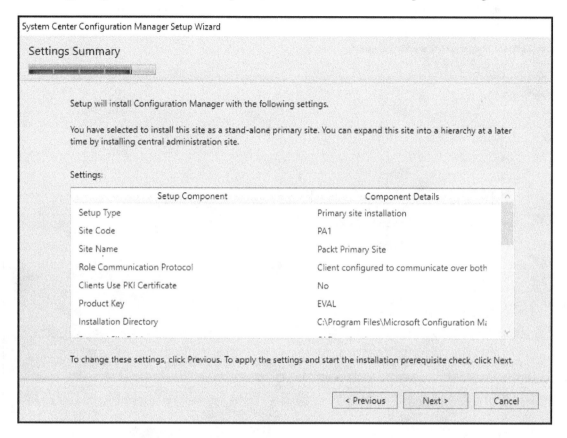

Configuration summary

After all of the required data has been provided to the installer, check all the prerequisites and requirements related to the operating system. There are two types of statuses that can be experienced:

- **Critical**: The error makes ConfigMgr unable to install, a situation that may cause an error, for instance, lack of Windows ADK

- **Warning**: The error does not influence the installation of the server, but its future operational status, for instance, lack of an installed WSUS server

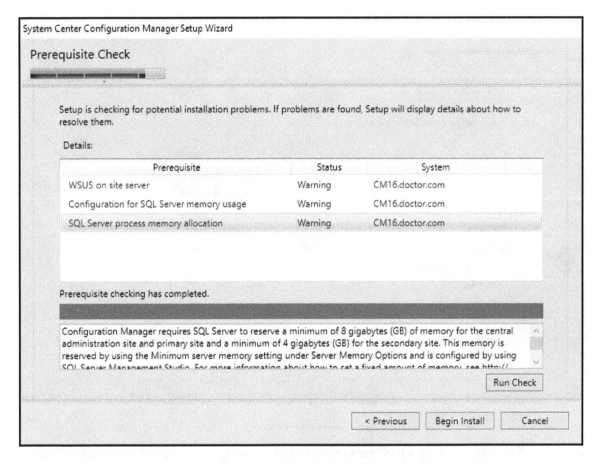

Configuration summary--checking for prerequisites

The actual ConfigMgr server installation shouldn't take longer than an hour:

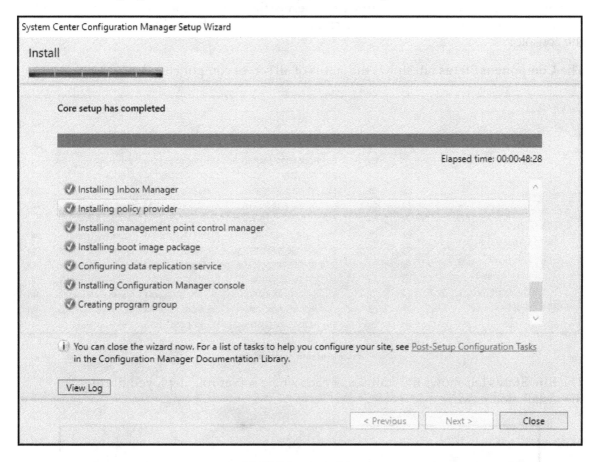

End of ConfigMgr server installation

After the server is fully installed, it is always good to perform a checkout and review whether all the components are working properly.

Checkouts after installation

Installation of the ConfigMgr server can be divided into two steps--installation of the core server functionalities and the rest of the components. Server console might be run after the first step of the installation is finished. However, shortly after the installation, the console will still show errors about some components that have not been configured--these will be resolved after the second step of the installation is finished.

Once the second step is finished, `setup.log` located on the `C:\` drive of the server might be reviewed for any errors. The first functional test of the server is console connectivity, and the health status of each single server's components may be checked once it's connected to the console.

The **Component Status** tab shows the status of all server components:

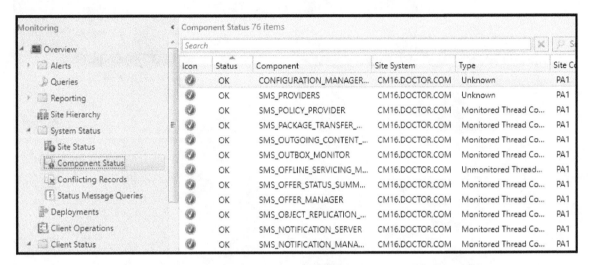

All ConfigMgr server components' states

The **Site Status** tab shows the statuses of each single server role deployed during the installation process:

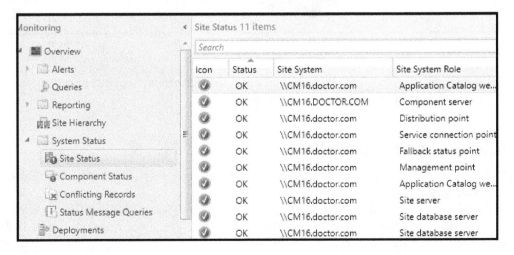

All ConfigMgr server roles' states

Green **OK** statuses on each tab mean that the ConfigMgr server deployment finished with success. Having properly installed the server, it is time to start the configuration of single server components.

Summary

This chapter covered how to properly go through the process of ConfigMgr 1706 installation, which is not a hard task if you're well prepared. Main tasks included installing the operating system, MS SQL Server, and the rest of the prerequisites. Some configuration data also needs to be prepared, along with a few fundamental decisions that need to be made, which has been also covered in this chapter.

The next chapter covers configuring sites, boundaries, and boundary groups. Boundaries define networks for managed devices, while boundary groups are logical groups of boundaries. Proper configuration of these components is a cornerstone for successful installation and communication between server and clients.

3
Configure Sites and Boundaries

Before ConfigMgr clients are able to perform any tasks, server roles, as well as features, need to be configured according to the project prepared. As the previous chapter covered the topic of ConfigMgr installation, this chapter covers the following topics:

- ConfigMgr server role types
- Installation modes on ConfigMgr server roles
- Server roles installed and configured for ConfigMgr server
- Installation and configuration of basic server role essentials in each ConfigMgr deployment
- Boundary types and their role in the ConfigMgr environment
- Boundary group types and their role in the ConfigMgr environment

This chapter should provide you with sufficient knowledge to configure the ConfigMgr server in a way that it is discoverable to clients so they can be properly managed.

There is a whole range of settings for particular ConfigMgr functions. All of them will be covered in later chapters, describing each server function. This chapter covers fundamental server configuration.

ConfigMgr server role types

Server roles used by ConfigMgr can be divided into three groups--default, mandatory, and optional roles. Default mandatory roles are ones that are deployed by the installer and cannot be uninstalled or added manually. Optional ones are the ones that the administrator installs on a chosen server system or, sometimes, client, to implement a certain functionality. Good examples of such optional features are a Software Update point and an Application Catalog.

Default roles

While installing ConfigMgr server or any of its particular roles, the default roles--mandatory for the environment--are installed. This is the list of default ConfigMgr server roles:

- **Site server**: This provides fundamental functionalities for the ConfigMgr server.
- **Site system**: This is the server that provides specific ConfigMgr functionalities. The role is automatically installed while installing some of the optional roles or when installing the ConfigMgr role.
- **Component system**: This is the server that runs the SMS Executive service, which means the server holds a site system role.
- **Site database server**: This is the role installed on a server that holds the SQL installed for the ConfigMgr server.
- **SMS Provider**: This is the role installed with the ConfigMgr server, and it enables communication between the server and the SQL database.

 The SMS Provider server role is not visible from the server console.

These roles are installed with some default settings, and the administrator has limited options for adjusting this setting. All other roles are optional ones, which means the administrator can install them on any system.

Optional roles

An optional role is one that should be installed along with the ConfigMgr server to add certain functionalities. The number of optional roles depend on the planned functionalities of the server. Each and every role needs to be properly configured. Some roles, such as a distribution point, might need to be configured differently on each server.

The following is the list of optional server roles that are added to the environment after the server is installed:

- **Application Catalog website point**: A role handling the communication between software library and Application Catalog website point; a website where users can browse applications that have been published for them.
- **Asset Intelligence synchronization point**: A server role that gains data from the Asset Intelligence catalog and sends all application signatures to the Asset Intelligence catalog. It is installed only on a central administration site or standalone primary site server.
- **Certificate registration point**: The server role that provides and maintains certificates used by the ConfigMgr client.
- **Distribution point**: The server role that provides source files with clients for tasks that have been created by an administrator. It's one of the roles that might be automatically installed when installing ConfigMgr server.
- **Endpoint Protection point**: The server role that manages the endpoint system protection system.
- **Fallback status point**: The role that saves data about the status of the ConfigMgr client's installation. Thanks to this, it is possible to find clients that are not able to connect to the management point.
- **Management point**: The server role that enables communication between clients and the server.
- **Data Warehouse service point**: The server role that synchronizes data from Configuration Manager database to Data Warehouse database.
- **Cloud management gateway connections point**: The server role that manages the endpoint system protection system.
- **Enrollment point**: This provides complete mobile device enrollment.
- **Enrollment proxy point**: This manages enrollment requests from mobile devices.
- **Reporting services point**: This provides reporting from the SQL server database.
- **Software update point**: This provides integration of the ConfigMgr server with WSUS, which enables you to manage patching from the ConfigMgr server.
- **State migration point**: This keeps user profiles during the operating system deployment.
- **Service connection point**: This connects to Microsoft Cloud. Thanks to this role, the server is instantly informed about new updates and new server versions. This role can be installed directly during server deployment or later.

The following are the roles that might be automatically installed when installing the ConfigMgr server:

- **Distribution point**: The server role that provides source files with clients for tasks that have been created by an administrator.
- **Management point**: The server role that enables communication between clients and the server.
- **Service connection point**: This connects to Microsoft Cloud. Thanks to this role, the server is instantly informed about new updates and new server versions. This role can be installed directly during server deployment or later.

 Please note that at least one distribution point and management point need to be installed in the environment in order to enable client management.

Now let's take a closer look at roles that are configured during server deployment.

Roles installed during server deployment

What follows is the description of all the server roles that might be installed during the ConfigMgr server deployment.

Site server

The site server role is always installed during ConfigMgr deployment. It is not possible to change preferences of this role or remove it.

Site system

The site system role is always installed on a computer that provides specific functions for the ConfigMgr environment. It is installed by the ConfigMgr server installer and if any ConfigMgr server role is going to be installed on an operating system.

It happens, for instance, when the administrator installs a Reporting Service point. During role installation, the installer configures the site system role as well as the Reporting Service point role:

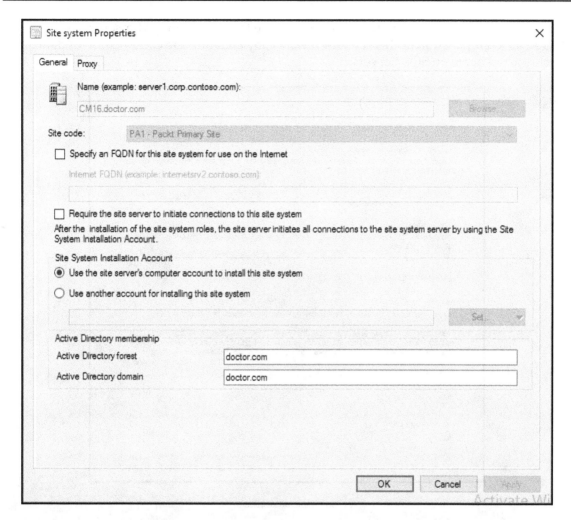

Site system role configuration

The role might be installed on more than one operating system. It is most common in larger environments where each server role is on a separate operating system. In certain circumstances, we might change the configuration of this role.

Site database server

The site database role is automatically installed during the deployment of each ConfigMgr server type, as each saves data in the database. This role cannot be uninstalled.

Administrators managing environments with more than one ConfigMgr server might change the configuration of this role, for instance, by enabling the compression of data synchronized between SQL Servers:

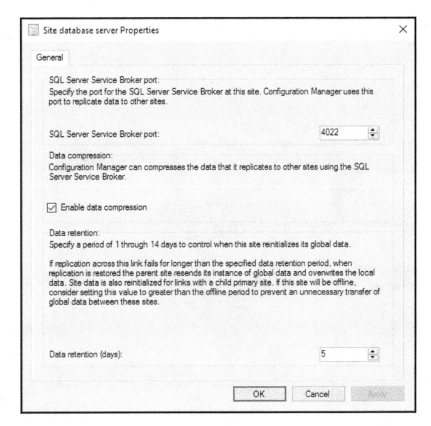

Site database role configuration

The administrator can also change the port used by the SQL service broker for connection between SQL Servers. There is also a possibility of moving ConfigMgr SQL database to another machine after the server is installed.

Service connection point

The service connection point is a fundamental role, but it's still optional. Why, though? The administrator might install it during server deployment or after. It can be removed anytime and the server will continue to work properly.

The role connects to Microsoft Cloud service and checks for any new updates that might be applied and whether a new version of the system is available. This role works under two modes. One is where the system checks for updates automatically and the second where it needs to be triggered by the administrator manually. The mentioned role is needed also for mobile device management when using Microsoft InTune (it replaces the older, already depreciated Windows Intune Connector role) and to manage on-premise devices with Mobile Device Management. This role is installed for the whole hierarchy.

Distribution point

A distribution point provides source files to clients for tasks that have been created by an administrator. These files are needed for operating system installation, releasing patches, and software deployment. To make use of this functionality, at least one distribution point server, assigned to proper boundary groups, needs to be installed in the environment:

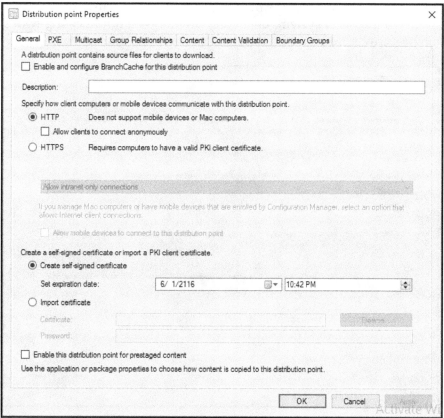

Distribution point default settings

This role is configured depending on the functions distribution points needs to provide. Additional configuration is also needed if the role is to support Windows Deployment Services. The server might be installed and configured during ConfigMgr deployment or later, being added to an existing deployment.

Management point

The management point role is the most important role in the whole ConfigMgr environment. It enables communication between ConfigMgr and its clients. If management point, or IIS, which handles the communication--is not working correctly, clients instantly become unmanageable. Clients won't be able to download policies or send any data to the server.

For this reason, it is an important administrator task to check whether the management point works properly on a regular, daily basis. The verification method is very easy--if at least one client communicates with the management point, it ensures the role works correctly. If some of the other systems encounter problems communicating with the server, the resolution needs to be searched on the client side, not the management point:

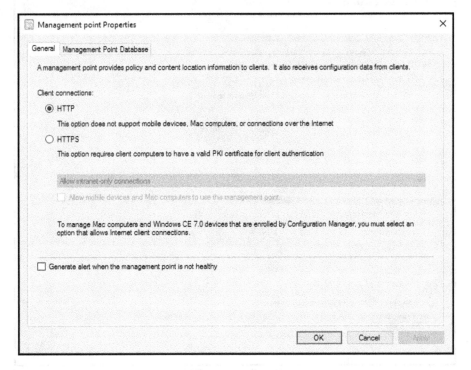

Management point default settings

To get alerts about management point accessibility issues, the administrator might want to select the **Generate alert when the management point is not healthy** option.

Each management point might have a different configuration; for instance, when publishing a management point in the DMZ zone, it needs to be secured with a certificate to work in the HTTPS mode. It might be installed and configured during ConfigMgr deployment or added to the existing ConfigMgr server later.

Methods of installing server roles

Server roles might be added to an environment at any suitable time. The same roles might be removed in the same way if the administrator no longer plans to utilize them or the concept of usage of ConfigMgr has changed.

Adding new server roles isn't problematic; however, the installation of a new role requires providing an account with local administrator rights; just having access to the ConfigMgr console is not enough, and installation will not be successful.

There are two installation methods:

- **Create the site system role**: The wizard used to install server roles on a computer that is not already handling any roles in the ConfigMgr environment
- **Add site system role**: The wizard that enables the installation of a new role on a computer that already provides some roles in the ConfigMgr environment

 Whether the role installation has been successful or not can be confirmed in the ConfigMgr console or by reviewing certain log files.

Wizards differ among themselves, usually only with the first screen. In all further settings, starting from proxy settings, all the steps are identical regardless of which wizard has been run.

All of the wizard steps will be described later in the book.

Create site system server

The **Create Site System Server Wizard** that is used to install roles on the newly added environment server, can be found in the tab under `Administration\Site Configuration\Sites`.

As this wizard installs roles on the new server, there is a need to identify which computer will provide the role and assign it to the appropriate site. This wizard can be run on the standalone primary server, central administration site server, as well as a primary site server working in a hierarchy:

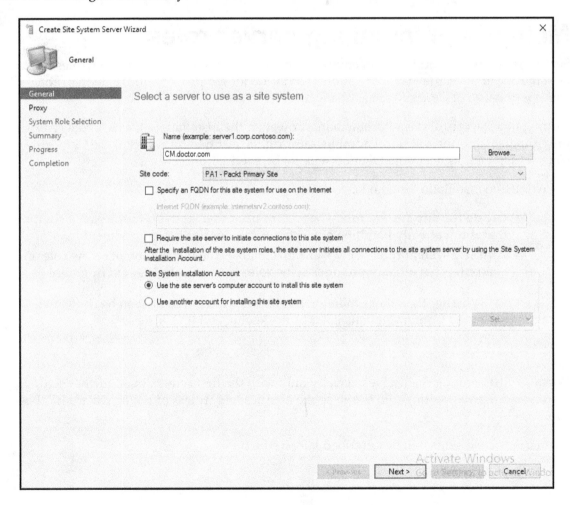

Pointing computer on which certain server role will be installed

The **Site System Installation Account** option is used to provide the Active Directory account that has appropriate permissions on the remote computer needed to perform an installation. Clicking on the **Next** button moves the wizard to the **Proxy** settings. The next steps, are to choose the server role and its installation.

Add site system role

The **Add Site System Roles Wizard** can be run from the `Administration\Site Configuration\Servers and Site System Roles` tab. The first step is to mark the chosen server and chose the **Add Site System Roles** option.

In this particular case, there is no need to point to a specific server name on which a role will be installed or assigned to a site; as this data is automatically populated when choosing an existing ConfigMgr server already assigned to a site, and this has been done in this example:

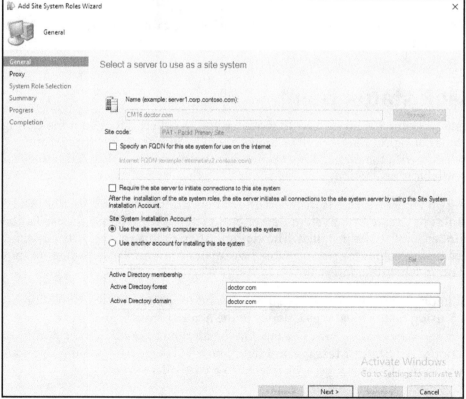

Installing a server role on a server already existing in a hierarchy

The **Site System Installation Account** option is used to provide the Active Directory account that has appropriate permissions on the remote computer needed to perform an installation. Further steps look exactly the same as when choosing the **Add Site System Roles** option.

Fundamental optional server roles

There are a few optional server roles that should always be installed. ConfigMgr will be fully functional without them; however, administration and reporting will be much more difficult.

These roles are as follows:

- Fallback status point
- Reporting service point
- Application Catalog

Description and installation steps for the aforementioned roles are presented in the upcoming section.

Fallback status point

Fallback status point is a server role that allows you to collect data about the ConfigMgr client installation's progress as well as issues about assigning clients to sites and communication with the management point. For these reasons, this role is always highly recommended for installation.

Depending on where the role is installed, the administrators need to pick the **Add Site System Roles** or **Create Site System Server** option in the wizard and choose **Fallback status point** as a role to be installed. The configuration of this role is fairly easy and comes down to choosing values for two options--how many communications the role should process, and in what time intervals.

The installation of this role process is quite fast, and the status of the installation process can be checked using Status Messages Queries in the `Administration\System Status\Status Message Queries` tab. On the aforementioned tab, the administrator needs to choose **All Status Message** and then **Show Messages**; the ConfigMgr console should now show all status messages related to a particular server.

To check the status of `SMS_FALLBACK_STATUS_POINT`, the administrator needs to find this component and then look for information that the component has been successfully started.

> The mentioned method might help in diagnosing a single server and all its components.

Reporting service point

A reporting service point is an optional ConfigMgr server role; however, it is hard to imagine daily work with a server without reporting the capability. The console of ConfigMgr 1706 shows a lot more than what used to happen on ConfigMgr 2007; however, it would still be difficult to operate with reports.

Reports have data that's useful not just for administrators or server operators; often, default reports and reports created by administrators, in particular, are shared with other employees. This is possible thanks to the option of providing permissions for reading reports for Active Directory users or groups.

To install a role, the administrator should choose between **Add Site System Roles** or **Create Site System Server** option and then select **Reporting service point** as the desired role.

Information needed for the **Reporting service point** role installation is as follows:

- The name of the SQL Server
- The name of the ConfigMgr database for which **Reporting service point** is installed
- The folder name in which reports will be configured
- The instance of Reporting Services
- The username with permissions for Reporting service point installation

The **Verify** option helps in data validation, telling the administrator if all given pieces of information are correct and all components are accessible:

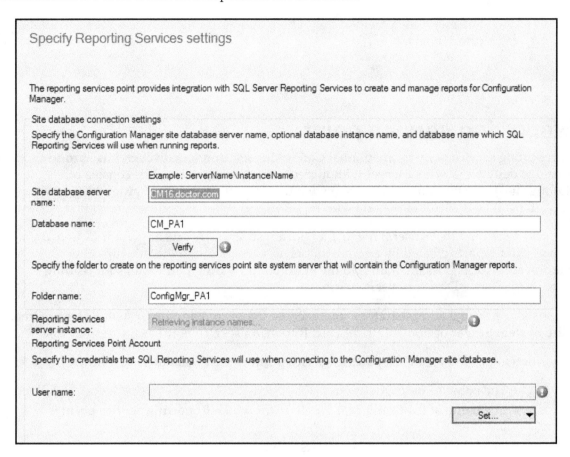

Reporting service point installation

After having all the data validated, the next step is the actual installation of the role:

Specify Reporting Services settings

The reporting services point provides integration with SQL Server Reporting Services to create and manage reports for Configuration Manager.

Site database connection settings

Specify the Configuration Manager site database server name, optional database instance name, and database name which SQL Reporting Services will use when running reports.

Example: ServerName\InstanceName

Site database server name: `CM16.doctor.com`

Database name: `CM_PA1`

Verify   Successfully verified.

Specify the folder to create on the reporting services point site system server that will contain the Configuration Manager reports.

Folder name: `ConfigMgr_PA1`

Reporting Services server instance: `MSSQLSERVER`

Reporting Services Point Account

Specify the credentials that SQL Reporting Services will use when connecting to the Configuration Manager site database.

User name: `DOCTOR\Administrator`

Set...

Settings for Reporting service point after validating data

The actual installation shouldn't take long. If the reporting services has been installed correctly, validation can be done by opening any report. Report accessibility on the ConfigMgr server console means that the installation of the Reporting service point role was completed successfully. All the reports are available in the `Monitoring\Reporting\Reports` tab. To verify a successful installation, any report should be run and checked for whether it contains any data.

When running reports with large amounts of data, in cases where the SQL Server shares the same machine with the ConfigMgr server, it might significantly degrade the performance of the ConfigMgr server. Separating Reporting Services is always worth considering.

Application Catalog

In version 2007, ConfigMgr server was granting permissions to users to install software based on collections. Starting with version 2012, this ability has been developed and has improved. Users can now install an application assigned to them using the server role called **Application Catalog**. It is an optional role; however, the implementation of the mechanism for application assignment management is important for company management. Therefore, this role--despite being optional--is automatically installed during each ConfigMgr server deployment.

To install a role, the administrator needs to choose **Add Site System Roles** or **Create Site System Server** to run the wizard; next, it chooses the desired role, which will be **Application Catalog web service point** and **Application Catalog website point**.

First, settings that need to be configured are for the **Application Catalog website point**. Usually, the protocol needs to be changed from **HTTP** to **HTTPS**:

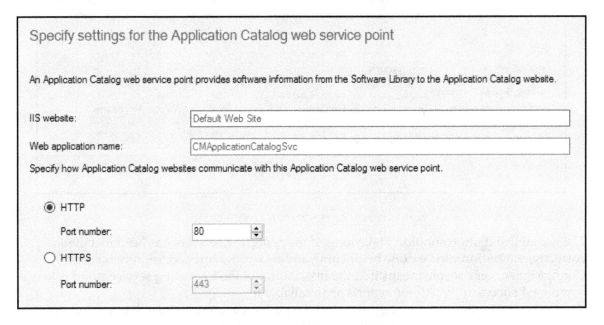

Application Catalog web service point settings.

The next step is to configure the settings of the **Application Catalog website point**. Here, similarly to the previous step, the **HTTP** protocol needs to be changed to **HTTPS**:

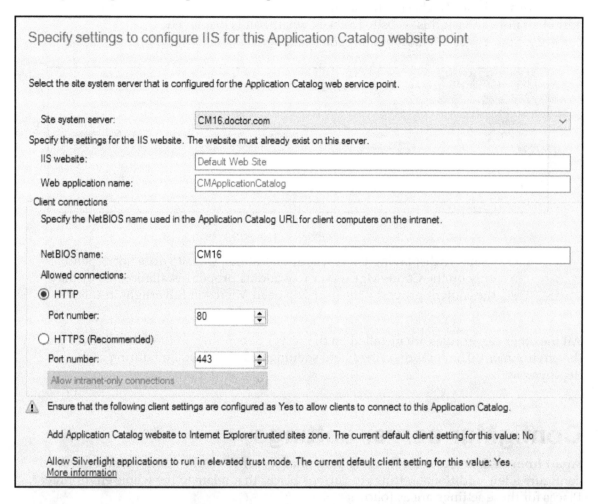

Specify settings to configure IIS for this Application Catalog website point

Select the site system server that is configured for the Application Catalog web service point.

| Site system server: | CM16.doctor.com |

Specify the settings for the IIS website. The website must already exist on this server.

| IIS website: | Default Web Site |
| Web application name: | CMApplicationCatalog |

Client connections

Specify the NetBIOS name used in the Application Catalog URL for client computers on the intranet.

| NetBIOS name: | CM16 |

Allowed connections:

◉ HTTP

| Port number: | 80 |

○ HTTPS (Recommended)

| Port number: | 443 |

Allow intranet-only connections

⚠ Ensure that the following client settings are configured as Yes to allow clients to connect to this Application Catalog.

Add Application Catalog website to Internet Explorer trusted sites zone. The current default client setting for this value: No

Allow Silverlight applications to run in elevated trust mode. The current default client setting for this value: Yes.
More information

Application Catalog website point settings

ConfigMgr cannot work with more than one Application Catalog role. It is acceptable to install one Application Catalog in the LAN network while having the second one in the DMZ zone for external clients. HTTP/HTTPS settings might differ for these two configurations.

The last step in configuring this role, before the installation, is setting up a name under which it will be published for the users in the Application Catalog, as well as the theme color of this website. To check whether the role has been installed correctly, the administrator can visit this website to check whether it is displayed correctly: `http://cm16/CMApplicationCatalog`:

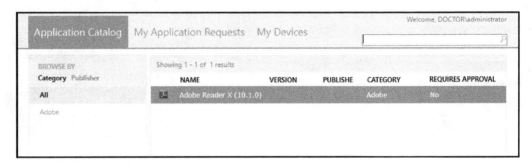

Application Catalog website with apps assigned to the user

 TIP

Properly displaying the Application Catalog website does not depend only on the ConfigMgr server role and its proper installation. To display the content properly, the user will need Microsoft Silverlight installed.

All the other server roles are installed on the server depending on the role they will play in the environment. The roles described here should always be installed during each deployment.

ConfigMgr server settings

Apart from installing and configuring particular server roles, the administrator needs to configure a few additional settings in various places that relate to the whole environment. Places for these settings are as follows:

- **Hierarchy site settings**: The place to configure settings related to hierarchy. These settings need to be configured even when the environment is contained from one primary site server.
- **Primary site settings**: The place to configure settings for a single primary site server.

The settings that are about to be discussed are important, not only from the functional point of view, but they also play important role in securing the system.

Hierarchy site settings

Settings for the hierarchy are placed under the `Administration\Site Configuration\Sites` tab. After choosing the site, the administrator needs to choose **Hierarchy Settings**. The **General** tab is used for setting up the way clients will cooperate with management points. The **Use a fallback site** option means that clients might automatically switch to another site if theirs is unavailable. The **Clients prefer to use management points specified in boundary groups** option means that clients will be using the preferred management point. The **Consent to use Pre-Release features** option means that, when installing a new version of ConfigMgr or installing upgrades, new features will be enabled by default, even if these features are still in the testing phase by Microsoft:

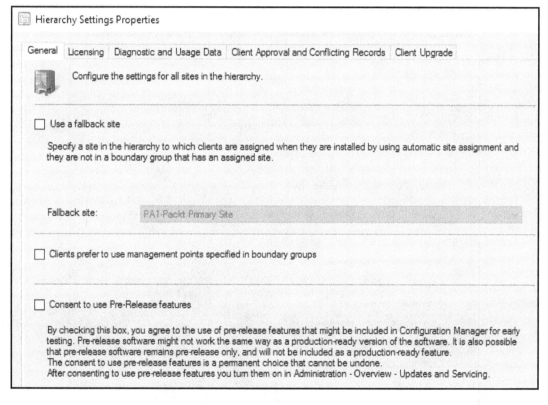

Settings for hierarchy

The **Licensing** tab provides the option of setting dates when Software Assurance is bought. Until the date is reached, the server will automatically check for any new version or updates and download them.

The **Client Approval and Conflicting Records** tab is very important for security reasons and computers managed by ConfigMgr clients. By default, if the client is in the same domain as the server, it connects to it automatically and will be managed. Client approval methods set up a way in which clients will be accepted by the server. The safest and most restrictive way is to set the manual acceptance method by an administrator. Until the administrator accepts a new client, communication will not be possible. The **Conflicting client records** is about published duplicated entries about the same ConfigMgr client.

The most secure as well as the most restrictive way is to set the acceptance to be performed manually by server administrators. Until administrators accept the client, it will not be able to communicate and be managed by the server. The **Conflicting client records** options are related to managing duplicated entries of the same client; these conflicts can be resolved by the server or by the administrator using the console.

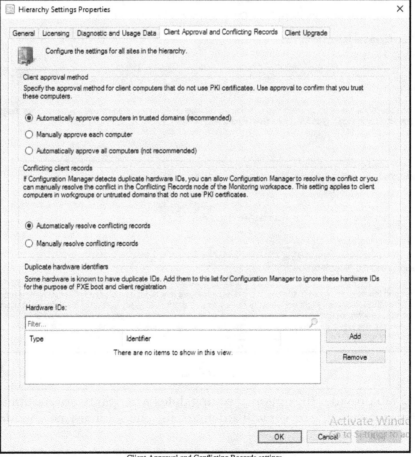

Client Approval and Conflicting Records settings

The last tab in the hierarchy settings is **Client Upgrade**. After installing new upgrades to the server or installing a new version, there is a need to install a new version of the client. This can be achieved in two ways, manually or automatically, after setting the proper configuration on the server. By default, the server does not install new client versions automatically. This kind of deployment needs to be prepared by the administrator. Settings for automatic deployment of the clients are under the **Client Upgrade** tab.

The **Upgrade all clients in the hierarchy using production client** option enables the automatic upgrade of all clients in the hierarchy. **Upgrade all clients in the pre-production collection automatically using pre-production client** enables the installation of new client versions on an endpoint based on a particular collection. The **Exclude specified clients from upgrade** option allows you to exclude specific computers from automatic settings. **Automatically distribute client installation package to distribution points that are enabled for prestaged content** allows you to send a package to the endpoint and the installation of the client even if the distribution point works in a prestaged mode. When installing a new client version, it is good to consider installing it first on the pilot group, and later--if the pilot was successful--deploy this new version to production:

Hierarchy Settings Properties   ✕

| General | Licensing | Diagnostic and Usage Data | Client Approval and Conflicting Records | Client Upgrade |

Configure settings that control how clients automatically upgrade.

Production client version: 5.00.8498.1711
Last modified: 6/25/2017 11:19:54 PM

☐ Upgrade all clients in the hierarchy using production client

    ☐ Do not upgrade servers

    Automatically upgrade clients within days: 7 ▲▼

Pre-production client version: 5.00.8498.1711
Last modified: 6/25/2017 11:19:27 PM

☐ Upgrade all clients in the pre-production collection automatically using pre-production client

    Pre-production collection :

    [   ]   Browse...

You can promote the pre-production client from Monitoring > Client Status > Pre-production Client Deployment.

☐ Exclude specified clients from upgrade

    Exclusion collection :

    [   ]   Browse...

These clients will not be upgraded via any method such as automatic upgrade or software update-based upgrade.

Client deployment status can be monitored in console and using reports.

ⓘ   Applied to Windows operating systems only. You can download clients for additional operating systems from the Microsoft Download Center.

☐ Automatically distribute client installation package to distribution points that are enabled for prestaged content

Activate Windo

[OK   ]   [Cancel   ]

Client Upgrade settings

Remember that **Hierarchy Settings** work for a single primary site server as well as for the whole hierarchy if these are configured on a central administration site server.

Primary site settings

Primary site settings are settings for a particular ConfigMgr site. The settings are located under the `Administration\Site Configuration\Sites` tab; to view them, the administrator needs to pick the site and then choose **Properties**. The **Client Computer Communication** tab is used to configure a protocol that will be used for communication between the server and clients. By default, it is HTTP:

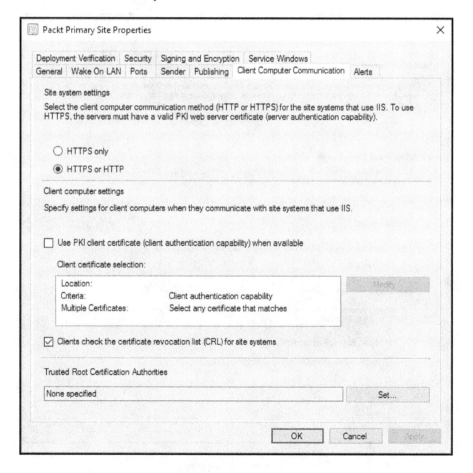

ConfigMgr communication protocol settings

The **Publishing** tab is used to check whether the server automatically publishes information about the management point in DNS. By default, this option is turned on, and it's better not to turn it off. Having it on will let clients find management point more easily.

The **Deployment Verification** tab lets us configure very useful settings for the server. ConfigMgr is a very useful and a powerful tool, but, if badly administrated, it may cause some real harm, especially when talking about operating system deployment. That is why the previously mentioned tab is so important. In the **Collection size limits** tab, the **Default size** option sets the limit for a collection beyond which the collection won't be visible when deploying operating systems. **Always hide collections that have more members than the maximum size** sets the maximum limit of the collection, beyond which it will be hidden. The **Collections with site system servers** option forbids you from deploying the operating system if at least one endpoint is a server:

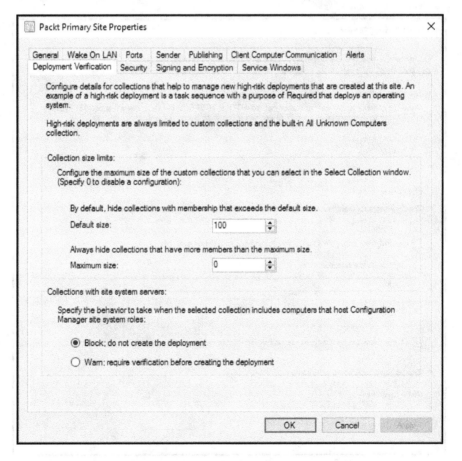

Deployment Verification settings

Deploying operating systems using ConfigMgr is one of the most dangerous server features. It is recommended that you perform all operations with due diligence.

Discovery Methods

All operations that clients perform are assigned to a collection. A collection is nothing but a set of objects (devices, computers, AD groups, and AD users) meeting the configured requirements. To use these objects to create a collection, the administrator first needs to create these from the console or configure the server in such a way that it will find the endpoints and save them in the database.

The database of the ConfigMgr server has nothing in common with the AD database. If an object is deleted in the ConfigMgr console, it will still remain in the AD database.

After installing the server, in the console, under `Assets and Compliance\Devices`, only devices with a ConfigMgr server role are visible. `Assets and Compliance\Users`, also, won't contain any objects.

The ConfigMgr server discovers objects based on built-in methods. Related to types of Active Directory, Heartbeat Discovery and Network Discovery. Heartbeat Discovery works a bit differently to other methods because it is the ConfigMgr client that sends information and updates about the system it works on. All the other methods are managed and run by the ConfigMgr server.

The following is a list of all the available methods:

- **Active Directory Forest Discovery**: Discovers the forest and all domains in the forest AD locations and sub-networks assigned to locations. It has the ability to publish information about the ConfigMgr server in the AD. It's turned off by default.
- **Active Directory Group Discovery**: Discovers AD security groups and basic information about these groups. It's turned off by default.
- **Active Directory System Discovery**: Discovers AD computer accounts and basic information about these accounts. It's turned off by default.
- **Active Directory User Discovery**: Discovers AD user accounts and basic information about these accounts. It's turned off by default.

- **Heartbeat Discovery**: According to a certain schedule, clients send information about the endpoint on which they are installed along with some basic information about this endpoint. Based on this, ConfigMgr can recognize that these clients are active. It's turned on by default.
- **Network Discovery**: Discovers devices in the network by the IP address and saves them in the database. As this method is rarely used, we won't focus on it in this book. It's turned off by default.

Active Directory Discovery Methods

Discovery Methods related to Active Directory have a common configuration set. All of these have the following settings:

- **Polling Schedule**: This sets the schedule that tells how often objects discovery should be performed
- **Active Directory Attributes**: This sets additional AD object attributes that will be saved in the ConfigMgr database

The **Polling Schedule** tab is used to set the schedule of the Active Directory discovery; there might be a different schedule for each and every AD object type. By default, the **Enable delta discovery** option is enabled; it means that the ConfigMgr server in a given schedule goes through AD and saves information about the objects it already knows, only for the attributes that it has changed:

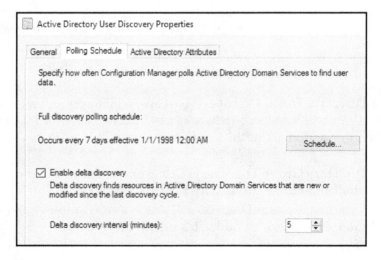

Active Directory scanning schedule setting

The **Active Directory Attributes** tab helps set additional AD object attributes that will be saved in the ConfigMgr data, apart from the ones saved by default:

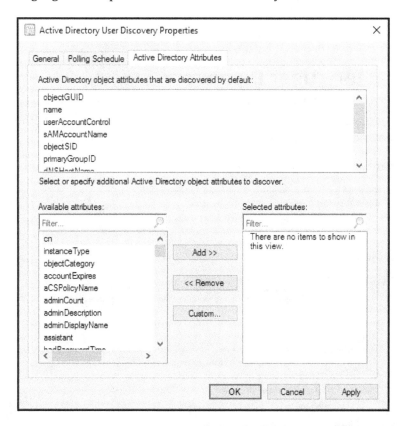

Active Directory Attributes settings

All remaining settings are different for each type of Active Directory object discovery.

Active Directory Forest Discovery

The **Active Directory Forest Discovery** method was introduced in ConfigMgr 2012. This method discovers the domain forest, all domains in this forest, AD locations, and sub-networks assigned to this location. After discovering these objects, the server might automatically create boundaries. It is possible to create a schedule of how often such discovery will be performed, so, if there were some changes in the environment, they would be included in the next scheduled discovery cycle.

Apart from discovering data, this method also has the ability to publish AD information for clients to let them find an assigned management point or distribution point. This capability is very useful if the ConfigMgr server manages clients from many different domains and AD forests--especially those that are not trusted.

Active Directory User Discovery

The **Active Directory User Discovery** method can discover Active Directory user accounts along with the set of attributes. The **General** tab is used to turn on the method as well as to set where--for instance in which OU--the server will discover objects.

The administrator can point to the whole domain, a certain OUs, or a couple of them:

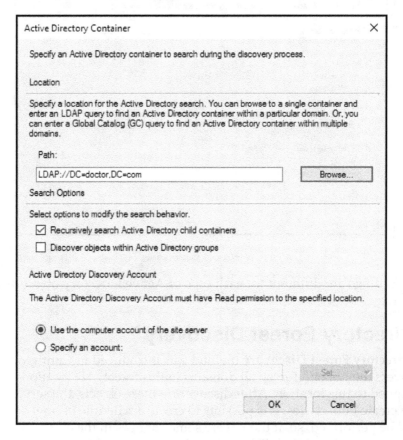

Active Directory Container settings

After configuring discovery, proper configuration can be confirmed by looking at the `adusrdis.log` log placed in the `C:\Program file\Microsoft Configuration Manager\Logs` folder. Immediately after objects are discovered, these should be visible on the console in `Assets and Compliance\Users`.

Active Directory User Discovery disregards disabled AD accounts; these accounts will not be saved in the ConfigMgr database.

Active Directory System Discovery

The **Active Directory System Discovery** method allows you to discover computer accounts in the Active Directory similarly to the previously described method; also, a scheduler needs to be set along with a location where objects will be searched. If the administrator would like to use this method, it needs to be turned on in the **General** tab.

The ConfigMgr server does not check whether the discovered object actually exists in the network. It just pools an AD controller for objects and attributes.

It is possible to specify the whole domain, a particular OU, or a couple of OUs.

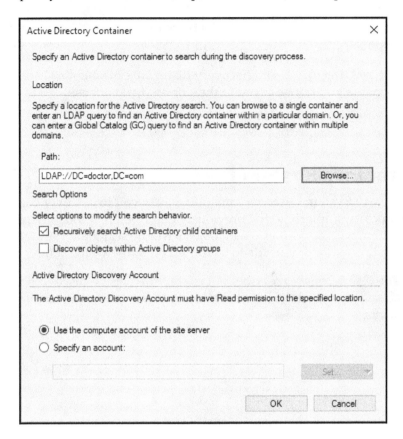

Starting from ConfigMgr 2012, some very important and useful sets of settings were introduced. The ConfigMgr database will save only those objects in the database that are actually used by users. In versions prior to 2012, the server was skipping objects that were turned off, but all other objects were saved in the database.

In the **Options** tab, it is possible to specify additional attributes and their values that need to be met to add an endpoint to the ConfigMgr database:

- The **Only discover computers that have logged on to a domain in a given period of time** option specifies the time span after which--if the endpoint hasn't logged in the meantime into a domain--a particular endpoint won't be added to the ConfigMgr database.

- The **Only discover computers that have updated their computer account password in a given period of time** option specifies the time span after which--if the endpoint hasn't changed the domain password in the meantime--a particular endpoint won't be added to the ConfigMgr database.

If both of these options are selected, then only endpoints that meet both requirements will be added to the ConfigMgr database:

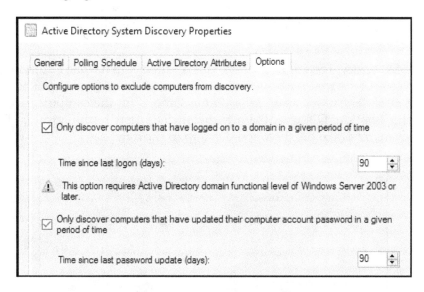

Options--Active Directory System Discovery settings

The same settings as for the **Active Directory System Discovery** apply to the **Active Directory Group Discovery** method. After its configuration is finished, the proper work can be checked in the `adsysdis.log` log file, placed under `C:\Program file\Microsoft Configuration Manager\Logs`. Immediately after new objects are discovered by the server, they are visible in the console under `Assets and Compliance\Devices`.

Active Directory System Discovery skips disabled computer accounts; hence, these objects won't be added to the ConfigMgr database.

Active Directory Group Discovery

The **Active Directory Group Discovery** method discovers security groups in the Active Directory. As with other methods, it is possible to set a schedule and a place where the ConfigMgr server will be looking for objects. In the case of this method, the way of identifying the lookup location is a bit different--in the General tab after clicking **Add administrator** can specify a group which will be searched or a location which will have a wider discovery scope. ConfigMgr might look for a certain place using the **Locations** option or some other groups using the **Groups** option; it is also possible to combine these two options.

As with **Active Directory System Discovery**, this method also has the additional ability of filtering by the conditions that the objects need to meet in order for them to be saved in the ConfigMgr database. The first two options are the same as for the computer accounts, and there is also a third option: **Discover the membership of distribution groups**. The third option also adds members of the discovered group to the database:

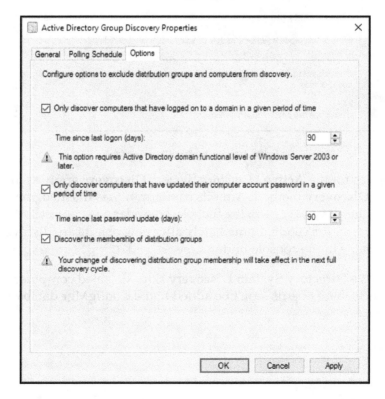

Active Directory Groups Discovery settings

To confirm that discovery is working as expected, the administrator can examine the `adsgdis.log` log file, located under `C:\Program file\Microsoft Configuration Manager\Logs`. Immediately after new objects are discovered by the server, they are visible in the console under `Assets and Compliance\Devices`.

Heartbeat Discovery

Heartbeat Discovery is a slightly different method compared to others. For all those managed by the server, it is a server that does all the queries and discovery in accordance with the settings. For **Heartbeat Discovery**, only the schedule can be set, and clients are the ones who--according to the schedule--send data to the server about them and their operating system state.

 Despite it being possible, **Heartbeat Discovery** should never be turned off. Turning it off will result in the absence of updates about clients and their operating systems.

Boundary and boundary groups

Boundaries and **Boundary groups** are very important configuration elements, as misconfiguration in this field will result in a lack of communication between clients and the server and the impossibility of deploying new clients. This part of configuration retains the same set of settings as it used in ConfigMgr 2007, with just one significant difference. Starting from ConfigMgr 1706, just after the server is installed, the default boundary group for ConfigMgr site is created. Each site has defined its own default boundary group.

In the case of a small deployment, or deployments with only one site, all clients can use only one boundary group. In the case of a larger number of endpoints or many locations, additional boundary groups will be configured to manage access to shares and client-server communication in a well-controlled manner.

The main objective of boundary groups is to tell clients about the server to which they have been assigned. Apart from that, they help in finding other assigned services/servers, such as the following:

- Distribution point for content location
- Software update point

- State migration point
- Preferred management point

The boundary group to which clients have been assigned is called **current boundary group**. The client always tries to use the site system server to which it has been assigned by the current boundary group. If it is possible, it will try to use the process called **fallback**.

If the administrator assigns many site systems to many boundary groups, this will provide an HA solution in case any of them are not accessible. For each boundary group, the administrator can create a one-way link to the other boundary group; this kind of link is called a **relationship**. A boundary group assigned to a current boundary group is called a **neighbor**. Each of the boundary groups might have many different **relationships**.

If servers in the current site system are not available, clients will try to communicate with these in neighbor boundary groups. This process is called fallback. The relationship can be configured in the **Relationships** tab, separately for each boundary group. When configuring a boundary group, the administrator can decide whether to allow a fallback mechanism or not.

Each boundary group created by an administrator has configured an implied link to `default-site-boundary-group`. That link has the default fallback set to **120** minutes. Clients who haven't been assigned to a boundary group always use `default-site-boundary-group` to identify servers they need to cooperate with.

Boundaries, on the other hand, are used to specify what IP addresses need to be managed by a particular ConfigMgr server, and by assigning them to the boundary group administrator, they specify which management point or distribution point is assigned to clients.

Configuring boundaries

When preparing for the creation of boundaries, the administrator needs to know in which way it needs to determine IP scopes that would be assigned to the boundary. There are a couple of boundary types, and each and every type has some advantages as well as some disadvantages.

After being assigned to a boundary group, the ConfigMgr client knows with which management point and distribution point it will cooperate. The following types of boundaries are available:

- **IP subnet**: This is a boundary defined with a subnet. It's easy in configuration, but if the network administrator changes IP addressing--it also brings changes to client assignment in ConfigMgr for the management point or distribution point. Additionally, ConfigMgr does not support some subnet types such as *supernet networks*.
- **Active Directory site**: This is the boundary defined by affiliation to the AD location. It has easy configuration, and its disadvantage is the same as that for IP subnets.
- **IPv6 prefix**: The boundary is defined based on the IPv6 prefix.
- **IP address range**: The boundary is defined based on IP address ranges. It's the most time consuming, but at the same time, it's the most precise as well.

It is possible to use all types of boundaries at once as well as using only one type--it is an individual case and very much associated with the environment where the deployment takes place.

In the majority of ConfigMgr deployments, the IP range method is used. This method is more time consuming than the others, but using it helps tell very precisely which IP address will be managed by which ConfigMgr server.

If the AD schema is extended when installing the ConfigMgr server, then the System Management container will store information about the following:

- Information about which servers have a management point role installed
- Information about the available domain/forest/sites for ConfigMgr
- Ports used for client-to-server communication
- Information about content deployment

Proper configuration of boundaries and boundary groups requires cooperation between AD and network administrators, especially if boundary ranges are set by a method other than the IP range.

In case clients are not doing their tasks or are facing communication issues and if the information stored in System Management was not deleted or changed/updated as an outcome of environment configuration changes, it is good to start troubleshooting from the boundaries configuration.

Manually created boundaries

Proper boundary configuration needs to be in place to ensure that clients can discover a management point, distribution point, or software update point correctly. Boundary creation is available under `Administration\Hierarchy Configuration\Boundaries`. In the **General** tab, the administrator selects the type of created boundary as well as filling in its **Description**. After choosing the right type, the administrator needs to specify the range accordingly:

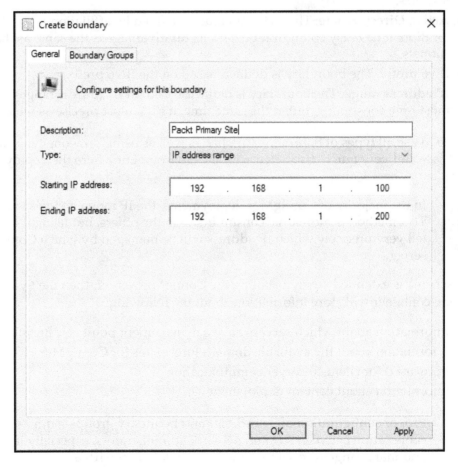

Setting up a boundary with an IP range.

In the **Boundary Groups** tab, the administrator can add boundary to boundary groups. This can also be done when creating a boundary group initially.

Even when there are a few ConfigMgr servers connected in one structure, they do not share information about the created boundaries on them. Because of this, it is not hard to set the same boundaries on two different servers, which will certainly cause clients to work incorrectly.

Automatically created boundaries

By turning on **Active Directory Forest Discovery**, boundaries will be created automatically by the ConfigMgr server. It scans AD, and, based on that, it creates the boundaries as well as updates them when a change is acknowledged. There are no differences between them, and these are created manually by an administrator; after boundaries are created, they need to be added to appropriate boundary groups.

Configuring boundary groups

After creating boundaries, the next step is creating boundary groups. Boundary groups are used to point the clients to their assigned management point, distribution point, and software update point.

There might be more than one boundary assigned to a boundary group. ConfigMgr 1706 introduces a new boundary group type: `Site-Default-Boundary-Group<site code>`. It is automatically created when a server is installed. When no boundary group is created, all boundaries are assigned to the default boundary group. For this reason, for this group, a management point, distribution point, and software update point should be assigned.

Default boundary group

For each ConfigMgr site, during installation, there is a default boundary group created: `Site-Default-Boundary-Group<site code>` and a management point and distribution point should also be assigned to it. As mentioned, when clients are in a boundary that is not assigned to any boundary group, it will allow them to connect to the ConfigMgr server.

Here is an example configuration of a ConfigMgr site with one default boundary group and three boundary groups created by administrators. For each additional boundary group, a distribution point has been assigned, including the default:

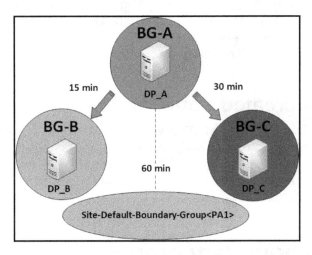

Communication between boundary groups

In this configuration, these are the points to remember:

- The client in the current boundary group (**BG-A**) will try to communicate with server distribution point (**DP_A**) from its own boundary group.
- If communication fails, after **15 min**--according to the set relationship--it will add distribution point from boundary group (**BG-B**) to the list of distribution points, and every 2 minutes, it will try to communicate with both distribution points (**DP_A**, **DP_B**).
- If there are issues still, after **30 min**, it will add a distribution point from boundary group (**BG-C**). Every 2 min, it will now try to communicate with three distribution points from the list (**DP_A**, **DP_B**, **DP_C**).
- Finally, if there is still no distribution point available, after the next **60 min**, the client will add a distribution point for the default boundary group to the list, under the condition that the fallback option is enabled.

In the **General** tab, the administrator can check what boundaries are assigned to a boundary group. The **References** tab allows you to add the site systems that are related to it. The **Use this boundary group for site assignment** option is always turned on for the default boundary group, which means that all endpoints within this boundary will be assigned to this site:

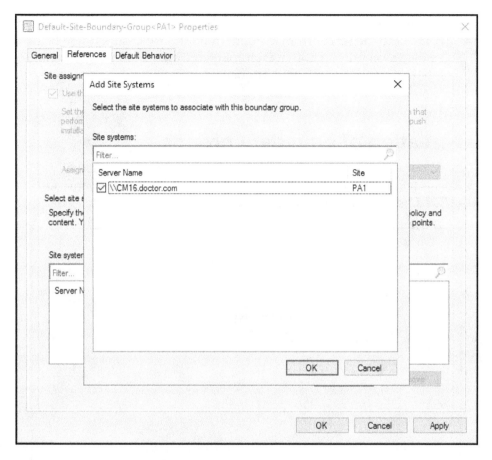

Adding site system server to the default boundary group

In the **Default Behavior** tab, the administrator can decide whether to allow fallback for the distribution point or management point and change the default fallback time.

By configuring many different boundary groups and connections between them, it is possible to decide precisely where a particular client will be looking for a distribution point or management point.

To enable a client to connect to a distribution point outside of the assigned boundary group, **Allow clients to use a fallback source location for content** needs to be enabled. If this option is disabled, clients not in a particular boundary will not connect to its distribution point.

If there is no boundary group created by administrators, clients will try to connect to the server from the default boundary group. It will be possible under the condition that in **Hierarchy Settings**, under the **General** tab, **Use a fallback site** will be enabled, and will point to the particular ConfigMgr site.

Manual creation of boundary groups

The creation of boundary groups is done from `Administration\Hierarchy Configuration\Boundary Groups`. In the **General** tab, the administrator adds the previously created boundaries, and more than one boundary can be added here:

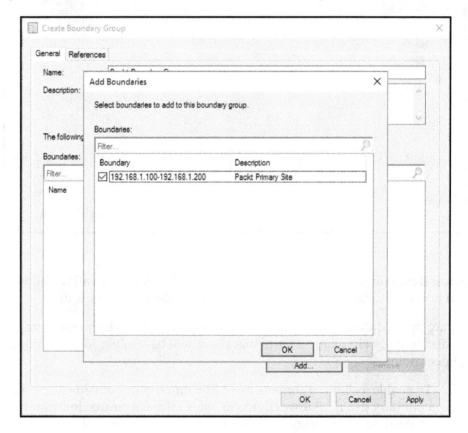

Adding boundaries to boundary group

In the **References** tab, the administrator adds the site system server that will be assigned to this boundary group; the administrator can select more than one site system.

After creating a boundary group, it is possible to change its settings in the **Relationships** tab by assigning a proper boundary. This is also the place where the administrator can enable fallback and change its time to wait; this setting can be provided separately for a **Distribution Point** and **Software Update Point**:

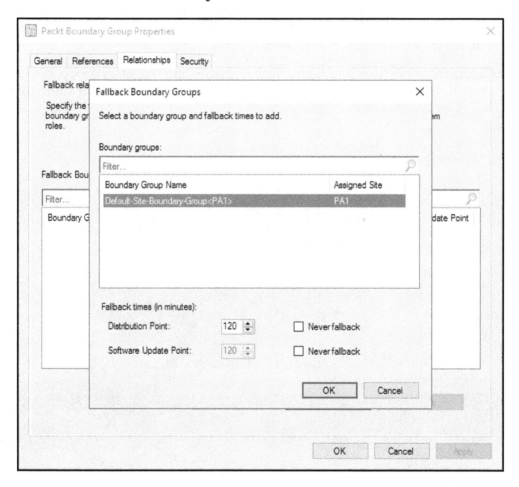

Fallback configuration for boundary group

Summary

This chapter covered topics such as ConfigMgr server role types and installation modes on ConfigMgr server roles. You could also learn about the server roles installed and configured for the ConfigMgr server, as well as the installation and configuration of basic server role essentials in each ConfigMgr deployment.

The chapter also covered topics related to the boundary and boundary groups such as boundary types and their role in the ConfigMgr environment and boundary groups types and their role in the ConfigMgr environment.

After installing the server and configuring its boundaries and boundary group, the next step is to install clients on operating systems that should be managed by the ConfigMgr server.

4

Configuration Manager Agent Installation

Previous chapters described the fundamentals of ConfigMgr server installation and configuration. To manage endpoints in the environments, the ConfigMgr server needs to have the client installed on these computers. This chapter covers how to prepare the environment to install ConfigMgr clients.

The list of the environment prerequisites when planning to install clients is as follows:

- Client operating systems need to meet all the prerequisites
- An installation account or accounts in the Active Directory need to have local administrator permissions on endpoints
- An appropriate **Group Policy Object** (**GPO**) should be configured if the plan is to deploy clients via GPO
- Properly configured boundaries and boundary groups
- At least one installed and working management point
- Management points need to have at least one boundary assigned

The installation of ConfigMgr clients is not difficult. The most important factors are to understand the process and check whether the installation of the clients has been successful.

 It is considered that the client's installation has been completed successfully when the computer is able to communicate with the assigned management point, which means that the endpoint is manageable.

Operating systems requirements

As has been mentioned previously, the installation of the client is not a difficult task. However, for installation to go smoothly, it is important to know one important detail--an operating system on which the ConfigMgr client will work needs to meet some prerequisites regarding the installed software.

The client installer checks for all the prerequisites; if these are met, the installer starts its work.

Prerequisites for the operating system as follows:

- Windows Installer version 3.1.4000.2435
- BITS version 2.5 or higher
- Windows Update Agent version 7.0.6000.363
- Microsoft Remote Differential Compression

Components that--if missing--are installed by the ConfigMgr client installer are as follows:

- Microsoft Core XML Services version 6.20.5002 or higher
- Microsoft Visual C++ 2013 Redistributable version 12.0.21005.1
- Microsoft Policy Platform version 1.2.3514.0
- Microsoft Silverlight version 4.0.50524.0 or higher
- Microsoft .NET Framework 4 Client Profile

 If the operating system is missing at least one of these components, the installation will fail.

ConfigMgr client installation

The installation of the ConfigMgr client always include three steps regardless of the chosen method:

1. Check whether the operating system meets all the initial requirements as well as the additional software requirements.
2. The next step is the ConfigMgr client installation. *Step 1* and *step 2* are completely separate tasks performed during installation.

3. Then, we find the assigned management point, which is searched based on the information found in the Active Directory, or the information given in the installer using the SMSMP switch.

Client installation is triggered by the `ccmsetup.exe` or `ccmsetup.msi` file when using GPO.

The `ccmsetup.exe` file performs the first step of installation. If it completes successfully, then it runs `client.msi`, which performs the actual client installation.

Installation methods

The ConfigMgr server provides various client installation methods.

This book describes the most common methods, which are as follows:

- Client push installation performed automatically by the ConfigMgr server
- Manual installation triggered by the administrator from the server console
- Manual installation

Client push

The Client push installation is a very convenient method of deploying ConfigMgr clients. As it is an automatic installation, it is important to configure settings in order to avoid accidentally installing the client where it shouldn't or mustn't be installed.

Client push installation is not enabled by default; it has to be enabled manually. To configure it, the following actions need to be performed:

1. Enable client push installation.
2. Configure installation accounts for the ConfigMgr server.
3. Configure GPO for endpoints.

GPO should enable two firewall exceptions to be configured--**File and Print Sharing** and **Windows Management Instrumentation (WMI)**.

Client push settings are located in the console under the `Administration\Site Configuration\Sites` tab and later **Client Installation Settings | Client Push Installation**. In the **General** tab, installation should be enabled as well as being placed to indicate the endpoints on which the client should be installed. The available options are as follows:

- **Servers**: Server systems
- **Workstations**: Client workstations
- **Configuration Manager site system servers**: Server systems with at least one ConfigMgr server role installed

By default, the **Never install the Configuration Manager client on domain controllers unless specified in the Client Push Installation Wizard** option is turned on. Thanks to that, ConfigMgr clients will never be installed on the domain controller:

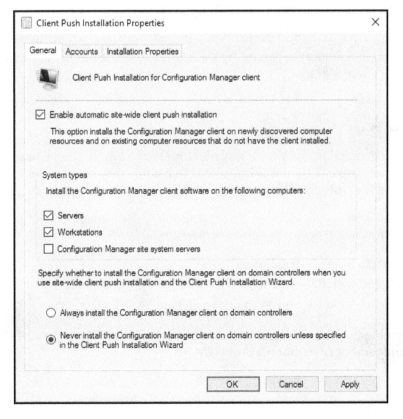

General client push installation settings

The **Accounts** tab has settings used to configure accounts used to install ConfigMgr clients on endpoints; there may be more than one account. The ConfigMgr server will try to connect to endpoints using given accounts, and it will use them one by one while trying to connect:

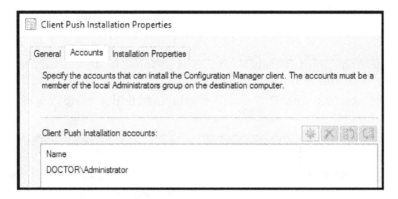

Accounts for client push installation

When providing credentials for installation accounts, these are not verified against domain controllers.

The **Installation Properties** tab is used to configure switches used for the installation. By default, there is only one switch here, `SMSISTECODE=<site name>`; in this example, it is `SMSSITECODCE=PA1`. It is always worth adding `SMSFPS=<Failback Status Point FQDN>`; in this example, it is `SMSFSP=CM16.DOCTOR.COM`. There are a lot of different switches used for client installation, but the two mentioned are the most important:

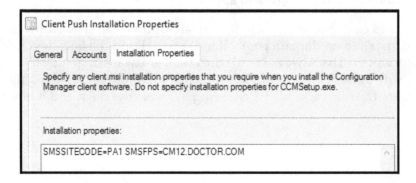

Installation Properties settings

After enabling client push installation, the ConfigMgr server starts installation of the clients according to the settings configured in **Discovery Methods** on endpoints that are still missing the client. It connects to the administrative share $ADMIN and copies the ccmsetup.exe file and runs it. This process can be monitored in the ccm.log log file, located in C:\Program files\Configuration Manager\Logs.

During client installation, the following server roles are leveraged:

- **Management point**: This is used by the installer to download the files needed for the prerequisites and the client itself
- **Fallback status point**: This discovers the installation status and saves it in the MS SQL database
- **Software update point**: This role is used if the client is installed by leveraging WSUS
- **Distribution point**: This is used by the client during client installation
- **Reporting service point**: This is used to generate the report

Client Push Installation settings work for the whole ConfigMgr site.

Installing from the console

Automatic client installation using client push is one of the available methods. Installation can also be triggered manually from the server console. To install a client, the administrator needs to highlight the endpoint (or endpoints) in the console and use the **Install Client** option--the client installation wizard will appear.

Installation settings can be configured in the **Install Options** tab. The **Allow the client software to be installed on domain controllers** option allows the installation of the client on a domain controller. The **Always install the client software** option installs the client even if it is already present in the endpoint--this method is often used to repair corrupted clients--it is one of the first methods when trying to repair the client and it often helps.

The **Install the client software from a specified site** option is always enabled. It is used to identify a site from which client installation will be performed:

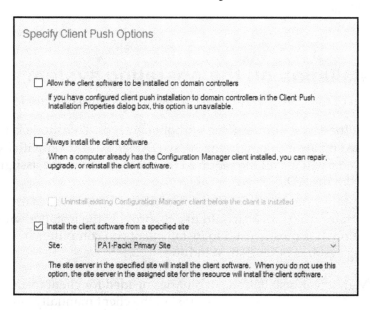

Install client options settings

The outcome of the wizard or client push installation can be viewed in the `ccm.log` file:

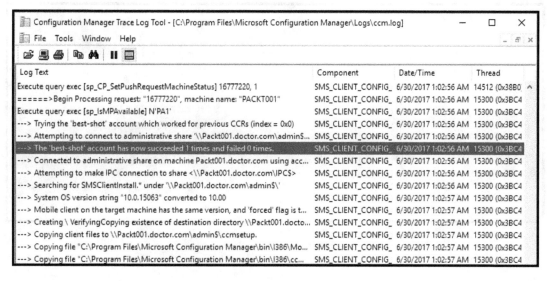

Outcome of client install wizard

If the ConfigMgr server cannot connect or find an endpoint in which the client needs to be installed, it will try to connect to it every hour for the next 7 days.

Manual installation on the operating system

Manual installation of the ConfigMgr client can be divided into two modes:

- Running the `ccmsetup.exe` file without switches: This mode is used if the client is installed on an endpoint in the Active Directory domain with extended schema. The installer will get all the required information about the assigned ConfigMgr server from the AD.
- Running the `ccmsetup.exe` file with switches: This mode is used when the administrator needs to, or would like to, provide the installer with the required information. It is mostly used to install clients on computers in a workgroup and operating systems other than Windows.

After the ConfigMgr server installation, all binaries needed for client installation can be found under `\\cm16\SMA_PA1\Client`. To install the client manually, all the administrator needs to do is run `ccmsetup.exe` from this share, and copy the whole folder to the destination endpoint and run it from there:

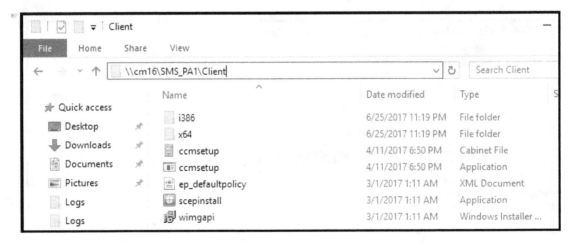

Folder with ConfigMgr client binaries

After running `ccmsetup.exe`, the installer copies the required files to `C:\windows\ccmsetup`. That folder remains unchanged for all Windows operating systems, servers, as well as clients:

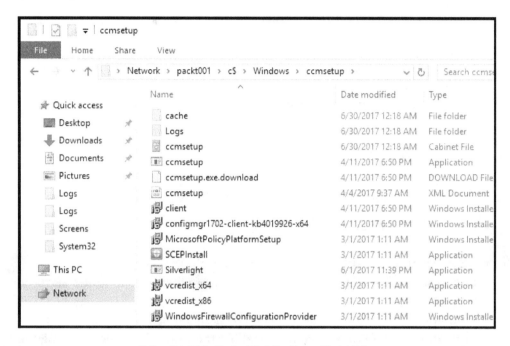

Folder with installation binaries of ConfigMgr client, used for installation

The `C:\windows\ccmsetup\logs` folder holds all logs related to client installation as well as installation of all the components needed for the client to work:

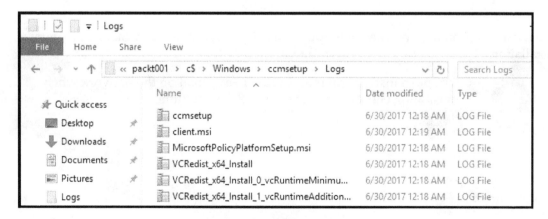

Folder with client installation logs

Client installation, depending on the speed of the client machine, can take up to 15 minutes. It might take a while for the client to find its server and connect to it.

By default, each client that works on the same domain, such as ConfigMgr, and is in the boundary accepted by the server, is approved to connect to it.

However, this behavior can be changed so that each new client would need to be approved for communication by an administrator in the ConfigMgr console, so if the administrator does not accept the endpoint, communication won't be available.

Other installation methods

There are a few more installation methods. Describing all of them is out of the scope of this book, so they will be mentioned briefly. These methods are a follows:

- **Group Policy**: Installation leveraging GPO and using `ccmsetup.msi` instead of `ccmsetup.exe`
- **Software update point**: Installation leveraging WSUS
- **Logon script**: Installation using a logon script when the computer starts and someone logs in
- **Upgrade**: Updating of already installed client using ConfigMgr server
- **Operating system deployment**: Installing the ConfigMgr client during the operating system deployment
- **Client Imaging**: Installation from a ready image with the ConfigMgr client embedded
- **Script**: Manual installation using the script

The most common methods are client push, installation from the console, and manual installation.

Client push installation might cause heavy load on the network when provisioning clients to many endpoints at one time.

ConfigMgr client installation checkout

During installation or after the client is installed, the administrator can check the status of the installation. As has been mentioned earlier, the installation process contains three steps. Steps 1 and 2 can be verified in log files under `C:\windows\ccmsetup\logs`. To verify that the third step, establishing communication with the server, was successful, the easiest way is to check it from the server console under `Administration\Device Collections\All Desktop and Server Clients`.

This collection contains all of the computers with the ConfigMgr client installed that have established connection and started to communicate:

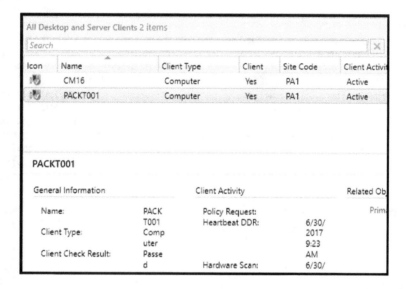

All Desktop and Server collection

Just after the installation, the client tries to find its ConfigMgr server and connect to it. Information about the discoveries clients have in finding their assigned systems, can be seen in two log files--`clientlocation.log` and `locationservices.log` located under `C:\windows\ccm\logs` on the client:

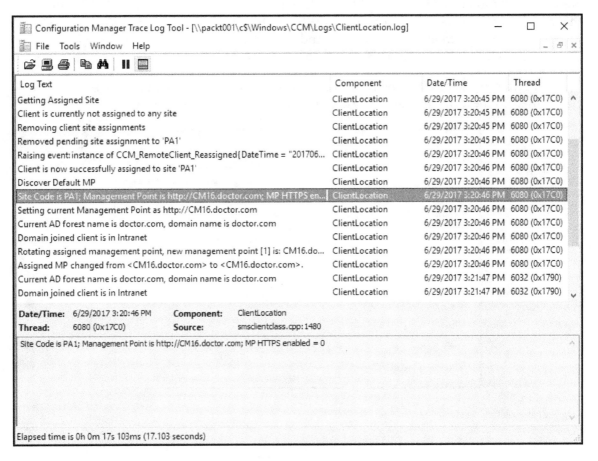

Information about the client finding the default management point

Each time the client gains information about the assigned management point server, it checks whether it is compatible. If the client has the same or a lower version than the discovered management point, it will try to connect to it. However, if the client version is higher than the version in the available management point, the client won't be able to communicate until both versions are the same. This process is called **compatibility check**:

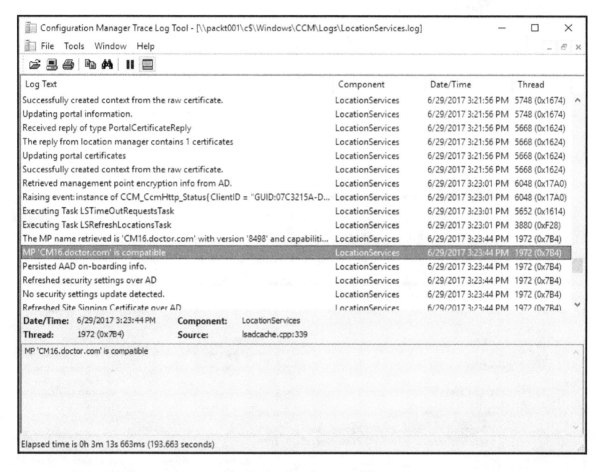

Information about client and server compatibility

After ensuring that the client has found its site and connected to it, the administrator can check whether the client sends data to the server. The administrator might also want to check whether the data from the hardware inventory and software inventory is collected and is properly visible from the console:

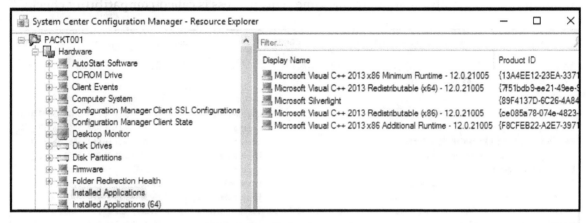

Outcome of hardware inventory task

Hardware inventory is enabled by default, so the first information about the inventory should be available in about 7 days starting from the installation date:

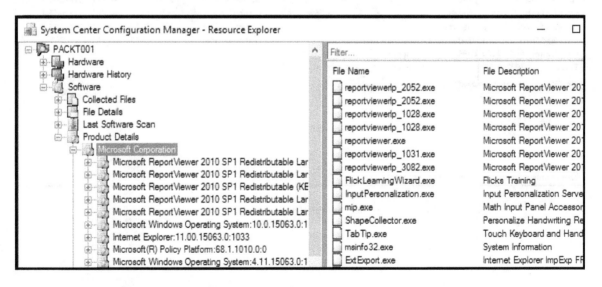

Outcome of software inventory task

The software inventory is disabled after installation by default, so the initial data appears as it is enabled in the console.

Troubleshooting client connectivity

The overall condition of the ConfigMgr server needs to be checked by the administrator on a daily basis. The same applies to the client side. There can be many reasons for the ConfigMgr client not establishing a connection. The most common reasons for such a situation are as follows:

- No boundary created
- No boundary group created
- Wrongly configured boundary or boundary groups
- No management point assigned to the boundary, boundary group, or default boundary group
- Changed AD location or network IP address
- Broken management point (operating system, IIS, corrupted files)
- No management point installed in a ConfigMgr site
- DNS errors
- A type in a switch when installing the client manually
- Deletion of the System Management container
- No access for the ConfigMgr server to a System Management container in order to save data
- The need for manual acceptance of clients from the console
- Blocking a computer on a console

> Server ConfigMgr and the client contain many components. The problem with the server or client can be due to various causes; hence, it is not feasible to even mention them all. Troubleshooting of client-server communication should always be started by checking boundaries and boundary group configuration.

Summary

This chapter covered topics such as the ConfigMgr client installation process and ConfigMgr client installation types. To properly maintain the installation process, the chapter also covered topics related to how to check whether the ConfigMgr client has been properly installed, and what the most common issues related to client-server communication are.

After client installation is complete and a proper final check has been conducted, it is important to configure what these clients will do, and when. This part is covered in the next chapter.

5
Creating Client Settings for Servers and Workstations

Previous chapters walked you through server installation and its basic configuration, as well as the installation of the client. The focal point of this chapter is the configuration of clients.

We will cover the following topics:

- Configuring client settings
- Deploying custom configuration to different collections
- Creating a maintenance window for each important collection

Client settings

Until version 2007, ConfigMgr was not supporting different settings for different computer collections of users. All of the settings were exactly the same for all of the clients assigned to a particular ConfigMgr site. Starting from version 2012, it has become possible to create your own set of settings and assign it to a certain collection. Thanks to this solution, there is no need to keep a few ConfigMgr servers, as it was once the only option to separate the scope of settings. This provides the ability to swiftly manage servers that are on one ConfigMgr server and have configurations different from each other.

Client settings are used for the following:

- Enabling various settings for different collections of computers or users (for instance, a different time for clients to pull policies)
- Enabling/disabling server features for different computer or user collections (such as software updates)

Creating your own configurations is not a hard task. In ConfigMgr 1706, it is possible to see all effective client or user configurations that have been set on an object. This possibility of viewing the permissions greatly eases administration and troubleshooting.

Default Client Settings

After the server is installed, there is already an available default configuration for computers and users. The administrator might continue using the default one or configure their own settings.

Default Client Settings can be found under `Administration\Client Settings`. This book will cover the most important options. Some of the additional options will be covered in future chapters. Here are the most important settings for every deployment:

- **Client Policy**:
    - **Client policy polling interval (minutes)**: By default, the client connects to the server every `60` minutes and downloads policies telling what, when, and how it ought to perform
- **Computer Agent**:
    - **Add default Application Catalog website to Internet Explorer trusted sites zone: Yes**
    - **Install permission: All users**
    - **Show notifications for a new deployment: Yes**
- **Hardware Inventory**:
    - **Enable hardware inventory on clients: Yes**
    - **Hardware inventory schedule**: A schedule that informs how often the client will be scanned regarding the hardware
    - **Hardware inventory classes**: The scope of data that will be collected by the Hardware Inventory

- **Software Inventory**:
    - **Enable software inventory on clients**: **Yes**.
    - **Schedule software inventory and file collection**: A schedule that informs how often the client will be scanned regarding the software.
    - **Inventory reporting detail**: Yes, **Software Inventory** will contain the exact data about the detected files.
    - **Inventory these files types**: This specifies which file types will be inventoried. The overall condition of the ConfigMgr server needs to be checked by the administrator on a daily basis.
- **Remote Tools**:
    - **Enable Remote Control on clients**: Yes
    - **Firewall exception profiles**: The firewall profiles on which **Remote Tools** will work
    - **Prompt user for Remote Control permission**: Yes; a user would need to explicitly confirm that he/she allows access to the workstation using **Remote Control**
    - **Grant Remote Control permission to local Administrators group**: **Yes**
    - **Permitted viewers of Remote Control and Remote Assistance**: A list with objects allowed to connect to the client using **Remote Control** or **Remote Assistance**
- **Software Updates**:
    - **Enable software updates on clients**: **Yes**
    - **Software update scan schedule**: A scheduled software update scan
    - **Enable management of the Office 365 Client Agent**: **Yes**

Of course, there are many more settings, but the ones pointed out here are the most important and fundamental. Include them all; exposing dependencies between them is out of the scope of this book.

Creating custom settings for a device

The creation of settings for the user as well as for the computer is not a hard task. To create your own settings administrator, go to `Administration\Client Settings` and choose the **Create Custom Client Device Settings** option to create custom settings for a device.

The settings creator will lead the administrator through all the configuration settings that are available:

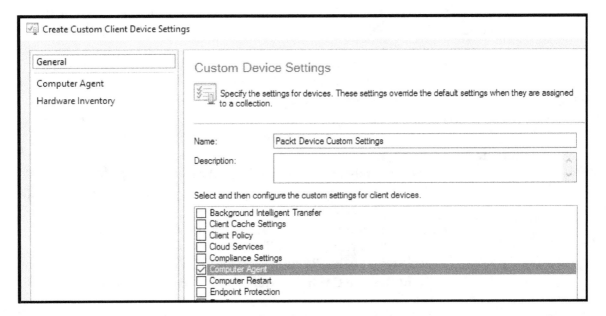

Deciding which parts of default policy will be changed

The next step will be to change the default settings to custom ones:

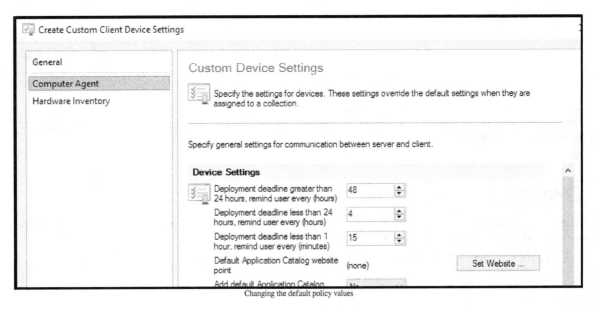

Changing the default policy values

Creating custom settings for a user

Creating settings for a user is as easy as it is for computers. To create their own settings, the administrator needs to go to `Administration\Client Settings` and choose the **Create Custom Client User Settings** option. The next steps would be similar to the computer settings.

Assigning to a collection

For settings to actually work on the objects, they need to be assigned to collections. This can be done by going to `Administration\Client Settings` and choosing the **Deploy** option, where the administrator selects the collection and assigns settings. As soon as the client downloads a new policy, it begins to work according to the new settings.

 By default, clients download policies from the server every 60 minutes.

Checkout of client settings

After assigning settings to a collection, it is possible to check the effective settings in particular. This can be achieved by going to `Assets and Compliance\Devices` on the server console, selecting a particular device, and choosing the **Client Settings | Resultant Client Settings** option.

A new window with effective permissions for this particular client should appear:

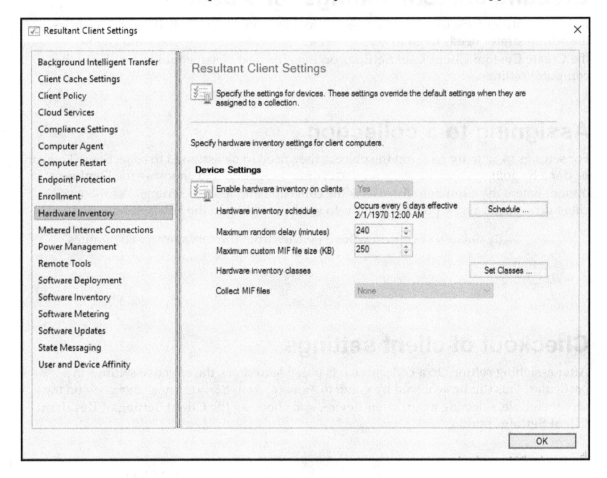

Resultant Client Settings

If the client has assigned more than one configuration, they are applied in a certain order. The default custom settings have a constant priority value, which is **10000**. Each next custom setting created has a number starting from **1**. The client applies settings starting from the one with the smallest priority to the one with the highest.

If you are removing any custom setting, each policy with a smaller number will automatically be given **1** for priority.

Collection settings

Effectively, many various settings configured in many different places affect ConfigMgr clients. Additionally, settings from collections where, computer or users belong also apply to them. To check these settings, the administrator can go to `Assets and Compliance\Device Collections`, select a collection, and choose **Properties**. The **Power Management** tab relates to the computer energy settings:

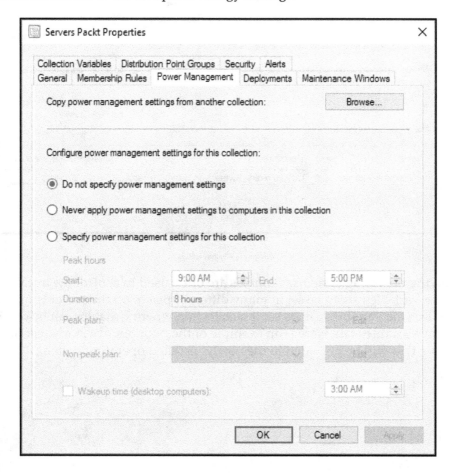

Power Management settings

The **Maintenance Windows** tab is for setting a suitable time when any operation that interferes with an operating system, such as software deployment, updating, or operating system deployment, can occur:

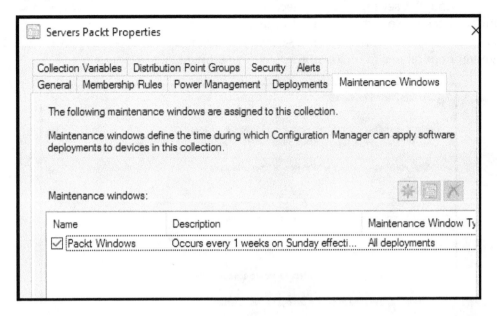

Maintenance Windows settings

When deploying operating systems, variables are often used to control the installation process. These variables are to be set in many different places on the server console. One of the places where the variables can be set is a collection where variables can be configured in the **Collection Variables** tab. Here is an example of the OSDComputerName variable, which defines a name that will be provided to the newly installed operating system:

Collection Variables settings

Starting from the ConfigMgr 2012 console, there is a feature of displaying alerts on a console related to the collection. Alerts can be configured in the **Alerts** tab. There are three types of alerts:

- **Client status**: Information related to client statuses
- **Endpoint protection**: Information about endpoint protection statuses

- **Membership**: Information about whether the allowed membership limit for a collection has been exceeded:

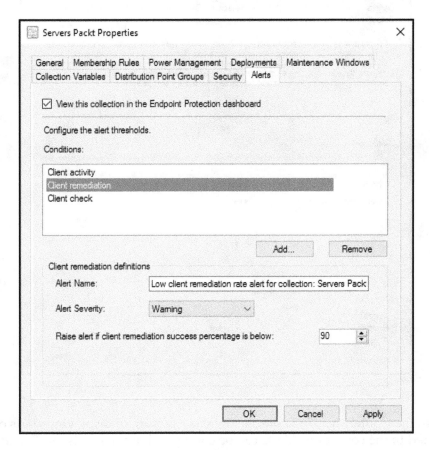

Alerts settings

When deploying settings to a client using a collection, it is recommended that you use a separate collection. It is not recommended to use a single collection for many purposes. Having separate collections significantly decreases the risk of having a configuration mishap and hence wrongly working clients.

Summary

This chapter covered ways in which settings can be applied to clients using a prepared set of settings and a collection to which these settings can be applied.

The next chapter covers topics related to compliance so that the administrator can ensure that clients are working according to the applied settings.

6
Compliance Settings

The previous chapter walked you through topics related to ConfigMgr client settings.

This chapter covers the following topics:

- Creating `Configuration Items`
- Creating baselines
- Deploying baselines to collections

Compliance feature

Starting from ConfigMgr 2007, the server can perform additional tasks to ensure whether the operating system status is correct, if the operating system is compliant with the policies, check the installed software against secure policies, or configure some settings of the operating system.

`Compliance Settings` have been divided into certain areas:

- `Compliance Settings`: Checking out the operating system or installed software compliance and status reporting
- `User Data and Profiles`: Managing user data as well as the user profiles
- `Conditional Access`: Managing conditional access to platforms such as Exchange and SharePoint
- `Company Resource Access`: Managing access to company resources
- `Windows 10 Edition Upgrade`: Managing the changing of the SKU for Windows 10

Two of the mentioned areas will be described in this book: `Compliance Settings` and `User and Data Profiles`.

`Compliance Settings` can be used for the following:

- Monitoring the installed operating systems
- Verification of installed operating systems and applications and getting them correctly configured
- Reporting whether company devices are compliant with security policies
- Checking out whether certain hotfixes have been applied to the operating system or installed software
- Setting up configuration on mobile devices
- Enforcing settings for mobile devices
- If possible, aligning the operating system and software settings to the operational standard
- Checking out the operating system and software settings against legal standards
- Configuration settings for the `User Data and Profiles` settings
- Configuration settings for `Company Resource Access`

All settings of `Compliance Settings` are assigned to a collection on a ConfigMgr server. Many of these can be applied by GPO as well, although configuration management would be much harder in cases where lots of different users need to have the same settings. It is much easier to create a collection for managing users and computers than to create an OU in AD and assign a GPO policy to it.

Compliance Settings

The `Compliance Settings` are mostly used to check the correctness of the operating system and application settings. Apart from Windows, this feature can be also used for operating systems such as macOS and various mobile operating systems such as Windows Phone, Windows RT, Apple iOS, and Android.

Capabilities of `Compliance Settings` are highly dependent on the operating system that is about to be configured. It is not only about different software vendors, but also about the differences between software versions that come from one manufacturer. Settings for iOS 10.3.2 would be different than for iOS 9.3; the same is the case with any other software vendor.

Active Directory allows you to configure a lot of settings via GPO, but not all. Of course, as GPO has many ready-to-use templates, it is highly recommended that you use it and not replace it with other tools. However, despite doubtless huge advantages, GPO has one downside. GPO policies are refreshed by the clients every 180 minutes, under the condition, of course, that there is a connection to a domain controller.

 Knowledge about Windows registry allows you to configure the system using compliance in any possible way. It may require some more work at the beginning; however, eventually, benefits in the form of a detailed view of system and software configuration will be more than helpful.

Nowadays, a significant number of computer users are rarely connected to the LAN network and do not have access to the domain controller. ConfigMgr clients can be managed not only when clients are in the LAN network, but also when clients are outside the local network--somewhere on the internet.

 The ConfigMgr server is a perfect solution for instant system management regardless of where a particular device is located. It relates to portable computers as well as mobile devices.

`Compliance Settings` deployment is composed of two phases:

- The creation of compliance `Configuration Items`
- The creation of the compliance `Configuration Baselines`, composed of compliance items, and assigning them to a collection of computers

 `Configuration Items` related to a registry and created on server 2012 have a remediation function. If the ConfigMgr client detects configuration that is noncompliant configuration, it might be replaced with one defined by the administrator. It relates to new registry keys as well as setting up a value on them.

Compliance Configuration Items

Compliance items are a unique value that will be compared with the pattern. When creating compliance items, it needs to be specified what and where they should be verified and which discovered values are considered the correct ones.

Compliance items can be created on Windows, macOS, and mobile devices. Each item might relate to something else, such as a different platform or even version of the operating system.

Items for Windows can be based on the following:

- **Active Directory query**
- **Assembly**
- **File system**
- **IIS metabase**
- **Registry key**
- **Registry value**
- **Script**
- **SQL query**
- **WQL query**

Items for macOS can be based on these:

- The macOS preferences
- Script

Items for mobile devices are used to configure settings that might relate to the following:

- Password
- Device
- Email management
- Store
- Browser
- System security
- Windows server work folders

New items can be created under `Asset and Compliance\Compliance Settings\Configuration Items` on the ConfigMgr console. The first step is a decision about what type of item will be created. The **Settings for devices managed with the Configuration Manager client** option creates a new item for systems managed by ConfigMgr, while the **Settings for devices managed without the Configuration Manager client** option creates items for mobile devices managed by the Microsoft Intune service:

Specify general information about this configuration item

Configuration items define a configuration and associated validation criteria to be assessed for compliance on client devices.

Name: Packt Item

Description:

Specify the type of configuration item that you want to create:

Settings for devices managed with the Configuration Manager client
○ Windows 10
○ Mac OS X (custom)
◉ Windows Desktops and Servers (custom)
☐ This configuration item contains application settings

Settings for devices managed without the Configuration Manager client
○ Windows 8.1 and Windows 10
○ Windows Phone
○ iOS and Mac OS X
○ Android and Samsung KNOX
○ Android for Work

Assigned categories to improve searching and filtering:

[Categories...]

Choosing the type of configuration item

When choosing the type, the administrator needs to select a platform or an operating system version for this particular item. The next step is choosing which settings should be configured, for instance, password. The last step is configuring the actual values for requirements that would need to be met, such as the password length or when it expires, and so on:

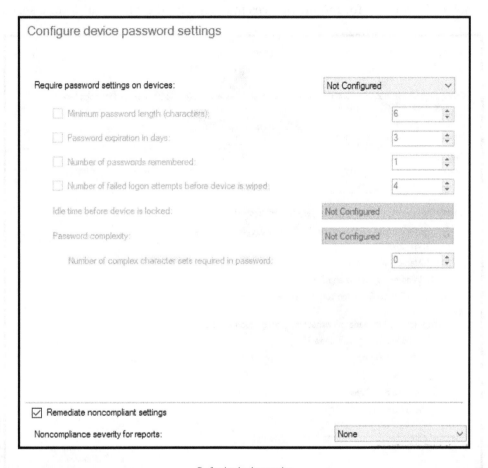

Configuring the chosen option

Both of the mentioned options allow you to edit the predefined settings available on the ConfigMgr server, whereas the **Settings for devices managed with the Configuration Manager client | Windows Desktops and Servers (custom)** option allows you to define your own configuration items based on predefined types:

- **Active Directory query**
- **Assembly**

- **File system**
- **IIS metabase**
- **Registry key**
- **Registry value**
- **Script**
- **SQL query**
- **WQL query**

This is a powerful tool in an administrator's hands. It allows you to examine almost all settings on the operating system as well as the software installed:

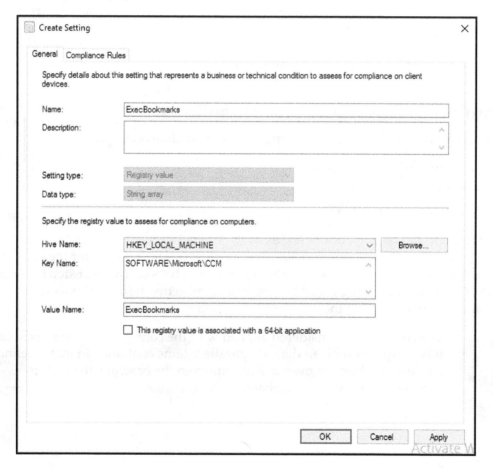

Defining checkout method for a registry value

The item created using **Settings for devices managed with the Configuration Manager client | Windows Desktops and Servers (custom)** needs to have configured the following information:

- Detection method information (only for Windows settings that check applications)
- Settings
- Compliance rules
- Supported platforms

 Most of the settings are available for Windows operating systems. Additionally, if the administrator has knowledge about the registry and where to set a particular configuration for the operating system or application, it is possible to use Compliance Settings to check almost the entire computer configuration.

Compliance Configuration Baselines

Each configuration baseline might be composed of more than one:

- Other configuration item
- Software update
- Configuration baseline

Baseline creation can be done under Asset and Compliance\Compliance Settings\Configuration Baselines. The baseline creator will ask for the name and configuration that a particular baseline should contain. That's it. The next step is assigning it to a collection. Only after assigning it to a particular collection will the clients start performing actions defined in the configuration baseline.

 The computer is considered aligned with the configuration baseline when it is compliant with all the configuration items contained in this baseline. If a computer does not meet at least one from the baseline, the state is reported as being noncompliant.

Configuration Pack

For ConfigMgr 2007 and 2012, there are sets of `Configuration Baselines` called **Configuration Packs**. These might be prepared by Microsoft and the community. Configuration Pack is nothing but the configuration baseline exported from the server; it can simply be imported and you can start using it right away.

Configuration Packs can be used as they are, can be aligned to your own needs, or can simply be used to learn and help in configuring custom configuration items.

Common tasks for managing compliance

Clients checking their status send information about the status of `Compliance Settings` to the server. This information can be used in two ways:

- **Reporting**: After the server is installed by default, there are over 20 reports available, showing data from `Compliance Settings` in a different way. It is also possible to use a default report as a baseline for your own custom report.
- **Create collections**: Based on the status data, it is possible to create collections containing, for instance, computers that have been reported as noncompliant for a particular configuration baseline assigned to a certain collection.

Collections are created based on the outcome of `Compliance Settings` and can be used for things such as triggering scripts that may correct inconsistency for computer settings in order to make them aligned back with company policies.

Client setting for compliance

Creating and assigning `Configuration Baselines` to a collection is not all that needs to be done. It is also necessary to configure the following two options:

- **Compliance Settings | Enable compliance evaluation on clients**: **Yes**
- **Compliance Settings | Schedule compliance evaluation**: Schedule reminders for how often the client will check configuration consistency. This schedule applies to computers that do not have contact with the ConfigMgr server. If the client has contact with the server, then the effective schedule will be the one set in a collection.

 Compliance after a server is installed is enabled by default.

Deploying the compliance baseline

When the compliance baseline is ready, it can be chosen from `Asset and Compliance\Compliance Settings\Configuration Baselines` and applied to a collection using the **Deploy** option.

As has been mentioned, starting from ConfigMgr 2012, there is the option of checking the configuration and, if it has drifted away from the standard, aligning it automatically.

The **Remediate noncompliant rules when supported** and **Allow remediation outside the maintenance window** options enable the repair of configuration drift by the server. Apart from what has been mentioned, there is also a need to select the collection to which the configuration baseline applies, and setting up a schedule defining how the other client will check against the configuration drift:

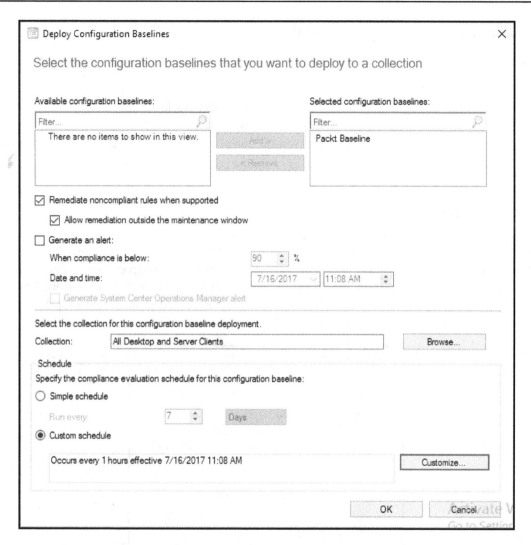

Configuration Baselines settings

The scheduler deployed with `Configuration Baselines` has a higher priority than the scheduler set with `Client Settings` if the computer is on the LAN network and has a connection to the ConfigMgr server.

Viewing compliance results

Statuses of `Compliance Settings` can be viewed in four different places:

- On the tested computer
- On the server thanks to the default reports accessible under `Monitoring\Reporting\Compliance and Settings Management`
- On the server if a collection based on `Compliance Settings` has been created
- Under the `Monitoring\Deployments` section for `Configuration Baselines`

Client reporting

A status can be viewed directly on the client computer. Client properties show all `Configuration Baselines` assigned to this computer on the **Configurations** tab. This includes checking the computer status and enforcing the client to do certain actions thanks to the **Evaluate** option and later viewing the report using the **View Report** option. The option mentioned, together with the **Evaluate** option, can be very useful for helpdesk support to review the computer configuration:

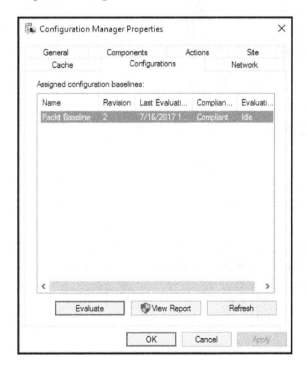

Configuration Baselines results

Running `Configuration Baselines` directly on a client computer is the fastest way to control whether a certain computer is aligned with the requirements defined by the administrator.

Console reporting

After installing Reporting Status Point server role, a few default reports are created. Among them, there are over 20 reports related to `Compliance Settings`. These can be found under `Monitoring\Reporting\Compliance and Settings Management`.

Creating collections based on the compliance result

To control the statuses of computers, collections can be created based on the `Compliance Settings` data sent by the client to the server. There can be four different statuses:

- **Compliant**: The computer is aligned with the requirements from `Configuration Baselines`
- **Error**: The computer has issues with checking requirements from `Configuration Baselines`
- **Non-Compliant**: The computer is not aligned with the `Configuration Baselines`
- **Unknown**: The client has not reported the status of `Configuration Baselines` yet

Administrators can create collections by themselves or with the user for whom this option has been enabled on the console. To do that, the administrator needs to select a configuration baseline, choose **Create New Collection** under **Deploy**, and select a status based on which collection will be created. The created collection will be automatically updated accordingly with the schedule.

Managing resource and data access

`Compliance Settings` not only check out the operating system or enforce mobile devices, configuration, but they also have the ability to configure the following areas:

- Redirecting user data from a particular collection to a network share
- Configuring offline files so users can work on the network share, while offline with no connection to the file server

- Configuring connections to the company network for company computers being outside of the Active Directory domain or working from the internet
- Configuring VPN profiles, certificates, Wi-Fi networks, email profiles, and Windows Hello for Business.

Remote Connection Profiles

`Remote Connection Profiles` allow users to connect to the company network, not being domain joined or working from the internet. Connection profiles can be created from the console under `Asset and Compliance\Compliance Settings\Remote Connection Profiles`:

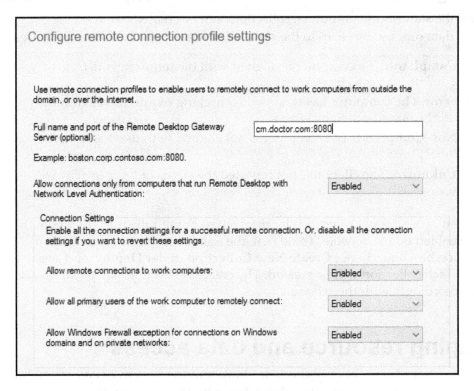

Remote Connection Profiles

The profiles mentioned work for the following systems:

- Windows
- iOS
- Android

Company Resource Access

`Company Resource Access` profiles are used to configure the connection to a company network or configure some required components to a network connection. Elements that can be configured are as follows:

- `Certificate Profiles`: Used for automatic certificate deployment
- `Email Profiles`: Automatically configured ActiveSync profiles on the Exchange Server for Intune service
- `VPN Profiles`: Automatic VPN profile configuration; transparent for the user
- `Wi-Fi Profiles`: Automatic Wi-Fi profile configuration; transparent for the user
- `Windows Hello for business Profiles`: Configuration of two-factor authentication for computers and mobile devices:

Specify general information about this Wi-Fi profile

Network name: Packt Wi-Fi

SSID: Packt Wi-Fi

☑ Connect automatically when this network is in range
☑ Look for other wireless networks while connected to this network
☑ Connect when the network is not broadcasting its name (SSID)

Configuration Wi-Fi Profiles

User Data and Profiles configuration

`User Data and Profiles` are used to configure settings responsible for user data or the whole user profile. The following actions can be performed:

- Redirecting particular folders to another location
- Setting the configuration of offline files
- Synchronizing user profiles on the network share after the user is logged off

Specify general information about this user data and profiles configuration item

Use these settings to configure folder redirection, offline files and roaming profiles for computers that run Windows 8 and later versions in your hierarchy.

Name: Packt Redirection

Description:

Select user data and profiles to configure

☑ Folder redirection

☑ Offline files

☐ Roaming user profiles

Configuration User Data and Profiles

Summary

`Compliance Settings` are a very useful and helpful server feature, thanks to which, ConfigMgr server administrators know exactly whether all of the computers are aligned with company requirements and whether all the users got the required configurations.

All you need to do for managing is to create a collection containing certain computers or users and associate appropriate settings for the collections.

Keep in mind that a computer with the ConfigMgr client installed can be managed by the ConfigMgr server, regardless of whether it is in LAN network or\on the internet. A lot of these settings can be configured using GPO. However, GPO configuration will only be applied if the computer is in the LAN network with a connection to the domain controller. If the computer is managed by the ConfigMgr server, only a connection to the management point is needed.

 All of the `Compliance Settings` are saved in policies accessible in the management point, and there is no need to send anything to the distribution point, so it is enough if the management point is accessible to ConfigMgr clients.

The next chapter covers software deployment. It contains information about:

- How to properly prepare software deployment
- How to configure server roles used for software deployment
- How to configure software deployment and advanced options used for software deployment

7
Software Distributions

Software distribution is an important role for the ConfigMgr server. Starting from ConfigMgr 2012, it has been possible to deploy applications with different settings for different platforms and users. The ConfigMgr server might also check for requirements, and the deployment will take place only if these are met. The server also discovers the operating system the user is working on and is capable of releasing appropriate binary files on that computer.

Software distribution provides the following capabilities:

- **Applications**: Deploy applications for operating systems such as Windows, macOS, Android, and iOS
- **App-V virtual environments**: Deploy applications App-V and manage the virtual environment
- **Packages**: Deploy packages to be compatible with earlier server versions
- **Approval requests**: Manage the approval of applications requested by users
- **Global conditions**: Manage conditions that need to be met when deploying applications
- **App configuration policies**: Manage iOS application profiles
- **Application management policies**: Manage profiles for iOS and Android systems
- **Windows sideloading keys**: Manage keys used for Windows Store application installation
- **License information for Store Apps**: Provide information about licenses used when deploying applications from Windows Store for Business

This chapter covers the fundamental configuration of application deployment with ConfigMgr.

Starting with ConfigMgr 2012, there is a possibility of deploying applications on collections of computers as well as collections of users. The ability to deploy applications on users' collections makes administration much easier nowadays, as it provides a possibility to ensure that the user will have the same applications available regardless of the platform they are logged into.

Main topics covered in the book are:

- Create an application from `.msi` or `.exe`
- Create deployment types
- App detection methods for `.exe`
- How to deploy apps
- Troubleshooting software distribution

Before configuring an application, it is crucial to get to know how the installer for that particular application works, what the available switches are, and what prerequisites need to be met for the installer to work. Lack of this information would make it really hard to investigate the real root cause of the problem--whether it is the system's fault, or maybe the application's.

Software distribution is not the only application deployment. With packages and programs, it is possible to not only deploy a program but also to run any script or program with a purpose other than it being installed. For this reason, the software distribution function is a great solution for any task--not just software deployment.

Users can install applications from various places--**Software Center**, **Application Catalog**, and **Company Portal**. The availability of an application depends on how it is deployed. An application that is deployed for mobile devices is available under Company Portal, applications for computers are available under Software Center, and applications for users are available under Application Catalog.

Applications versus packages

Each previous ConfigMgr version had its own method of being deployed when using *packages*. Starting from ConfigMgr 2012, there is a new mode, *applications*, which is the deployment of applications based on application installation files, such as `.msi`.

This chapter focuses on this second mode, and thanks to it, the administrator can significantly ease daily deployment administration. However, it won't be possible to leave out packages mode completely.

The packages mode is made mainly for running installations of Windows systems. It is not always possible to run an installation using the `.msi` file. A lot of applications use `.exe`, `.bat` scripts, or PowerShell scripts to get installed. In these cases, there is a need to use the packages mode instead of applications.

> The administrator should always try to use the application mode whenever it is possible, but the packages option should always be kept in mind, as in some circumstances, it might be the best choice.

Software distribution server roles

Usually, two standard roles are engaged in software distribution. The first is the management point, of course, and the second is the distribution point. Both of these roles are used along with all server features that are used for the installation of operating systems, applications, or updates.

When talking about application deployment, there is one more role, which enables users to access applications assigned to them personally and not to the workstations. This role name is Application Catalog, and the installation of this role has been covered in Chapter 2, *Installing Configuration Manager*.

Application management features

Starting with ConfigMgr 2012, when application management was introduced, administrators could use many new features dedicated to application deployment.

Application management features include the following:

- **Requirements**: Checking before the installation whether requirements were met
- **Global conditions**: Checking before the installation whether the required global conditions were met
- **Detection methods**: Checking whether the application has already been installed on the computer

- **Supersedence**: The ability to automatically replace one application with another
- **Deployment action and purpose**: The ability to install or uninstall an application, as well as set whether a particular deployment is mandatory or not
- **State-based deployment**: The ability to re-install the required application if it is uninstalled by the user
- **User device affinity**: Installing various types of the same application depending on the logged on user
- **Monitoring**: The possibility to check the console for deployment statuses
- **Installation per-user or per-device**: The ability to use .msi files attributes and install them on computers or for the user
- **Deployment types**: For each application, it is possible to configure different installation files depending on the operating system the user is working on

Creating applications

Applications can be created in two ways:

- Automatically, based on files such as .msi
- Manually, using the built-in creator

The second option allows you to create applications even when using the .exe files and scripts, which is not possible in an automatic way.

Automatic application creator gets the required information about the application from the installation file, such as the .msi file. There is always a need for checking whether all application properties have been configured. It is a common scenario that, for instance, an uninstall command is missing; in such cases, it needs to be added manually.

Automatic application creation

Automatic creation of an application is possible under Software Library\Application Management\Applications when clicking on the **Create Application** option. The next choice is between automatic or manual application creation. The default choice is the **Automatically detect information about this application from installation files** option. After selecting the appropriate option, there is a need to precisely specify what application types will be created and select the installation file by specifying a UNC path:

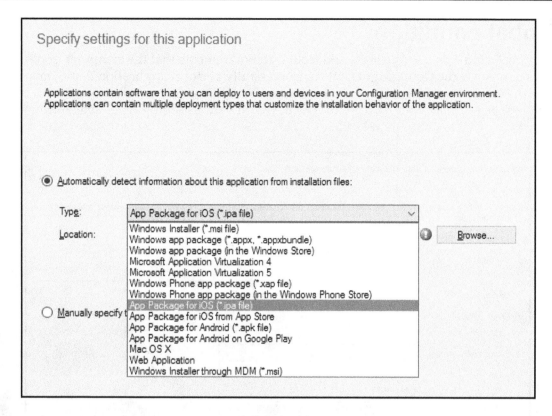

Application type choice

After selecting the installation file, the administrator is just a few clicks away from the creator's end. All settings that were read from the file by the creator can be changed later.

After the application is created and set up, it can be sent to a distribution point and installed with the configuration accordingly.

Manual application creation

The manual approach is not as easy as the automatic one. All the required settings to create an application need to be manually filled in. The most important factors are that it is possible to create an application from the .exe file and scripts. A complete review of the entire process of the manual approach is out of the scope of this book.

Global condition

The global conditions are business and technical requirements that the computer or user needs to meet so the ConfigMgr client can successfully perform application deployment. After the server is installed, there are a few global conditions that are already defined. It is also possible to create your own conditions based on various setting types available in the wizard:

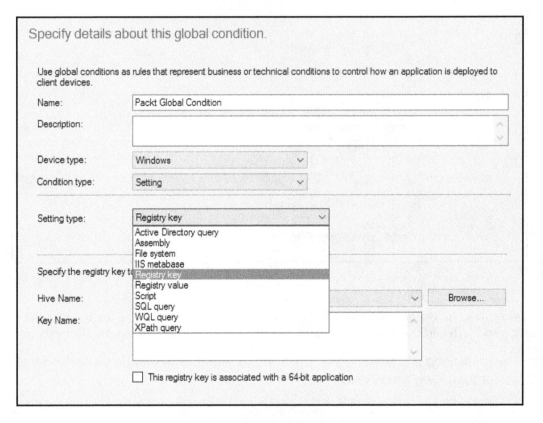

The available global condition setting types

It is possible to assign global conditions to applications using the requirements option after specifying exactly what ConfigMgr needs to check before application deployment.

The global condition is checked by the client directly on the working system and not on the ConfigMgr database. Using global conditions can allow you to eliminate the need for creating a collection, as an application--when using global conditions for deployment--will be installed only on the systems that meet these requirements.

Configuring application features

After creating an application, the next step is configuration. All the required settings allowing installation have been read by the wizard when creating the application on the server console. Information saved in the installation file, as well as that saved by ConfigMgr, can be edited later, after the application is created. The features described here are the new ones, and they are available in this ConfigMgr version.

Supersedence

Thanks to the settings placed under the **Supersedence** tab, the administrator can automatically replace one application with another. It is not important if the newly installed application is the newer version of the old one or is a completely different application. The following screenshot shows how to configure application uninstallation before installing a new one.

In older versions of ConfigMgr, the administrator needed to prepare two completely separate deployments. The first was uninstalling the application and the second was with the installation. Usually, the client needed to wait until the old application was uninstalled before the installation. Now it is possible to combine two applications and prepare a new application deployment; the ConfigMgr client will know that the deployment is combined out of two phases:

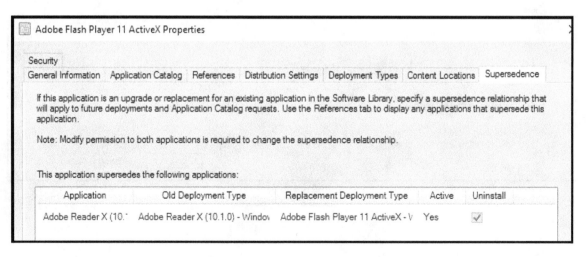

Supersedence application

Application Catalog

The **Application Catalog** tab keeps configurational information for an application when it is installed by **Application Catalog**. Here, the administrator can set the application name, keywords for easier searches, and links to the documentation, the manufacturer website, or the application icon:

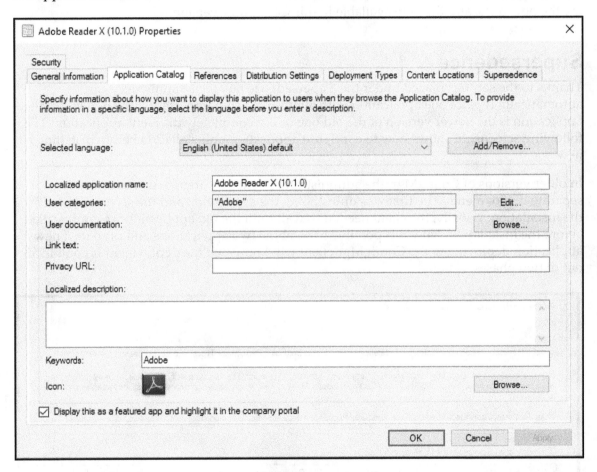

Application Catalog settings

Application Catalog distributes applications that are deployed for users as available applications, not mandatory ones. The deployment of mandatory applications is done by Software Center.

References

The **References** tab is used to verify whether:

- The application is related to any other application using **Supersedence**
- The application depends on other applications
- The application is deployed in the same App-V environment

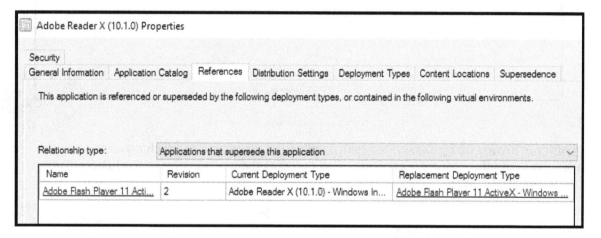

References application tab

Revision history

It might happen that some applications get wrongly configured and saved. If the administrator has no knowledge or has forgotten what has been changed, it is possible to use the history option. The option mentioned allows you to do a rollback to previous application settings.

It is also possible to review the settings in order to ensure that settings that are just about to be set are correct:

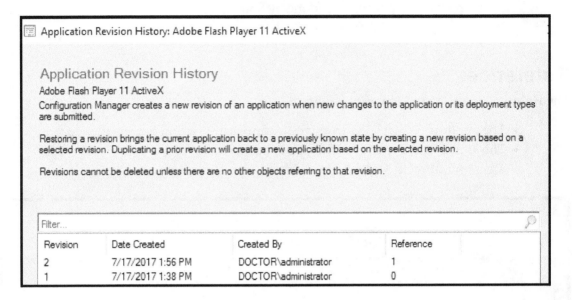

History of application version configuration

History is turned on by default for each application. Each and every change made on the application on the console is automatically saved as the new version in the history for this particular application.

Deployment Types

The most important feature of the applications mode is a capability to prepare installation files for the application in such a way that the user can use the same application regardless of the device or platform they have logged on. The ConfigMgr client is able to recognize the operating system the user is working on and check whether proper application installation files have been prepared.

Performing the mentioned configuration is possible under the **Deployment Types** tab, where different installation types can be configured for one application. If properly configured, the application can be deployed for a user regardless of whether they work on Windows, Windows Phone, or an Android system:

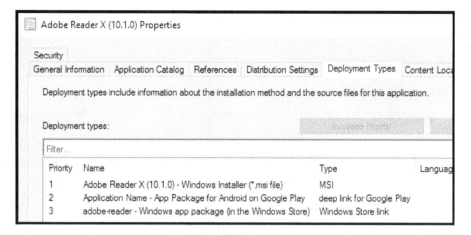

Different installation types for one application

Additional application types are created using a built-in wizard. This is the final result of the wizard mentioned with detailed requirements of what needs to be met for the client to start installation:

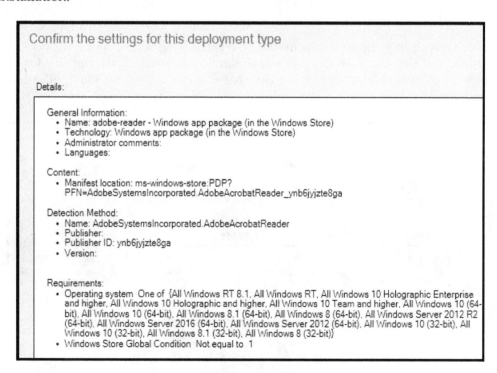

Final results of the wizard used to create a new deployment type for application

Assigning one application to many different deployment types is a very good idea and very easy to maintain.

Detection Method

The *packages* deployment mode, which was available in previous versions of ConfigMgr, was getting by pretty well; however, it had some disadvantages that have been removed for the *applications* mode. Previously, there was a need for deploying a package to a collection, and the administrator needed to ensure that the collection contained only computers that met the defined requirements. That model is also possible now, and the administrator can still create a collection and assign a deployment to them, but it's not necessary. It is possible to assign the deployment of an application to a root collection, and the application will be deployed only on those systems where it is missing. This kind of approach is called **Detection Method**.

 For each application, at least one **Detection Method** rule needs to be created. If there are none, the wizard won't allow you to save an application on the ConfigMgr console. Each application can have more than one rule configured.

The rule for **Detection Method** is automatically created when deploying an application. It can be edited, and the administrator can add their own rules, check the registry for certain keys, check for folders or files, or pass a script that will check whether the application has been installed properly:

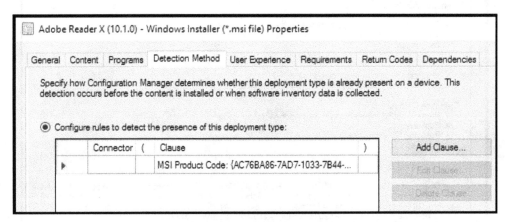

Detection Method for an application

Thanks to **Detection Method**, the ConfigMgr client always checks whether a particular application is installed on the operating system, and there is no possibility to uninstall it by mistake during a deployment.

> **Detection Method** rules are run by the ConfigMgr client. If the workstation meets the requirements, the client downloads the files and starts the installation. If the workstation does not meet the **Detection Method** rule, no action will be taken, and the application won't be installed.

Dependencies

Dependencies can be configured for each application. It is a common scenario when, before installation and application, some additional software is required by the application to work correctly. Back in ConfigMgr 2007, there was a need for performing at least two deployments to cover such scenarios. After installing all of the required components, it was possible to deploy an application. It is not a secret that this approach significantly extended the time required for application deployment.

Starting from the 2012 version, it was possible to install an application and all the prerequisites using only one deployment:

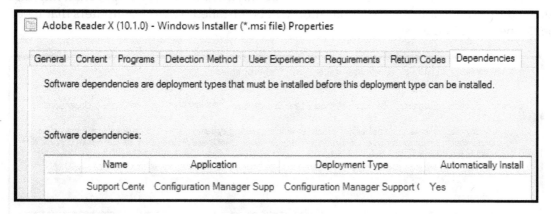

Dependency settings

An application can have one or more dependent applications. For each such application, the administrator needs to define whether it should be automatically installed. If an additional dependent application is being added, there is a need for choosing between the AND and OR conditions to properly associate these two dependent applications.

When deployment is done by the client, the installation of at least one dependent application installation ends with a failure, and the whole deployment will be reported as failed and the application will not be installed.

Requirements

Until ConfigMgr 2007, there was no easy way to tell the client what requirements needed to be met in order to start application deployment. As a workaround, there was a need for creating a collection with all the computers that met the requirements and deploying the application on that collection.

It is still possible to deploy an application as mentioned; however, it is worth noting that the collection might contain computers that do not meet the requirements, as the collection has its refresh interval, which may be shorter or longer; such situation can cause a real concern sometimes.

To remediate the problem, in the **Requirements** tab, it is now possible to set conditions that need to be met by the client for installation.

Here is an example application, which will be installed only when the operating system is detected as a Windows 10 64-bit version. The deployment of such an application might be assigned to a collection and the application will be installed only on computers that meet the defined requirements:

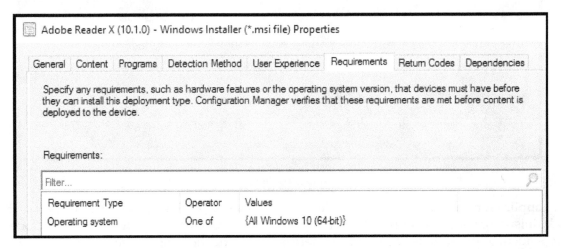

Example of application requirements

As has been mentioned, after the server is installed, there are some predefined global conditions that contain requirement definitions.

There are three main reasons why it is worth using **Requirements**:

- To ensure that the application will be installed only on a primary device computer and will not be installed for a user if they use something other than a primary device computer
- To check whether the computer meets the hardware requirements for an application
- To check whether the operating system meets all the defined requirements for the application to be installed

> The ConfigMgr client first checks whether all the requirements are met by the client computer, and only after the checkout is positively completed does it download files from the distribution point and then start the installation. Thanks to this, there is no chance of deploying an application on a computer that does not meet the requirements, as each such try will result in a failure.

Application deployment

When deploying applications, there are some new features that were not available until now. The administrator can choose between many deployment types depending on how the installation should be done.

There are three available deployment types:

- **Simulate Deployment**: A test deployment to check the condition set on an application. It is used to check whether the ConfigMgr client that meets the application requirements would be able to start the application installation. It is a very useful feature in terms of checking whether the conditions set on the application are correct.
- **Available Deployment**: A deployment without a deadline. Hence, the application will not be installed automatically on the computer. Users can run such installation or not; it depends on them. All the available deployments are available for users under Application Catalog and for computers in Software Center.

- **Required Deployment**: The application will be installed at a scheduled time in the deployment or after the computer is on after being off for some time. The user cannot stop the deployment of the application unless the administrator allows the installation earlier than the deadline. All the required deployments are available in Software Center.

The simulation of application installation does not actually install the application on computers. The system only checks on which computers the installation of the application is feasible.

Available reasons of deployments are as follows:

- **Install**: Application installation
- **Uninstall**: Application uninstallation--earlier, there was no such option

As each application has an installation string configured, installation deployments are always available. However, not every application has an uninstall string configured that would allow you to uninstall it.

There are additional installation types when using the .msi files:

- **Per-user installation**: The application will only be available for the user on the account on which it has been installed
- **Per-device installation**: The application will be installed on the computer so all logged-in users will be able to use it

Each application can have different per-user and per-device installation settings. It is recommended that you check them on the console after each time the application is created.

Simulating a deployment

Each application and application type can have a requirement set, where requirements need to be met for the application installation to start. This is always good to ensure that the installation of a particular application will take place. In earlier versions, there was a need for creating collections containing users or computers that met the requirements. Membership of this collection is based on data from the ConfigMgr database, as this data may be outdated or not full. Since version 2012, there is a very easy way to check on how many computers the application will install: an option that is called **Simulate Deployment**. The option mentioned allows you to check whether an application will be installed or uninstalled:

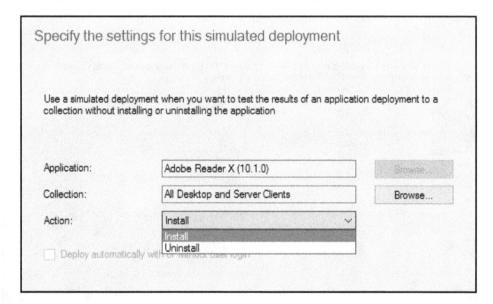

Specify the settings for this simulated deployment

Use a simulated deployment when you want to test the results of an application deployment to a collection without installing or uninstalling the application

Application: Adobe Reader X (10.1.0)   Browse...

Collection: All Desktop and Server Clients   Browse...

Action: Install

Install
Uninstall

Deploy automatically with or without user login

Simulated deployment settings

Simulated deployment cannot be converted into a regular deployment. It needs to be deleted and regular deployment needs to be assigned to a collection. There is no technical possibility to run simulated and regular deployment for the same application simultaneously on a collection.

Available deployments

ConfigMgr has always had two application deployment modes available. **Available Deployment** is one of them. This deployment type specifies which application and which collection need to be deployed. The **Schedule the application to be available at** option is used to specify the time from which the application is available for users. There is no deadline set, apart from one exception--if there is another application specified in **Supersedence**, then the deadline set as a deployed application will replace the other one. To set this deadline, the **Installation deadline to upgrade users or devices that have the superseded application installed** option will be used:

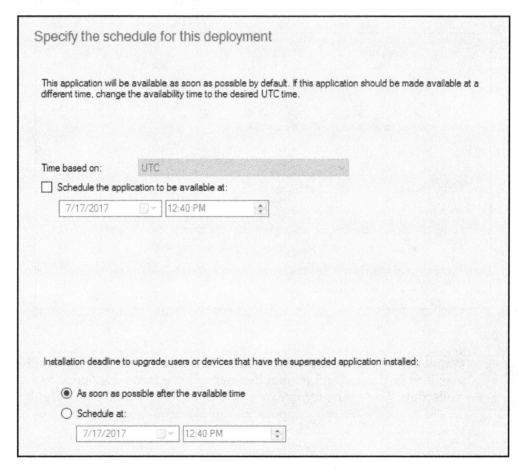

Schedule settings for available deployment

User notifications is used to inform users whether there is a new application available for them to install. There is a choice between informing users about each application deployment or only about those that require the restarting of your PC:

Specify the user experience for the installation of this software on the selected devices

Specify user experience setting for this deployment

User notifications: | Display in Software Center, and only show notifications for computer restarts ∨
Display in Software Center and show all notifications
Display in Software Center, and only show notifications for computer restarts

When the installation deadline is reached, allow the following activities to be performed outside the maintenance window:

☐ Software Installation

☐ System restart (if required to complete the installation)

Write filter handling for Windows Embedded devices

☑ Commit changes at deadline or during a maintenance window (requires restarts)

If this option is not selected, content will be applied on the overlay and committed later.

User notification settings

Deployments assigned to users are available in Application Catalog, while deployments assigned to computers are available under Software Center.

Required deployments

A **Required Deployment** is the one with a configured deadline; deadline refers to the time when an application will be installed without interfering with the user. The **Purpose** option is used to set a type of installation that is supposed to be performed. When deciding on this type of deployment, there are some additional and useful options available. The **Pre-deploy software to the user's primary devices** option forces the ConfigMgr client to download the required files from the distribution point after receiving information that the application is assigned to the user. The benefit is that the client that's not connected to the LAN network can install the required software without the need for connecting to the distribution point, as it already has files pre-deployed.

The **Send wake-up packets** option is used to wake the computer on using the Wake On LAN feature. The ConfigMgr client starts the installation instantly after being turned on. However, to use this option, Wake On LAN needs to be properly configured in the first place.

The **Allow client on a metered Internet connection to download content after the installation deadline, which might incur additional costs** option allows the ConfigMgr client to download files from the distribution point over a paid internet connection:

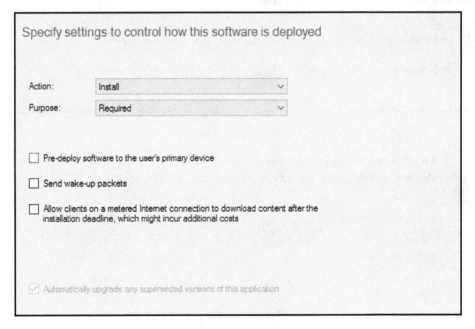

Required Deployment settings

Required deployments force setting a deadline, after which the ConfigMgr client performs installation automatically; the date is set using the **Installation deadline** option. It is possible to set **As soon as possible after the available time** or **Schedule at**. The second option allows you to set the start of installation on a certain date and time. The first option is used when there is a need for installing an application as quickly as possible, which means as soon as the ConfigMgr client receives any information about the new deployment:

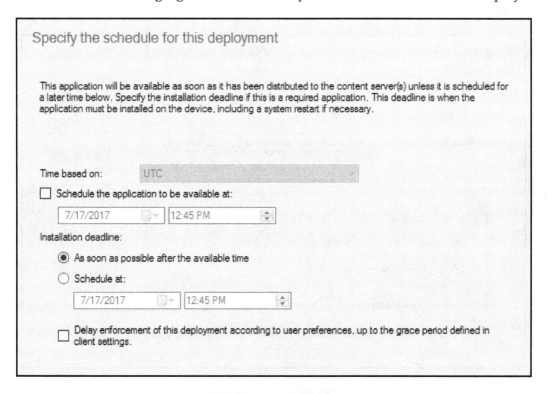

Specify the schedule for this deployment

This application will be available as soon as it has been distributed to the content server(s) unless it is scheduled for a later time below. Specify the installation deadline if this is a required application. This deadline is when the application must be installed on the device, including a system restart if necessary.

Time based on: UTC

☐ Schedule the application to be available at:

7/17/2017   12:45 PM

Installation deadline:

◉ As soon as possible after the available time

○ Schedule at:

7/17/2017   12:45 PM

☐ Delay enforcement of this deployment according to user preferences, up to the grace period defined in client settings.

Required Deployment schedule settings

The **As soon as possible after the available time** option does not work instantly. Remember that the ConfigMgr client communicates with the management point on a certain schedule with intervals. By default, intervals are 60 minutes, as only after 60 minutes will the clients start to download the files, and after the download is done, they will start the required deployments.

Similar to the previous deployment type, there is a need to configure **User notifications**. There are three options available; the first two are exactly the same as in the **Available Deployment**, and there is also one additional--**Hide in Software Center and all notifications**. The third option allows you to hide all the notifications about downloading and installing the application; it is used mainly to not distract the user at work. The **System restart (if required to complete the installation)** option allows the client to restart the computer if required by the application:

Specify the user experience for the installation of this software on the selected devices

Specify user experience setting for this deployment

User notifications: Display in Software Center and show all notifications   ⌄

Display in Software Center and show all notifications
Display in Software Center, and only show notifications for computer restarts
When the installation deadline | Hide in Software Center and all notifications
window:

☐ Software Installation

☐ System restart (if required to complete the installation)

Write filter handling for Windows Embedded devices

☑ Commit changes at deadline or during a maintenance window (requires restarts)

If this option is not selected, content will be applied on the overlay and committed later.

Required Deployment user experience settings

Starting from version 2012, it is impossible to create a deployment for an application that hasn't been sent on at least one distribution point. It is a significant enhancement, as in version 2007, it was possible to create a deployment of an application that was not available on any distribution points, and hence clients were actually not able to perform such deployment.

Triggering an installation

Applications that are deployed are visible in two places. One of them is Software Center, which is a part of the ConfigMgr client and allows users to run the installation of applications available for the client computer or the applications required for the user:

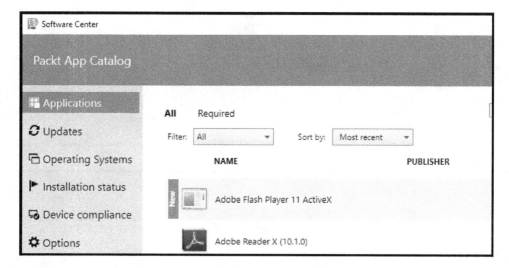

Available applications in Software Center

Application Catalog, on the other hand, is a server role, where the user sees all the available applications and not only those available for the user or computer:

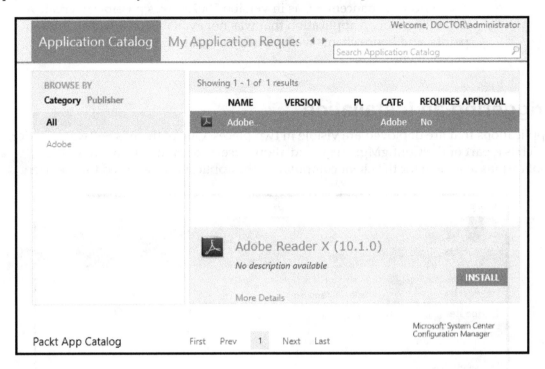

Application Catalog view

Reporting

Along with the introduction of `Application Management`, Microsoft has significantly improved the reporting feature related to application deployment. For each deployment, it is possible to review client statuses in live mode. Apart from three already known statuses, there is a fourth, **Requirements Not Met**, which presents computers that haven't met the requirements:

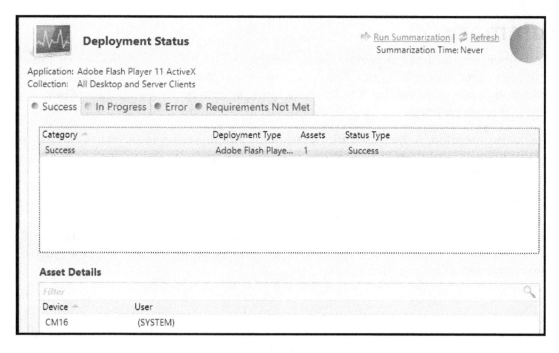

Deployment Status

Invoking scripts on devices

Packages and applications are not the only way for invoking scripts on devices managed by ConfigMgr server. On the ConfigMgr console under `Software Library\Scripts` it is possible to configure PowerShell scripts, and without the need of creating a package or application--run it on the managed device.

The mentioned scripts need to be written leveraging PowerShell 3.0 or newer and need to be approved by the server administrator prior to running them on the devices. In this case, simplicity is a big plus--administrator imports script to the console, approves it and creates deployment or certain collection. There is no need to create package o application and sent it to a distribution point.

Summary

This chapter covered most important topics related to deploying an application by the ConfigMgr client. If possible, it is always recommended that you use `.msi` files for application deployment for the Windows operating system or the installation of binaries in the case of other platforms.

A new way of working with applications has many advantages compared to what has been available before ConfigMgr 2012. Options available for application deployment can significantly speed up and enhance the application deployment cycle.

The next chapter covers topics related to patching deployments, such as configuring server roles responsible for update deployment, ConfigMgr and WSUS synchronization, the process of scanning for missing patches, and the updates installation process. There will also be a section on configuring features such as updates deployment, automatic patch deployment, and Windows 10 servicing.

8

Software Update Management

The deployment of updates is a very important process, allowing you to protect the managed environment. Administrators often use the **Windows Server Update Services** (**WSUS**) server to deploy patches to the operating systems and software.

Integrating the WSUS server with the ConfigMgr server significantly broadens capabilities for software and operating system patching. And if there is a need, it is possible to deploy patches not just for Microsoft software solutions using System Center Updates Publisher. The mentioned solution would allow you to publish third-party software updates on the WSUS server.

 When managing updates, it is not that important what software is used-- whether it is WSUS, ConfigMgr, or Patch Manager. What is important is knowledge of patches and when they need to be deployed and on which workstations--this task is much harder than knowing the technology.

This chapter will mostly be concentrated on deploying patches to Windows systems, as it often happens that errors in patch deployment are the outcome of lack of knowledge about the handled process. Of course, the essential topics about preparing update deployment using ConfigMgr integrated with WSUS will also be covered.

The administrator working on update deployment needs to know the three basic phases of working with updates:

- Synchronization of data between Microsoft Update and WSUS server and between WSUS and the ConfigMgr server
- Scanning systems by Windows Update Agent and saving this data in WSUS as well as ConfigMgr database
- Update deployment by the ConfigMgr client and Windows Update Agent

Getting to know these three processes makes update deployment much easier, as well as speeds up any further troubleshooting.

 The ConfigMgr client does not scan or install updates; it just has a supervisor role. The scanning and installation operation is done by Windows Update Agent, which the ConfigMgr client supervises.

We will cover the following topics in this chapter:

- Creating a software strategy
- Approving required updates
- Distributing and deploying software updates
- Automating the entire patching process

Software update features

Managing deployment using ConfigMgr provides a number of features that are not available for the WSUS server alone. Additional available features are as follows:

- The outcome of update scanning can be used to deploy updates or used for other tasks, such as `Compliance Settings`
- An easy and straightforward way to install updates only on maintenance window for each collection separately
- Automatic deployment of updates that match the criteria set by the administrator
- Monitoring and reporting of scanning results as well as the deployment of updates based on data from the ConfigMgr server
- The capability to create your own reports related to update deployment
- The capability to use Wake On LAN and power plans for deployments
- Deployment of updates even on computers with no domain joined and working on the internet
- Deployment of updates using Windows Update for Business
- Publishing updates for third-party software using System Center Updates Publisher
- Support for express installation files for Windows 10
- Deployment of upgrades for Windows 10 using service plan

Before starting deploying updates, it is important to get to know some requirements; otherwise, it will not be possible to use all of the features that the integration of WSUS with ConfigMgr provides.

Initial requirements

There are some initial requirements that need to be met in order to update deployment without an issue. The mentioned requirements need to be met on both the server side as well as on the managed endpoints side.

Server requirements

The base requirement is to use the WSUS server in version 4.0, which is available only on Windows Server 2012 or higher. The 4.0 version of WSUS works properly when it comes to updating and upgrading Windows 10 and Windows Server 2016.

> Server WSUS (3.0), available on Windows Server 2008 R2, is not capable of working with Windows Update deployments. It will not be possible to deploy feature upgrades to new Windows 10 versions.

If this requirement cannot be met, it will not be possible to deploy all update types available on Microsoft Update.

> To properly deploy Windows 10 feature upgrades on WSUS installed on Windows Server 2012 or 2012 R2, it is essential to install two updates: KB3095113 and KB3159706.

Another requirement is to install the WSUS server console; it is always installed with the console. After installing the software update point on the WSUS server, the requirement is met by default. If the software update point is installed on some other, separate server, there is a need for installing the WSUS console on that server as well.

Of course, apart from the mentioned server features, the administrator also needs at least one management point, distribution point and optionally a reporting point.

Client requirements

The basic requirement for updates deployment to work correctly is proper work of Windows Update Agent on the client machines, as well as proper settings allowing to connect to WSUS server integrated with ConfigMgr. Stopping Windows Update Agent service using GPO, for instance, causes the deployment of updates to stop instantly.

System scanning for missing updates and their installation is done by Windows Update Agent. The ConfigMgr client manages the start time of scanning or deploying, but it does not run it. Hence, Windows Update Agent always needs to be on, up and running.

GPO policies can configure the WSUS server address and port it is working on. All the other settings need to be set to the **Not Configured** state.

Client settings

Integrating WSUS with the ConfigMgr server is not enough for ConfigMgr clients to manage update deployment. One thing that needs to be checked is whether software updates are enabled in Clients Settings; this option should be enabled by default; however, it is always good to ensure this fact:

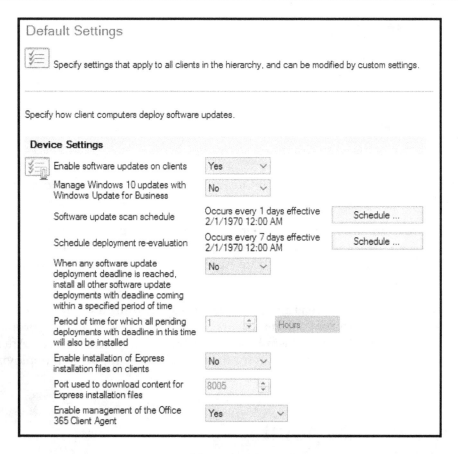

Software update settings

Additionally, **Software update scan schedule** needs to be configured, so the ConfigMgr client knows how often Windows Update Agent needs to initialize operating system scanning.

Preparing ConfigMgr site for software updates

Preparation of the environment to manage updates deployment consists of two phases:

- Installation and configuration of the WSUS server
- Installation and configuration of the software update point server role

Installing WSUS

WSUS is a part of the server operating system. Its database can be installed on the SQL server or using Windows Internal Database.

 The WSUS server installed on Windows 2012 or higher uses 8530 and 8531 port numbers.

When installing the WSUS server, the administrator needs to point a local folder where the server will store license information for updates.

 There are many updates where it is necessary to get to know the license agreement. Specifying the mentioned folder is not a must; however, it is required for Windows Update Agent to also deploy these updates that require accepting of license terms.

After the server is installed, there is a need to perform synchronization of the server with Microsoft Update. The synchronization might take a while, and it is very important to wait patiently until it ends, as this is the last phase of configuring the WSUS server. After the synchronization is done, it is time to go in for the next phase of application deployment--installation of the software update point server role.

Software update point

Software update point is a server role that integrates both WSUS and the ConfigMgr server. Depending on where the role will be installed, there are two options that install this role: **Add Site System Roles** or **Create Site System Server**. After running one of them, the next step is choosing the **Software update point** role. If the ConfigMgr environment uses the central administration site, software update point should be installed on the server holding the mentioned role.

 ConfigMgr allows you to assign software update point to boundary group. Thanks to that, clients of a boundary group will know which server they shall connect to.

Installation of software update point is an easy task:

1. The first step is to point to a WSUS server that will be integrated with the ConfigMgr server. If WSUS is installed on a Windows Server 2012 or higher, the **WSUS is configured to use ports 8530 and 8531** option should be chosen:

Specify software update point settings

A software update point integrates with Windows Server Update Services (WSUS) to provide software updates to Configuration Manager clients.

⚠ For Configuration Manager to use a software update point that is not installed on the site server, you must first install the WSUS administration console on the site server.

WSUS Configuration

○ WSUS is configured to use ports 80 and 443 for client communications (default settings for WSUS 3.0 SP2)

◉ WSUS is configured to use ports 8530 and 8531 for client communications (default settings for WSUS on Windows Server 2012)

☐ Require SSL communication to the WSUS server

Client Connection Type

○ Allow intranet-only client connections

○ Allow Internet-only client connections

◉ Allow Internet and intranet client connections

Configuration of ports used by the WSUS server

2. The second step is specifying a proxy server used for the internet connections, if it is used, and providing an AD account that will be used to connect to the WSUS server. Specifying an AD account is important if the WSUS server is installed on a separated machine, and the given account needs to have administrative permissions on the WSUS server.

3. The third step is configuring the way in which data synchronization from the WSUS server will be done. Software update point connects to the WSUS server and asks it to perform Windows Update synchronization. The default configuration is **Synchronize from Microsoft Update**, so the WSUS server performs synchronization directly with the Microsoft Update website. It is also possible to specify a different WSUS server that will be used as a source for the synchronization automatically or the administrator triggers it from the console manually:

Specify synchronization source settings

Select the synchronization source for this software update point.

⦿ Synchronize from Microsoft Update
  When there is an upstream software update point, this option is unavailable.

○ Synchronize from an upstream data source location (URL)
  Example: http://WSUSServer:80 or https://WSUSServer:8531

  [   ]   Browse

○ Do not synchronize from Microsoft Update or upstream data source

  Select this option if you manually synchronize software updates on this software update point. Typically, you use manual synchronizing when the software update point is disconnected from Microsoft Update or the upstream software update point.

WSUS reporting events

You can configure the Windows Update Agent on client computers to create event messages for Windows Server Update Services (WSUS) reporting. Configuration Manager does not use these events, you should not create them unless you require them for other uses.

○ Do not create WSUS reporting events
○ Create only WSUS status reporting events
⦿ Create all WSUS reporting events

Setting up synchronization

4. The fourth step is configuring the synchronization schedule; however, the installer will allow you to finish the installation without having it set up. If the scheduler is not set, there is a need to manually run the synchronization from the ConfigMgr console.

5. The fifth step is configuring the time after which updates will be replaced with new versions and will not be available for deployment. This is an example of such updates:

Select behavior for software updates that are superseded

You can configure a software update to expire as soon as it is superseded by a more recent software update or to expire after a specified period of time when it is superseded by a more recent software update.

Supersedence settings do not apply to System Center Endpoint Protection definition updates or to software updates that are superseded by Service Packs. These software updates never expire when they are superseded.

Changing this setting will force a full software update point synchronization.

Supersedence behavior

○ Immediately expire a superseded software update

◉ Do not expire a superseded software update until the software update is superseded for a specified period

Months to wait before a superseded software update is expired: 3

☑ Run WSUS cleanup wizard.

Behavior for software updates that are superseded settings

It is worth enabling the **Run WSUS cleanup wizard** option. The wizard makes the server block the deployment of any old and superseded, by Microsoft, updates. The mentioned option is available only for first software update point installed on the ConfigMgr site.

6. The sixth step is configuring the file types, which will be downloaded from the Microsoft Update website by the ConfigMgr server. Selecting the **Download full files for all approved updates** option will force the ConfigMgr server to always download the full version of installation files. The **Download both full files for all approved updates and express installation files for Windows 10** option will make the ConfigMgr server download the full version of installation files for all updates apart from cumulative updates for Windows 10. If a cumulative update from the previous month has been already downloaded, ConfigMgr will download only those files that were not downloaded the previous time, so that's the only the difference between both packages:

Specify configuration for software update content

Express installation files provide smaller download and faster installation on computers because only the necessary files are downloaded and installed. They are larger files and will increase download times for your site servers and Distribution Points.

Select the following options when downloading update files to your servers:

◉ Download full files for all approved updates

○ Download both full files for all approved updates and express installation files for Windows 10

Express files usage configuration

To fully use the express file, an administrator should enable support for it in `Client Settings\Software Updates`.

7. The seventh step is specifying classifications of updates that will be synchronized. If you're planning to use WSUS for Windows 10 upgrades, there is a need for installing relevant KBs, and this task needs to be done before initial synchronization with Microsoft Update. The wizard will specify which KBs need to be installed. There is no need to install them if the WSUS server is installed on Windows Server 2016:

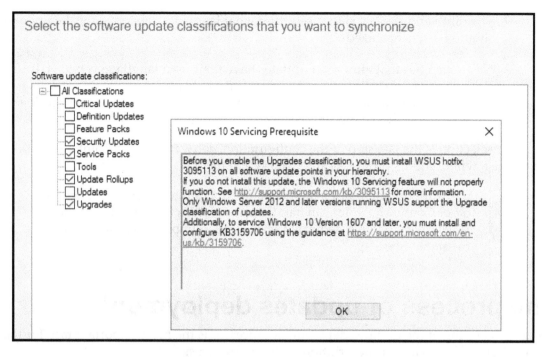

Settings of classifications that administrator wants to synchronize

8. The eighth step is specifying products that need to be checked for available updates:

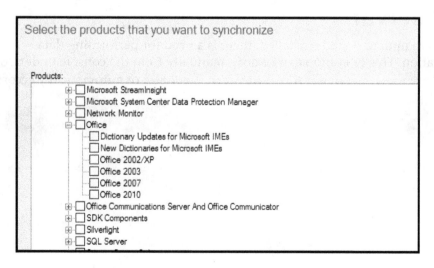

Specifying products for synchronization against updates

9. The ninth and the last step is selecting what language version(s) for the updates should be synchronized.

Remember that almost all updates have their own language versions. If 10 languages are selected, each update is downloaded from the Microsoft Update website in 10 different, separate files. This can cause a serious load with unnecessary files in a distribution point.

Language selection is the last step of the configuration, software update point installation might take a while, and its progress can be tracked in the wcm.log log file.

Software update point installed on the operating system along with the other ConfigMgr roles can handle up to 25,000 clients simultaneously. When installed on a dedicated server, this number increases to 150,000 at the same time.

The process of updates deployment

An understanding of the updates deployment processes is the most important task for the administrator. Here is a short description of these processes.

The process of synchronizing data with the WSUS server

After software update point is installed, there is a need for performing data synchronization. This operation can be done manually from the console under Software Library\Software Updates\All Software Updates or automatically according to the schedule:

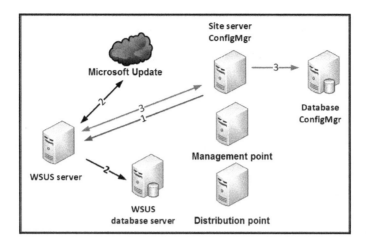

Process of synchronizing information about updates

The installation process looks as follows:

1. On the ConfigMgr server, the administrator chooses product classes that should be synchronized with **Microsoft Update**. The ConfigMgr server connects to the **WSUS server** and triggers the synchronization.

2. The **WSUS server** connects to the **Microsoft Update** website and performs synchronization according to the settings saved in the ConfigMgr console. Synchronized data is saved in the database.

3. After WSUS synchronization is done and data is saved in the **WSUS database server**, ConfigMgr performs synchronization with the **WSUS server** and saves the data in its own database.

The synchronization status between these two servers can be checked in the `wsyncmgr.log` log file.

There are two types of synchronization:

- **Synchronization according to the schedule**: Complete data synchronization. If classification or products are changed, this change is saved in the WSUS database. After the synchronization is performed, there might be more or fewer products or classifications for which synchronization of updates is performed.

- **Manual synchronization**: Synchronization is done only for products and classifications that are visible to the ConfigMgr server. Synchronization can be much faster as it is performed only for known, ConfigMgr products and classifications. Newly added products or classifications are not synchronized.

The process of scanning for compliance

After synchronizing updates with the WSUS server, the ConfigMgr console provides information about these updates. At this point, the administrator can perform system scanning.

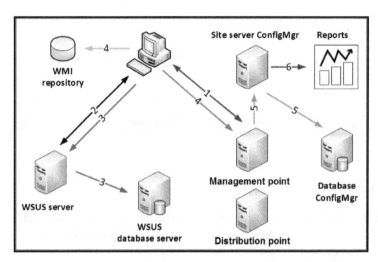

System scanning process

The process of system scanning is as follows:

1. The client, according to the schedule, downloads a policy from the ConfigMgr server that specifies when the client needs to initiate system scan using Windows Update Agent.

2. Operating system scan begins. Windows Update Agent communicates with the **WSUS server**, which is integrated with the ConfigMgr server and downloads data about available updates.

3. By default, information about scanning is not saved in the **WSUS database server**; it can be saved if the administrator configures it.

4. The ConfigMgr client saves data about scanning locally in the Windows Management Instrumentation database. It sends it out also to a **management point** as a *state message*; these messages are sent by default every 15 minutes.

5. **Management point** sends data to the ConfigMgr server, which saves the data in its own SQL database.

6. Data related to system scans can be viewed using the ConfigMgr console, **Software Update--D Scan** and **Software update--A Compliance** reports.

The most important fact is that scanning is performed by Windows Update Agent, not by the ConfigMgr client.

Scanning statuses

After the scan is performed and all relevant data is sent to a management point, there are four statuses that the scanning result can get:

- **Required**: An update is available for the operating system or software but is not installed on the machine
- **Installed**: An update is installed on the machine
- **Not Required**: An update is not relevant for a particular machine operating system or installed software
- **Unknown**: The site server has not received any data about this particular update

The status of the scanning can be seen on the ConfigMgr console or using default reports.

Updates deployment process

The process of updates deployment is the last phase for managing updates. Luckily, some of the tasks performed here by the ConfigMgr server are the same as for the operating systems or application deployment, which at the same time makes it easier to understand:

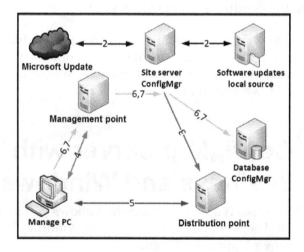

Process of updates deployment

The process of updates deployment is as follows:

1. On the ConfigMgr server console, the administrator creates a deployment using the **Deploy Software Updates Wizard**.

2. The site server downloads installation files from the catalog specified in the wizard. These files have been earlier downloaded from the **Microsoft Update** website or from the local source.

3. The site server copies installation files to a **distribution point**, adding them to the already existing software packages or by creating a new package.

4. The ConfigMgr client, according to schedule, downloads policies that inform you about updates that are deployed for the client.

5. If some new updates were discovered since the last scan, the client triggers Windows Update Agent, which performs a scan. If a deployment is **Required**, the client downloads the installation files for relevant updates from **distribution point** to a local cache folder. If the deployment is **Available**, the client performs a download operation only after the user triggers it manually.

6. After downloading files, the client sends a state message to **management point**, and that one sends it further to the site server, which saves it in the database.

7. If the deadline is reached, the client performs scanning again, checking whether all updates marked as **Required** still have the same status. If there are such updates, Windows Update Agent performs the installation of updates, and ConfigMgr client sends information about the installation status. If there is a restart required by an application, **management point** is given the status that the machine is in the **Pending system restart** state.

 The ConfigMgr client downloads only those update files that are required on that particular client machine (it does not download updates for all software on that machine). This significantly speeds up an installation process and lowers the load on the network.

Integrating ConfigMgr server with Windows Update for Business and Windows 10

Windows Update for Businesses is a set of features that allows you to deploy updates and upgrades for Windows 10. The deployment of updates in Windows 10 can be managed by the WSUS server or Windows Update for Business.

To enable Windows Update for Business for computers, the following requirements need to be met:

- A device needs to have Windows 10 Pro, Enterprise, or Education installed
- Windows needs to be connected directly to Microsoft Update
- Windows 10 needs to work in Current Branch for Business mode

Windows Update for Business enables the following deployment types:

- **Upgrades**: Windows 10 version 1511 to Windows 10 version 1703
- **Updates**: The deployment of regular updates for Windows 10
- **Other/not deferred**: Updates, for instance, for Endpoint Protection and Windows Defender

The ConfigMgr server can recognize which workstation is managed by Windows Update, which is managed by business, and which is managed by WSUS. Computers connected to Windows Update will always have the **Unknown** status and will also not be contained in statistics related to updates deployment.

If computers managed by ConfigMgr are connected to Windows Update for Business, some of the ConfigMgr features will not work properly:

- All of the computers connected to Windows Update for Business have **Unknown** status, which significantly constricts troubleshooting and reporting
- It is impossible to deploy updates for Office, IE, Visual Studio on these workstations
- It is not possible to deploy third-party software updates published on the WSUS server
- It is impossible to install the ConfigMgr client using software update point

Supporting non-Microsoft Updates

Since a long time ago, ConfigMgr has enabled the deployment of third-party software updates using the WSUS server. These updates can be published on the WSUS server using System Center Updates Publisher. It is an additional software licensed along with the ConfigMgr server.

Thanks to the update, publisher administrator can do the following:

- Import third-party software updates
- Create and modify the updates definition
- Export the updates definition to a catalog
- Publish updates or updates catalogs on the WSUS server

Some of the vendors, such as Adobe, HP, Fujitsu or Dell, prepare ready-to-use catalogs with updates that can be imported.

Maintenance setting on collection

All kinds of deployments are assigned to the collections. There is, however, one important setting the administrator needs to remember, which significantly affects performing deployments by clients--this setting is **Maintenance Windows**. This option allows you to control at what time and day clients can do tasks that interfere with operating systems, such as installing updates, software, or operating system installation.

There are situations where the installation needs to be performed out of scheduled **Maintenance Windows**. The client may disregard configuration of **Maintenance Windows** when the **Ignore maintenance Windows and install immediately at deadline** option is used when preparing the deployment. In such a scenario, deployment will be performed as if there were no **Maintenance Windows** configured for a particular client.

For **Required** deployments, if **Maintenance Windows** are configured on the client, deployment will not be performed according to the deadline but at the first suitable time, according to the **Maintenance Windows**, unless it covers the deadline time; then, it will be deployed as configured.

Update search

Since always, the list of the system updates has been measured in thousands. Managing them can be considered really hard without the ability to filter them out. Updates can be filtered by categories and classifications assigned to them by Microsoft.

These two mentioned attributes allow you to filter updates that ease administration, as the ConfigMgr console shows all updates together by default. Here is an example of such a query, which searches only updates with particular parameters:

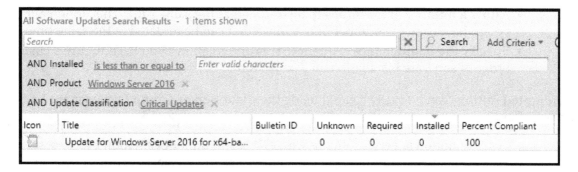

An example of searching updates on the ConfigMgr console

There is no need to create queries each time from scratch. Each query can be saved, so it can be used later if there is a need.

One of the most common queries is one regarding updates where the release date is less than 1 month. It is an easy way to get the newest Microsoft updates released in the current month.

Server group

When managing server updates, it is important to know whether servers can be restarted and in what order. The order of restart is sometimes essential when dealing with applications on managed servers.

Previous ConfigMgr versions didn't provide such granularity in managing updates, such as setting up the server restart order. Version 1706 allows you to manage the order of software installation as well as restart within a server group. It can be configured in collection properties by choosing the **Server Group** option and later in the **General** tab using the **All devices are part of the same server group** option and choosing **Settings**.

Settings contain three different ways in which a service group can be maintained:

- **Allow a percentage of machines to be updated at the same time**: This option specifies what percentage of machines can be updated at the same time
- **Allow a number of machines to be updated at the same time**: This option allows you to hardcode the number of machines that can be updated at the same time
- **Specify the maintenance sequence**: This option allows you to configure a custom order of software installation on a collection

Configured settings can be easily cleared using the **Clear Server Group Deployment Locks** option after choosing the collection.

 This option is very useful; however, it is still under evaluation by Microsoft. To start using it, **Consent to use Pre-Release features** needs to be enabled under hierarchy settings.

Deploying software updates

After getting familiar with all the processes that occur when deploying updates and understanding them, the next step is deployment. The deployment phase has two main modes:

- **Manual**: All objects that require the deployment of updates are created manually.
- **Automatic**: Creating an automation, which will later be deploying updates by itself. The wizard creates `Software Update Groups` as well as `Deployment Packages`.

The manual mode in WSUS has had the ability to deploy updates in an automated way and now, so does ConfigMgr.

Deployment always consists of the same objects, regardless of the mode:

- `Software Update Groups`: An object that returns updates. The software update group is assigned to a collection, which means all items assigned to it will be deployed to a collection computer. A software update group can be created using the console under `Software Library\Software Updates\All Software Updates` where, after adding relevant updates, they can be added to an existing software group or create a new one.

- `Deployment Packages`: A package containing all binaries for updates that are available on the distribution point. The ConfigMgr client downloads data from it only for those updates that are installed. These are visible on the console under `Software Library\Software Updates\Deployment Packages`; however, it is impossible to create them from there as these are created when creating a deployment. It is possible to assign updates to an existing deployment package, though.

 Adding updates to an existing software update group should be done with due diligence, especially when considering a group that already has some deployments assigned. Adding an update to such a software update group creates the deployment of this update to all other deployments assigned to this software update group.

To deploy updates, three different types of wizards can be used:

- **Download**: A wizard used to download installation files, for instance, from Microsoft Update, and saving them in the local repository, creating deployment packages with these updates, and sending them to the distribution point. At this point, binaries are not assigned to any collection; all it does is just download the installation files.
- **Deploy**: A wizard used to deploy updates to collections of devices. It is possible to deploy only those updates that were downloaded to the server. This wizard goes through the same tasks that **Download** wizard does; after these steps, it is possible to go directly to the creation of a deployment.
- **Automatic Deployment Rules**: A wizard used to create automatic update deployment.

Deployment preparation

Software update deployment will be presented using a feature that has become available in ConfigMgr 2012, `Automatic Deployment Rules`, as it fills the previous gap in maintaining updates using ConfigMgr. At the end of this section, the main differences between manual and automatic deployments will be outlined as well. Automatic updates are always deployed in the **Required** mode, so there is a deadline after which the deployment will be triggered. The user can only postpone installation for certain short periods of time. There is a reason why it is important to precisely specify what application types are going to be deployed using this feature.

The most important difference between manual and automatic update deployment is available installation modes. For the automatic deployment type, it is not possible to choose the **Available** mode. As for the manual deployment type, it is possible to deploy updates in the **Required** and **Available** modes.

Of course there are products for which updates are deployed automatically; otherwise, it would be a time-consuming task, such as Endpoint Protection. Virus database updates are published a couple of times a day by Microsoft, and manual installation, in this case, would be a big challenge for the administrator. Therefore, automatic deployment is something that helps in such cases.

When creating an ADR, there are a few default templates that can be used for automatic deployment.

The creation of `Automatic Deployment Rules` is not hard; the wizard for this can be run from `Software Library\Software Updates\Automatic Deployment Rules`.

There are 12 main steps when creating an ADR:

1. The first step is naming the ADR, choosing whether it will be deployed using one of the default templates, and assigning a collection to it. It is possible not to run ADR straight after creation; the **Enable the deployment after this rule is run** option is used to tell whether ADR should run automatically after the wizard is done or not:

Specify the settings for this automatic deployment rule

Name: | Packt ADR

Description:

Select a previously saved deployment template that defines configuration settings for this deployment. You can save the current configuration as a new deployment template on the Summary page of this wizard.

Template: | Office 365 Client Updates | | Manage Templates...

Specify the target collection for the software update deployment.

Collection: | All Desktop and Server Clients | | Browse...

Each time the rule runs and finds new updates.

○ Add to an existing Software Update Group

◉ Create a new Software Update Group

Choose whether to enable the deployment after this rule runs for the associated software update group. When this setting is not selected, you must manually deploy the software update group.

☑ Enable the deployment after this rule is run

Initial configuration of Automatic Deployment Rules

2. The second step is the configuration of license agreements for updates. Some of the updates require acceptance of the license agreement, hence it is possible to approve them automatically, or not, but then only updates without the need for accepting the agreement will be deployed.

3. The third step is a choice of which updates will be deployed automatically. If default templates are used, this settings site is already configured. It is worth checking, using the **Preview** option, how many this particular rule is going to deploy:

Select the property filters and search criteria

The software updates that meet the specified criteria are added to the associated software update group.

Property filters:

- ☐ Article ID
- ☐ Bulletin ID
- ☐ Content Size (KB)
- ☐ Custom Severity
- ☑ Date Released or Revised
- ☐ Description
- ☐ Language
- ☑ Product
- ☐ Required

Search criteria:

Date Released or Revised Last 1 day

Product "Office 365 Client"

Choosing update types for the rule

Using the **Preview** option has two purposes. The first is checking for the number of updates affected by the rule, and second is ensuring that the rule is configured for updates that are supposed to be deployed.

4. The fourth step is checking how many updates are covered by this rule. If there are too many of them, the rule will never work as its constraints have been exceeded:

Title	Article ID	Bulletin ID	Product	Vendor	Update Classification
2017-07 Security Update ...	4025376		"Windows 10 LTSB","Windows 10"	Microsoft	"Security Updates"
2017-07 Security Update ...	4025376		"Windows 10 LTSB","Windows 10"	Microsoft	"Security Updates"
2017-07 Security Update ...	4025376		"Windows 10"	Microsoft	"Security Updates"
2017-07 Security Update ...	4025376		"Windows 10"	Microsoft	"Security Updates"
2017-07 Security Update ...	4025376		"Windows 10"	Microsoft	"Security Updates"
2017-07 Security Update ...	4025376		"Windows 10"	Microsoft	"Security Updates"
2017-07 Cumulative Upda...	4025338		"Windows 10 LTSB","Windows 10"	Microsoft	"Security Updates"
2017-07 Cumulative Upda...	4025338		"Windows 10 LTSB","Windows 10"	Microsoft	"Security Updates"
2017-07 Cumulative Upda...	4025344		"Windows 10"	Microsoft	"Security Updates"
2017-07 Cumulative Upda...	4025344		"Windows 10"	Microsoft	"Security Updates"

Preview updates

Configuration Manager returned 22 updates.

Filter...

Preview of updates that are covered by the rule

`Automatic Deployment Rules` will not work if there are more than 1,000 updates applied.

5. The fifth step is the configuration of the synchronization schedule with the WSUS server. A schedule is needed to automate synchronization and to cyclically search for new updates published by Microsoft. The **Run the rule on a schedule** option enables setting a separate schedule for each rule. When the rule starts, it triggers synchronization with a software update point about updates. This synchronization is independent of the synchronization schedule set on software update point. The **Run the rule after any software update point synchronization** option provides the ability to run synchronization each time after finishing synchronization on software update point. The **Do not run this rule automatically** option will work only when triggered manually from the ConfigMgr console by the administrator:

Specify the recurring schedule for this rule

Current software update point synchronization schedule:

No SUP synchronization schedule is set, or Admin does not have sufficient permissions to view this setting.

○ Do not run this rule automatically

○ Run the rule after any software update point synchronization

◉ Run the rule on a schedule

Occurs every 30 days effective 7/19/2017 7:53 PM

[Customize...]

Rule run schedule settings

6. The sixth step is setting up a deadline for deployed updates. The assumption of automatic deployment is that updates have to be installed on the operating system. Because of this, there is a need for defining the time for deployment. The **Software available time** option specifies the time scope within which updates will be available for installation, and **Installation deadline** is used to specify the ultimate time for installation:

Configure schedule details for this deployment

Schedule evaluation
Specify if the schedule for this deployment is evaluated based upon Universal Coordinated Time (UTC) or the local time of the client.

Time based on: Client local time

Software available time
Specify when software updates are available. After this rule is run, software updates are distributed to the content server. Then the software updates are available to install as soon as possible or scheduled to install at a configured period of time after the rule is run.

Note: You must enable this deployment before software updates are available to install.

○ As soon as possible
● Specific time: 4   Hours

Available time: 7/19/2017 11:53:00 PM

Installation deadline
Specify a deadline for required software updates. The deadline is determined by adding the deadline time to the installation time. When the deadline is reached, required software updates are installed on the device and the device is restarted if necessary.

○ As soon as possible
● Specific time: 7   Days
Deadline time (from deployment available time):

7/26/2017 11:53:00 PM

☐ Delay enforcement of this deployment according to user preferences, up to the grace period defined in client settings.

Update installation time settings

7. The seventh step is specifying whether the user will be notified about updates installation; this is controlled by the **User notifications** option; when deploying updates automatically, it is worth selecting the **Hide in Software Center and all notifications** option. Thanks to this, the user will not be shown any notifications. There are two more important options, and set **Device restart behavior** if automatic restart is required after applying updates; it is possible to postpone such updates on both the server and workstations. **Deadline behavior** specifies whether updates in this deployment can be installed out of configured **Maintenance Windows**:

Specify the user experience for this deployment

User visual experience

User notifications:

Display in Software Center and show all notifications

Display in Software Center and show all notifications
Display in Software Center, and only show notifications for computer restarts
Hide in Software Center and all notifications

Deadline behavior

When the installation deadline is reached, allow the following activities to be performed outside of any defined maintenance windows:

☐ Software Update Installation

☐ System restart (if necessary)

Device restart behavior

Some software updates require a system restart to complete the installation process. You can suppress this restart on servers and workstations.

Suppress the system restart on the following devices:

☐ Servers

☐ Workstations

Write filter handling for Windows Embedded devices

☑ Commit changes at deadline or during a maintenance window (requires restarts)

If this option is not selected, content will be applied on the overlay and committed later.

Software updates deployment re-evaluation behavior upon restart

☐ If any update in this deployment requires a system restart, run updates deployment evaluation cycle after restart

Settings for notifications and automatic restart after updates deployment

8. The eighth step specifies when the ConfigMgr client will download installation files. By default, binaries are downloaded from distribution points assigned to the default site boundary group if the client is not able to download files from the current or neighbor boundary group distribution point. If the client computer is out of LAN network, it might download binaries directly from the Microsoft Update website if the **If software updates are not available on distribution point in current, neighbor or site boundary group, download content from Microsoft Updates** option is set:

Specify the software updates download behavior for clients on slow site boundaries.

Select the deployment option to use when a client uses a distribution point from a neighbor boundary group or the default site boundary group.

Deployment options:

○ Do not install software updates

◉ Download software updates from distribution point and install

When software updates are not available on any distribution points in current or neighbor boundary group, client can download and install software updates from distribution points in site default boundary group

Deployment options:

○ Do not install software updates

◉ Download and install software updates from the distribution points in site default boundary group

☑ Allow clients to share content with other clients on the same subnet

☑ If software updates are not available on distribution point in current, neighbor or site boundary groups, download content from Microsoft Updates.

☐ Allow clients on a metered Internet connection to download content after the installation deadline, which might incur additional costs

Installation files download settings

9. The ninth step is the creation of deployment packages or adding downloaded files to the existing deployment package:

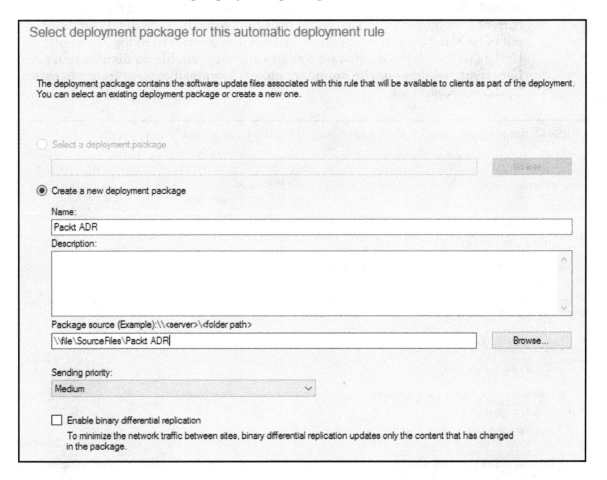

Deployment packages settings

Deployment packages might contain binaries for more than one software update group. The ConfigMgr client downloads only the required files from the distribution point, not the whole deployment package.

10. The tenth step is specifying a distribution point to which deployment packages will be sent.
11. The eleventh step is specifying from where binaries should be downloaded. The administrator can choose between Microsoft Update or a local resource if it has been added earlier.
12. The twelfth step is configuring language packs in which binaries will be downloaded.

When creating your own ADR, it is possible to create a template for later use.

Manual update deployment

There are no major differences between manual and automatic software updates deployment. All of these settings need to be configured manually, but eventually, many of the settings will be the same in both deployment types.

Two basic actions need to be done to deploy updates manually:

- Create a software update group and assign updates to it
- Create a deployment for proper software update group assigned to a certain collection

In the next step under `Software Library\Software Updates\All Software Updates,` the administrator needs to select updates and create software update point. Then, similar to automatic deployment, the **Download** or **Deploy** creator needs to be used; there are three main differences between them. The first is choosing how the updates should be deployed--in the **Required** or **Available** way:

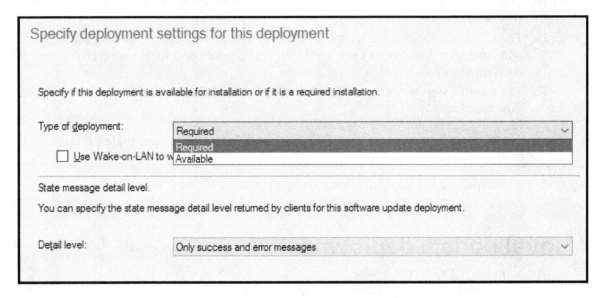

Deployment type settings

The second difference is in the schedule settings. If **Required** is chosen, then settings will be the same as for automatic deployment. For **Available**, it is necessary to set the date for which updates are available for the computer to download:

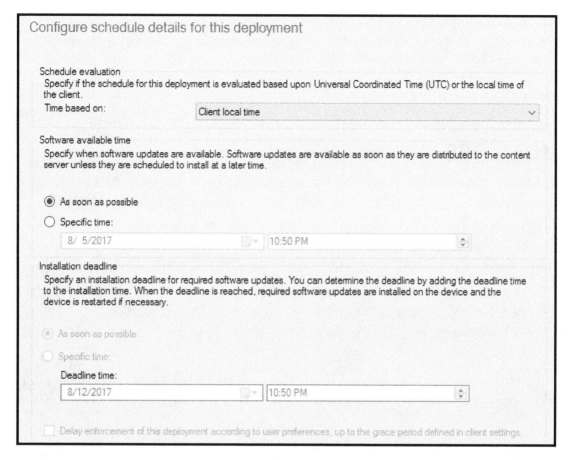

Schedule update

The third difference is the possibility of enabling updates installation for the user. **Display in Software Center and show all notifications** needs to be set in this case.

Windows 10 as a service

Along with Windows 10, Microsoft introduced a new way of installing updates. Apart from regular updates, as usual, there are updates called upgrades: these updates increase the system version. At the time of writing this, the newest version for Windows 10 is 1703, so the upgrade will be updating it from, for instance, 1607 to the 1703 version.

Updates can be deployed using new the ConfigMgr feature, which is a service plan. In short, it is an `Automatic Deployment Rules` for Windows 10 upgrade deployments. A service plan can be created under `Software Library\Windows 10 Servicing\Servicing Plans`. These rules will be discussed later in `Chapter 10`, *Operating System Deployment*.

Office 365 Client Management

An important factor to secure systems and user data is to update Office 365. Updating application Office 365 has been separated on the ConfigMgr server in order to ease the management of this process.

Deployment for Office 365 can be created under `Software Library\Office 365 Client Management`, and there are three options to choose from:

- Creating a deployment of the Office 365 client
- Creating `Automatic Deployment Rules` for Office 365 updates
- Creating `Client Settings`

 Managing updates for Office 365 is not enabled by default in Client Settings. To make it available, **Software Updates | Enable management of the Office 365 Client Agent** in the `Client Settings` option should be enabled.

Monitoring software deployment

There are two ways to implement updates. The first is available on the ConfigMgr server reports on the various stages of implementation of the update. The second is the use of this way to show the status of the update--**Software Update Dashboard**.

Software Update Reports

The advantage of integrated ConfigMgr with the WSUS server is reporting, as the WSUS server doesn't have nicely developed reporting. After the server is installed, there are a few available default reports divided into the following categories:

- **Software Updates--A. Compliance**: Reports that show data regarding compliance based on a certain collection, software update group, or update

- **Software Updates--B. Deployment Management**: Reports that show data about updates in certain deployments
- **Software Updates--C. Deployment States**: Reports that show data regarding the status of each deployment
- **Software Updates--D. Scan**: Reports that show data regarding clients scanning for updates
- **Software Updates--E. Troubleshooting**: Reports that show data about errors regarding scanning or updates deployment

Apart from the default reports, there is a possibility to create your own reports.

Software Update Dashboard

On the ConfigMgr console under `Monitoring\Security\Software Updates Dashboard` administrator can find information about update deployment status.

Dashboards contain:

- Information about devices meeting the requirements
- Information about the number of missing updates on the managed computers, grouped by categories
- Number of critical--related to updates--alerts
- Information about missing updates
- Date of last successful synchronization with WSUS server

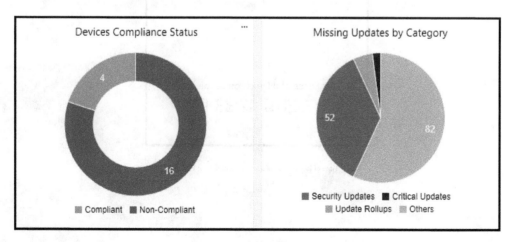

Information about computers meeting the requirements and number of updates grouped by categories

In order to configure **Devices Compliance Status**, the administrator needs to click ellipses (...) in the upper-right corner and configure available filters:

Compliance Status filter configuration

There is also information about the last successful synchronization of ConfigMgr with WSUS server:

Time of last successful synchronization with WSUS

Last information is a diagram showing--depending on the chosen category in **Missing Updates by Category**-- the number of computers which are missing a certain update:

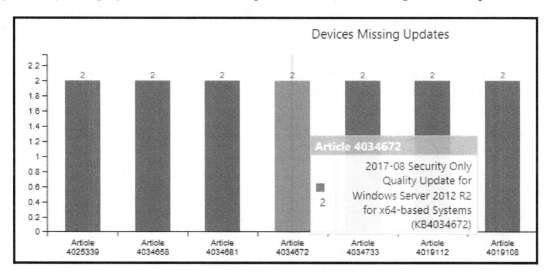

Missing security updates

If update rollup category is chosen, the diagram will show information about this particular update type:

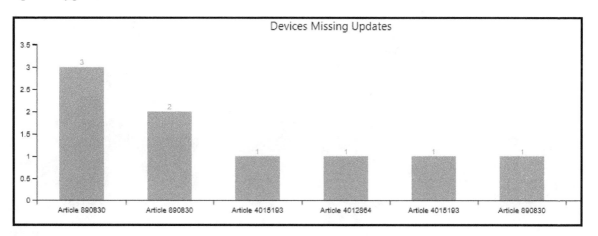

Missing update rollups

Summary

This chapter covered essential concepts related to updating deployment. The most important point is to understand the process of updates deployment; without it, it would be really had to manage updates and troubleshoot any issues.

Starting from the 2012 version, it is possible to deploy updates manually as well as automatically. Automatic deployment is very handy; however, it needs to be configured with due diligence to avoid any troubles.

The next chapter will show you how to secure managed computers that leverage Endpoint Protection.

9
Endpoint Protection

Previous chapters covered topics about the essentials of installing and configuring the ConfigMgr server, how to install clients, and how to deploy application updates on the system.

This chapter will cover important topics that are related to protecting a managed environment against `malware.scep`.

Specifically, we will cover the following topics:

- Understanding Endpoint Protection
- Deploying antimalware and firewall policies
- Creating a software update point for Endpoint Protection
- Monitoring Endpoint Protection

Understanding Endpoint Protection

Managing and configuring the environment are not all the capabilities provided by the ConfigMgr server; a great feature is also fundamental protection against unwanted software, and a component responsible for this is Endpoint Protection. It is a part of the ConfigMgr used for hardening the environment against malware threats and for firewall rules configuration.

The ConfigMgr server provides the possibility of performing deployments, central management, and monitoring statuses of managed computers. In fact, Endpoint Protection is Windows Defender, which is managed using the ConfigMgr console. Endpoint Protection and Windows Defender have similar interfaces and settings.

The ConfigMgr server license does not contain a license for Endpoint Protection; it is necessary to buy the subscription separately.

These are the steps that need to be taken in order to deploy the Endpoint Protection feature:

1. Installation of Endpoint Protection point.
2. Creation of the device collection and assigning it to Endpoint Protection.
3. `Client Settings` configuration for Endpoint Protection in order to install the Endpoint Protection client. By default, the Endpoint Protection client installation is disabled.
4. Creation of your own antimalware policies if not intending to use default ones.
5. Optionally, configuring firewall rules.
6. Optionally, configuring Windows Defender Advanced Threat Protection policies.

After deploying Endpoint Protection, it is possible to control the system state and the Endpoint Protection client.

The Endpoint Protection client is able to uninstall some antivirus programs when installing itself. It is not possible to install two different antivirus systems on one operating system.

Endpoint Protection capabilities:

- Detect and remediate malware, rootkit, network, and spyware vulnerabilities.
- Automatically download updates for virus definition and the Windows Defender engine.
- Basic management of firewall rules.
- Managing and monitoring Windows Defender **Advanced Threat Protection** (**ATP**). Windows ATP is a cloud service used to detect, track, and respond to threats found on the internet.

Integrating Endpoint Protection with the ConfigMgr server also provides the following benefits:

- An elastic way of distributing the Windows Defender definition and updates using a software update point
- Definitions can be downloaded from a software update point, from a local UNC path, or from Microsoft Malware Protection Center

- The Endpoint Protection client uses the ConfigMgr server infrastructure to download settings for clients and report about the operating system status
- Data sent to the ConfigMgr server can later be used in default reports available on the console or to create your own custom reports

Endpoint Protection point

The process for Endpoint Protection installation is very short. The first step is to choose between **Add Site System Roles** and **Create Site System Server** located under `Administration\Site Configuration\Sites`, and the next step is choosing the **Endpoint Protection point** role. Apart from the wizard, it is essential to provide the installation of definitions and updates to the engine using a software update point, and later automatic deployment rules:

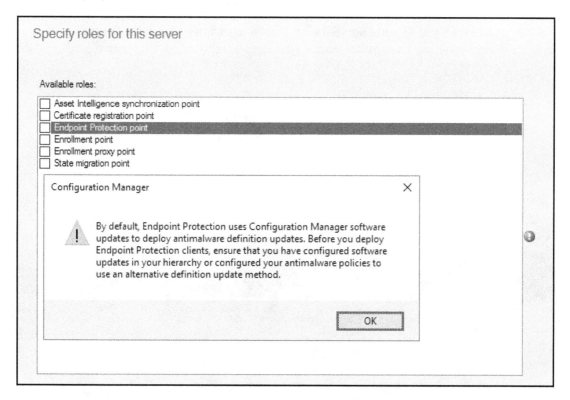

Choosing Endpoint Protection point role

Because Endpoint Protection needs an additional license, when installing the role, there is a need for accepting a license agreement for this product:

Endpoint Protection License Terms

Microsoft System Center Endpoint Protection

View the Microsoft System Center Endpoint Protection License Terms

View the Privacy Statement

☑ By checking this box, I acknowledge that I accept the License Terms and Privacy Statement.

Accepting of license agreement for Endpoint Protection

Microsoft provides Cloud Protection Service, which associates Endpoint Protection users. The wizard asks whether the administrator agrees to send data to the service, and it is also possible to decide how much data will be sent:

Specify Cloud Protection Service membership type

The Cloud Protection Service membership type you choose will be applied to all Endpoint Protection antimalware policies. Cloud Protection Service is a worldwide online community that includes System Center Endpoint Protection users. By joining Cloud Protection Service, System Center Endpoint Protection will automatically send information to Microsoft to help Microsoft determine which software to investigate for potential threats and to help improve System Center Endpoint Protection's effectiveness. This community also helps stop the spread of new malicious software infections.

You can choose to join the Cloud Protection Service community with either a Basic or Advanced membership. The type of information that is sent in reports to Microsoft depends on your level of Cloud Protection Service membership. In some instances, personal information might unintentionally be sent to Microsoft. However, Microsoft will not use this information to identify you or to contact you.

To learn more about Basic and Advanced Memberships and the information collected by the Reports, see the Privacy Statement at http://go.microsoft.com/fwlink/?LinkID=626987.

○ Do not join Cloud Protection Service

○ Basic membership (on Windows 10 and above, the behavior is the same as advanced membership)

◉ Advanced membership

Sending data to Cloud Protection Service settings

The installation of the Endpoint Protection role does not take a long time, and there are only three tasks that need to be done:

- `Client Settings` allow Endpoint Protection client installation
- Prepare and deploy a policy with custom Endpoint Protection settings if you do not intend to use a default one
- Deploy the automatic installation of Endpoint Protection definitions and engine updates

In the ConfigMgr environment managed by the central administration site, the Endpoint Protection role needs to be installed on a CAS server.

Client Settings for Endpoint Protection

As mentioned earlier, just installation of the Endpoint Protection role is not enough. It is necessary to allow ConfigMgr clients to install the Endpoint Protection client:

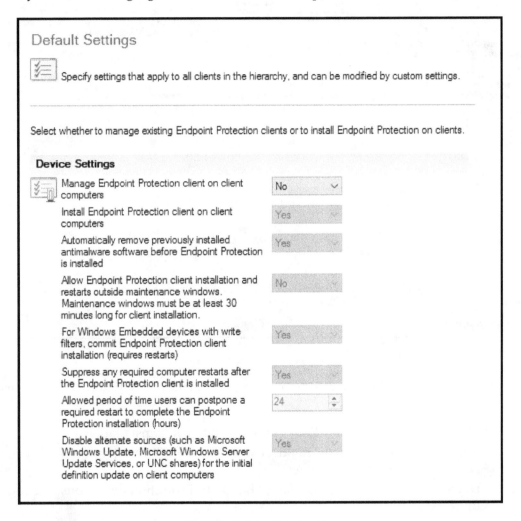

Client Settings for Endpoint Protection settings

The **Manage Endpoint Protection client on client computers** option enables the management of the Endpoint client.

The **Install Endpoint Protection client on client computers** option allows automatic installation of the Endpoint Protection client on managed systems.

The **Disable alternate sources (such as Microsoft Windows Update, Microsoft Windows Server Update Services, or UNC shares) for the initial definition update on client computers** option is used to reduce net flow traffic when definitions are downloaded for the first time. If this option is enabled, initially, only the ConfigMgr server is allowed to deliver virus definitions.

 There are three Endpoint Protection-related actions available from the ConfigMgr console, which are **quick scan**, **full scan**, and **download definitions**.

Configuring a software update point for Endpoint Protection

After Endpoint Protection, the client is installed and there are a few more configuration steps to be performed.

Microsoft prepares Endpoint Protection definition updates a few times a day. It is possible to imagine a situation where the administrator manually deploys these definition updates; however, it would be far too non-effective to work.

It is possible to configure automatic deployment using automatic deployment rules and prepared by the Microsoft template that is used when configuring rules for deploying definitions.

It is necessary to have the WSUS server integrated with the ConfigMgr server using the server role software update point. When configuring what will be synchronized, the administrator chooses certain classifications and products; in this case, classification would be definition updates and produces Forefront Endpoint Protection as well as Windows Defender.

After performing the synchronization, the automatic deployment rule needs to be created using the template given by Microsoft, or from scratch:

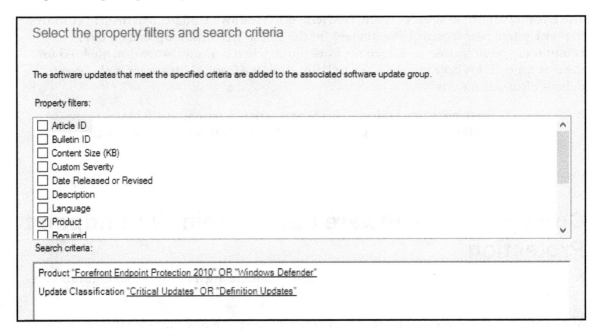

Select the property filters and search criteria

The software updates that meet the specified criteria are added to the associated software update group.

Property filters:

- [ ] Article ID
- [ ] Bulletin ID
- [ ] Content Size (KB)
- [ ] Custom Severity
- [ ] Date Released or Revised
- [ ] Description
- [ ] Language
- [x] Product
- [ ] Required

Search criteria:

Product "Forefront Endpoint Protection 2010" OR "Windows Defender"

Update Classification "Critical Updates" OR "Definition Updates"

Endpoint Protection classifications and product synchronization

It is important to remember that there are two options that need to be selected: Forefront Endpoint Protection as well as Windows Defender.

Antimalware policies

The last step of Endpoint Protection configuration is configuring antimalware policies for the Endpoint Protection client, which is also responsible for the client behavior. The policies can be created in `Asset and Compliance\Endpoint Protection\Antimalware Policies`.

Policies provide the following settings:

- The **Run a scheduled scan on client computers** option: Enabling the scanning schedule
- The **Scan type**, **Scan day**, and **Scan time** options: The scanning type and the day and hour of scanning
- The **Limit CPU usage during scan to (%)** option: The allowed CPU load when performing the scanning:

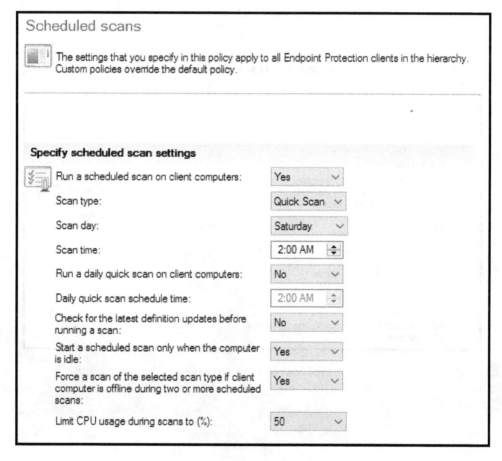

Options related to operating system scanning

- The **Check for Endpoint Protection definitions at a specific interval (hours)** option: How often the Endpoint Protection client will check for new definition versions:

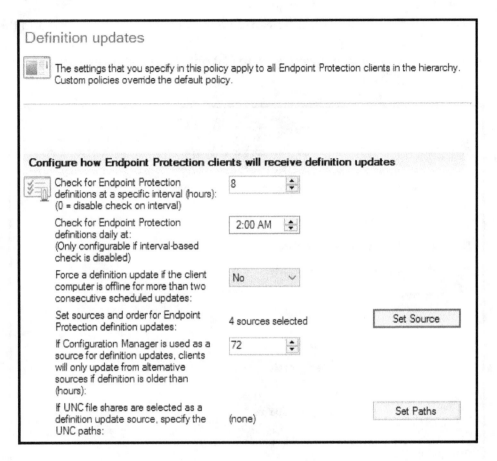

Endpoint Protection definition installation settings

- The **Set sources and order for Endpoint Protection definition updates** option: Selecting the location from which updates would be downloaded. Depending on environment configuration, the proper source should be chosen:

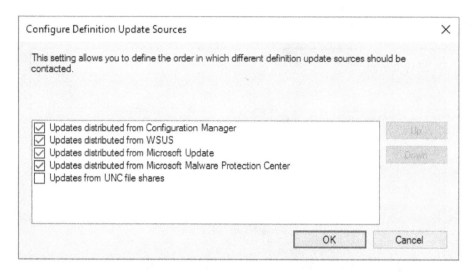

Endpoint Protection definition sources settings

Similar to `Client Settings`, there is an option to create custom policies and assign them to different collections. Thanks to that, depending on the need, it would be possible to change Endpoint Protection settings. These are created in the same way as `Client Settings` and further assigned to a certain collection.

 If there is an antivirus software installed on the distribution point, or any server containing binaries used by ConfigMgr server, it is necessary to exclude these folders from antivirus scanning. As for distribution point, it is necessary to exclude all folders used by this server role.

Firewall policies

Endpoint Protection, additionally, has the ability to manage firewall settings on the workstation. Firewall policies are created under `Asset and Compliance\Endpoint Protection\Windows Firewall Policies`.

When creating a policy, it is necessary to establish which firewall ports the policy will apply to. The **Block all incoming connections, including those in the list of allowed programs** option, is used to control the connection that can be made to the client. The **Notify the user when Windows Firewall blocks a new program** option is used to notify the user when the firewall blocks a certain software:

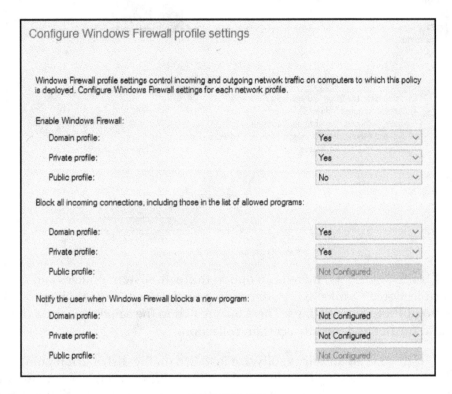

Configure Windows Firewall profile settings

Windows Firewall profile settings control incoming and outgoing network traffic on computers to which this policy is deployed. Configure Windows Firewall settings for each network profile.

Enable Windows Firewall:

Domain profile:	Yes
Private profile:	Yes
Public profile:	No

Block all incoming connections, including those in the list of allowed programs:

Domain profile:	Yes
Private profile:	Yes
Public profile:	Not Configured

Notify the user when Windows Firewall blocks a new program:

Domain profile:	Not Configured
Private profile:	Not Configured
Public profile:	Not Configured

Firewall policies settings

After creating a policy, similar to other policies, it is necessary to assign it to a certain computer collection.

Windows Defender Advanced Threat Protection

The last optional step of Endpoint Protection configuration is to apply proper settings on Windows Defender Advanced Threat Protection. These policies are created under `Asset and Compliance\Endpoint Protection\Windows Defender ATP Policies`.

To create policies, there is a need for purchasing access to the service after which it is possible to provide the configuration file when creating the policy.

Monitoring Endpoint Protection status

Just like how each deployment is required to monitor its state, the case is the same for Endpoint Protection as well.

The server provides a few ways to check operating systems' protection status:

- Under `Monitoring\Security\Endpoint Protection Status\System Center 2012 Endpoint Protection Status`, the console provides information about the operating system protection status
- Under `Monitoring\Security\Endpoint Protection Status\Malware Detected`, the console provides information about the malware detected
- Under `Monitoring\Security\Windows Defender ATP Status`, the console provides information related to Windows Defender ATP
- When selecting a device, the console provides information about current antimalware policy and detected threats
- Default reports created when installing the ConfigMgr server

Additionally, it is possible to configure alerts for Endpoint Protection separately for each collection.

Endpoint Protection state

The ConfigMgr server console, starting from 2012, provides a lot of priceless information. Previously, a lot of pieces of information were accessible only via reports, but now a lot of information is also available on the console.

The data from `Monitoring\Security\Endpoint Protection Status\System Center 2012 Endpoint Protection Status` is divided into two data types:

- Data **Security State** contains information about the Endpoint Protection client state:

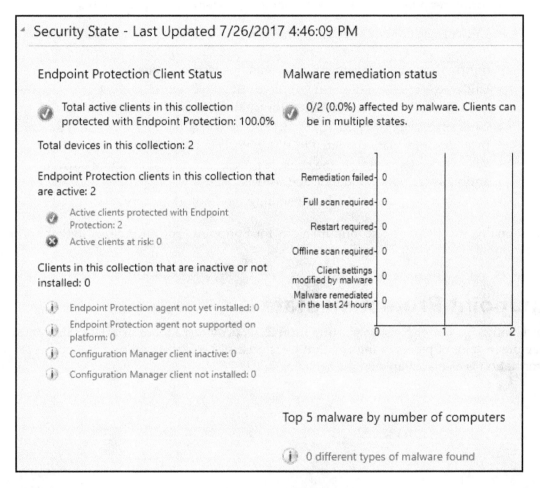

Data Security State Endpoint Protection

- Data **Operational State** relates to definitions installed on the Endpoint Protection clients and the ConfigMgr client state:

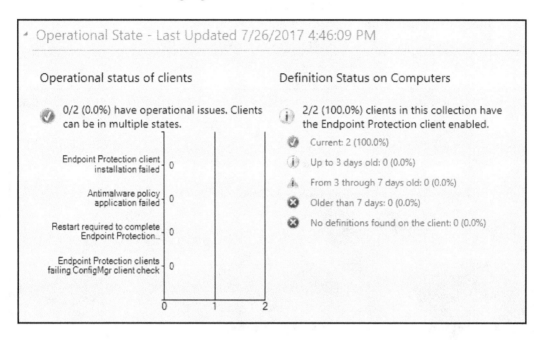

Operational State Endpoint Protection data

Data presented on the ConfigMgr console is only basic. Additional information can be found in the reports under `Monitoring\Reporting\Reports\Endpoint Protection`.

Data available under `Monitoring\Security\Endpoint Protection Status\System Center 2012 Endpoint Protection Status` is related to a particular collection. Thanks to this feature, it is possible to easily filter and display data.

Endpoint Protection alerts

Protecting the environment is a very important part of the administrator's work, hence it is always worth setting up alerts on Endpoint Protection. These alerts can be set in the collection properties under the **Alerts** tab.

There are three kinds of alerts:

- **Client status**: Related to the general ConfigMgr client state
- **Endpoint protection**: Regarding detected threats
- **Membership**: For a computer collection exceeding the assumed number of devices

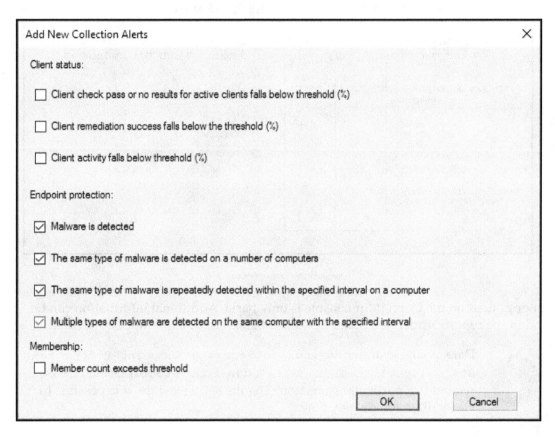

Choosing the alert type

After choosing the proper alert, there is a need to configure a threshold for it:

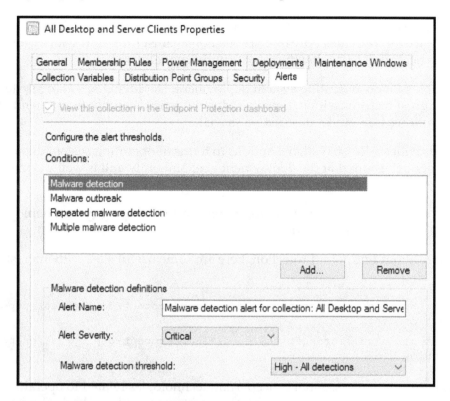

Alert threshold settings

Alerts can be viewed in two places on the console:

- `Monitoring\Alerts\Active Alerts` shows all active alerts

- `Monitoring\Alerts\All Alerts` shows all of the alerts that were triggered by the server

Alerts can be viewed not just from the console. After integrating the ConfigMgr server with the Exchange Server, an alert can be emailed to the administrators. This can be done using subscriptions available on the console under `Monitoring\Alerts\Subscriptions`.

Summary

This chapter covered how to protect the environment against malware. Endpoint Protection, however, provides only basic protection against threats. If wider protection is required, it is necessary to deploy third-party antivirus solutions.

The next chapter covers operating system deployment. Deploying operating systems can bring a lot of great features with it; however, due diligence is highly recommended as, if you're not cautious, it might be destructive as well.

ConfigMgr provides a lot of available options in terms of operating system deployment. Hence, in order to be sure that the deployment goes smoothly and is well-planned, it is essential to get familiar with all of them.

This chapter covers the most important topics related to operating system deployment security as well as available scenarios.

To know more about Endpoint Protection, here are some useful sites with interesting materials:

- `https://docs.microsoft.com/en-us/sccm/protect/deploy-use/endpoint-prot ection-configure`
- `https://docs.microsoft.com/en-us/sccm/protect/deploy-use/endpoint-prot ection`

The next chapter presents essential concepts and technologies related to operating system deployment, preparing and managing operating systems templates, basic ConfigMgr settings helpful for operating system deployment, and scenarios for operating system deployment.

10
Operating System Deployment

Previous chapters covered topics related to the installation and configuration of ConfigMgr server. Also, almost all available deployment types were described, such as application deployment, deploying updates, and compliance settings. This chapter will be fully dedicated to operating system deployment.

We will discuss the following topics:

- Operating system deployment
- Operating system deployment scenarios
- Task sequences
- Drivers
- Deployment types
- Windows 10 servicing

Operating system deployment

Deployment of operating systems is the most sophisticated feature available on the ConfigMgr server. To get all of the most useful functionalities out of that feature, one would need to know not only ConfigMgr server, but also some topics unrelated to ConfigMgr, such as:

- The operating system installation process
- Available possibilities of controlling the operating system installation process
- Creation and management of operating system templates

It doesn't really matter which operating system deployment tool we are talking about, be it Windows Deployment Service, Microsoft Deployment Toolkit, or ConfigMgr server--without having a knowledge base of the aforementioned topics, it would be really hard to do anything related to operating system deployment.

Only by having knowledge about the process itself is it possible to choose a tool for OS deployment. This chapter covers essential terms related to OS deployment and configuration, as well as, scenarios of OS deployment offered by ConfigMgr server.

 The methods of installing various versions of operating systems differ from each other, but whether for Windows 10, Windows 8, or Windows 7 deployments, there are still many things these deployments have in common.

Straight after being installed, the ConfigMgr server is ready to deploy operating systems in a basic scope. All the administrator needs to do before starting to prepare operating system deployments is to import an OS template that has been prepared manually or taken from an installation CD.

Of course, if there would be a need to use more advanced functions, such as starting the installation using a network card, you would need to set additional configurations on the ConfigMgr and Windows Deployment Services servers, network, and firewalls.

Operating system deployment terminology

It is not possible to manage an operating system deployment without getting to know terms related to it. An administrator without this knowledge won't be able to prepare any OS deployment.

As has been mentioned earlier, many topics related to OS deployment haven't changed over the years. Administrators that already used to deploy operating systems--even if it was Windows XP--will have it easy, as some phases of the process are exactly the same.

 The most important change in operating system deployment since Windows XP is deploying operating systems using images. Installation with images was introduced with Windows Vista. Since then--regardless of the deployment method--it is always done using the OS image.

We need to know the appropriate tools to properly deploy operating systems. Almost all of them have nothing in common with ConfigMgr, and this might be kind of an obstacle for administrators. The most important tools used for operating system deployment are:

- Windows Assessment and Deployment Kit
- Windows **Preinstallation Environment** (**PE**)
- Deployment Image Servicing and Management
- Windows System Image Manager
- System Preparation Tool
- User State Migration Tool

Windows Assessment and Deployment Kit

Windows Assessment and Deployment Kit is a set of tools essential to operating system deployment. Some of the tools described shortly are part of this package.

Windows PE

When deploying operating systems manually, one may not be aware that for OS deployment, one thing that is needed is Windows PE. The CD installer is prepared in such a way that Windows PE is loaded at the beginning, and in the next step, it runs the OS installer.

Hence, when deploying operating systems, the administrator needs to prepare the Windows PE image as well as the operating system image. During the installation process, ConfigMgr automatically creates images with Windows PE x86 and x64. As has been mentioned earlier in the first chapter, Windows Assessment and Deployment Kit is a required set of tools to install the ConfigMgr server. Thanks to this toolkit, we can install prepared Windows PE images. It is also possible to create your own custom images and add them to the ConfigMgr console. Windows PE images are available under `Software Library\Operating Systems\Boot Images`. These boot images are nothing different from bootable CDs with Windows PE.

When preparing a task sequence for operating system deployment, it is important to choose the proper Windows PE version for deploying the operating system. For an x86 operating system, Windows PE x86 or x64 can be used, but for deploying on an x64 operating system, Windows PE needs to be x64.

It might happen that the administrator needs to change the default Windows PE configuration. This operation can be done manually using dism.exe or using the ConfigMgr server console. The most common change is adding drivers to Windows PE, mostly network card related. Windows PE has some default network drivers, but there are situations where drivers need to be added manually:

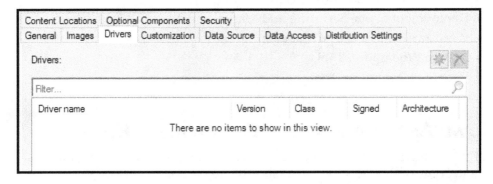

List of drivers added to Windows PE

The second reason for such a change in the Windows PE configuration is for adding components that are used for operating system deployment, and which are not present in the default Windows PE configuration:

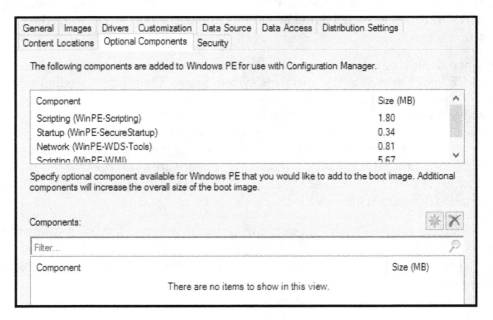

Available optional components for Windows PE

Regardless of the chosen operating system, Windows PE, and the operating system are both needed for deployment.

Operating system image

With Windows Vista, Microsoft completely changed the way of installing operating systems. All the previous versions of operating systems were installed by copying files to the hard drive and extracting them, and only after this was done did the installer start. Since Windows Vista, each operating system is installed from the OS image prepared by Microsoft and placed on the installation CD in the `\Sources` catalog.

While deploying operating systems using ConfigMgr, we might use the default operating system or a custom one. To use a custom image, it needs to be imported under `Software Library\Operating Systems\Operating System Images` in the ConfigMgr console:

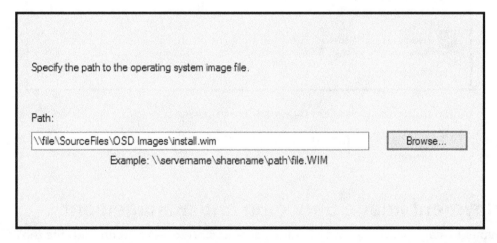

Selecting a .wim file to be imported

After the file is imported to the ConfigMgr server, the most important information about the operating system image can be viewed, including information about the type of operating system, partition architecture, and size:

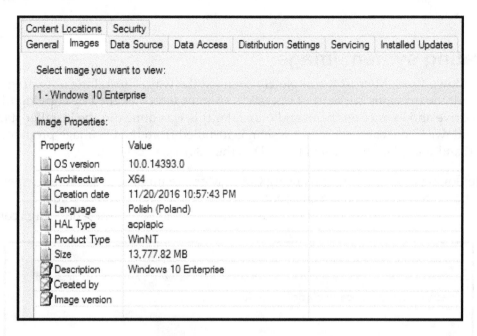

Information about the operating system image contained in the .wim file

Information about what a particular `.wim` file contains might also be pulled out using the `dism.exe` application.

Deployment Image Servicing and Management

Deployment Image Servicing and Management--`dism.exe`--is a command-line tool. The `dism.exe` file is a part of the Windows Assessment and Deployment Kit package that has superseded `imagex.exe`, which was used to create OS images until Windows 8.

While working with `dism.exe`, the following operations are available:

- Capture and apply Windows images
- Edit the `.wim` files, adding or removing operating systems from it
- Prepare a Windows PE boot image
- Mount images
- View lists of drivers and information about drivers
- View information about enabled features in the image
- Enable/disable features in the image
- Apply settings from an `unattend.xml` file

The `dism.exe` file is the most commonly used tool to create and modify operating system images, as well as to add drivers to Windows PE.

 Windows ADK is a required component for installing ConfigMgr server. Unfortunately, it is possible to uninstall it after ConfigMgr is installed. After Windows ADK is uninstalled, all functions on the ConfigMgr console responsible for Windows PE image modification and update installation will stop working.

Windows System Image Manager

Windows System Image Manager is a major part of Windows Assessment and Deployment Kit and is leveraged to create the `unattend.xml` files which can be used to control operating system installation and to change settings of the operating system.

While deploying operating systems, the installation may vary depending on the computer type--even if the OS installed is the same. For instance, when installing the operating system on a computer with a Wi-Fi network adapter, the installer will ask to which detected network it should connect. At such a moment, the installer waits for user interaction and stays pending; tools like ConfigMgr are supposed to automate the process and perform it without user interaction.

The following is an example of an unattend file for Windows 10 installation that skips the Wi-Fi connectivity step so installation can be performed automatically unattended to the very end:

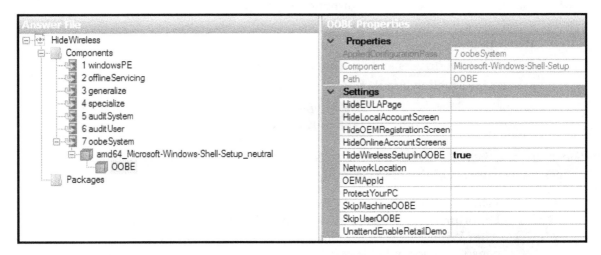

Unattend file settings example

The unattend.xml file might be used to control the installation processes of all operating systems deployed using ConfigMgr. The unattend.xml file can also be used to change the configuration of the installing system, such as adding some system components.

There is no need to create a separate OS image for each and every operating system and all the possible configurations. For instance, if the firm is international and the operating system language is English, regional configurations for each country can be changed via the unattend file or GPO.

Windows image file format

Windows image files allow for saving data in operating system image files. One .wim file can contain one instance of a regular or Windows PE operating system.

The .wim files contain the structure of saved files and folders from the template machine. To reduce used space, all operating system files are saved in a .wim file only once, so even if one file appears twice in the system, the .wim file will contain only one copy of the actual file.

During installation, files are installed where they are supposed to be on the template machine. Thanks to this deduplication process, the `.wim` files are much smaller than the actual operating system.

> Windows 10 contains a file called `install.esd` instead of `install.wim`. ConfigMgr does not support `.esd` files, but they can easily be exported using `dism.exe`.

System Preparation Tool

System Preparation Tool--`syspre.exe`--is a tool used to prepare a template VM to be an operating system template. The whole process of template creation can be done manually or in an automated way using ConfigMgr. The automated way is possible after preparing a special CD on the ConfigMgr console, under `Software Library\Operating Systems\Task Sequences`; the administrator should choose the **Create Task Sequence Media** option and later **Capture media**.

If the console runs on a machine where a USB drive is inserted, the administrator may select it and wait until all needed files are copied over. If the console runs on the server, it is possible to choose a place where the server saves its ISO files and choose that file instead, to be saved on the USB drive:

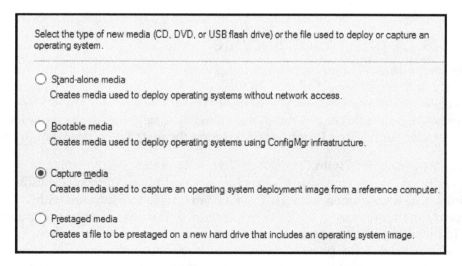

Select the type of new media (CD, DVD, or USB flash drive) or the file used to deploy or capture an operating system.

○ Stand-alone media
Creates media used to deploy operating systems without network access.

○ Bootable media
Creates media used to deploy operating systems using ConfigMgr infrastructure.

◉ Capture media
Creates media used to capture an operating system deployment image from a reference computer.

○ Prestaged media
Creates a file to be prestaged on a new hard drive that includes an operating system image.

Capturing operation system settings

The USB drive can be plugged into the template machine, to process with the creation and saving of the image.

Creation of the image consists of four phases:

- Installing and configuration of a template machine
- Running `sysprep.exe`
- Running the Windows PE operating system
- Creating the operating system image using `dism.exe` and saving it on the network share

Using the capture media CD, all steps--apart from the first one--can be performed automatically. All that needs to be done is to specify where the `.wim` file should be saved and which credentials will be used.

Of course, if someone wants to, it is possible to perform the whole operation step by step. It is not important how the OS image is prepared; it is important to have it. However, using capture media, the operation is much easier.

> The ConfigMgr client needs to be uninstalled before running `sysprep.exe` on a template machine.

Windows Deployment Service

One of the methods used to install the operating system is starting the PC using the network card and downloading all needed files over the network. The service responsible for that is called **Windows Deployment Service (WDS)**. It allows you to send Windows PE over the network on the target computer, and in the next step, the machine does a reboot and the computer starts using Windows PE, starting the installation process.

WDS very easily integrates with ConfigMgr. To use it, on the console under `Administration\Distribution Points`, after choosing one of the distribution points, the administrator should open settings. The **PXE** tab is used to configure with WDS. **Enable PXE support for clients** is used for WDS integration. **Allow this distribution point to respond to incoming PXE requests** is used to enable PXE requests. Once these two options are enabled, the distribution point starts supporting the installation of operating systems with network cards. ConfigMgr is able to install the operating system on a computer that is not in the database. It is a very useful function, but can also be harmful.

The option allowing such installations is **Enable unknown computer support**. If the administrator decides to enable this function, it is worth considering enabling the **Require a password when computers use PXE** option, which enforces the administrator providing a password on the computer where the installation will take place. If the password is not provided, the installation won't be started. **Specify the PXE server response delay (seconds)** should always be set to a value lower than on the WDS server. If the value is lower, it will be WDS performing PXE installation in the first place, instead of ConfigMgr:

PXE settings

After integrating the WDS server with ConfigMgr, it is ConfigMgr that takes control over the WDS service. There is no need for any additional configuration on the WDS side after integrating it with ConfigMgr.

While installing the WDS server, a `RemoteInstall` catalog is created, which--after integrating with ConfigMgr--contains the additional catalogs and files needed for PXE deployments:

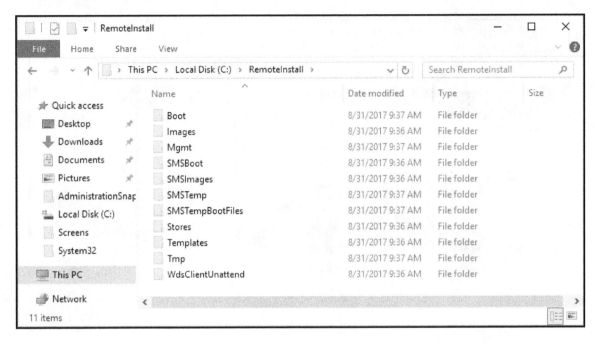

WDS installation folder, along with ConfigMgr files

Microsoft Deployment Toolkit 2012

Microsoft Deployment Toolkit 2012 (**MDT**) is a free tool used to deploy operating systems. It is always worth integrating ConfigMgr with this tool--it is very easy. After installing Microsoft Deployment Toolkit, the administrator needs to run a script prepared by Microsoft, available in the Start menu:

Specify the actions to perform.

(•) Install the MDT extensions for Configuration Manager

    ☐ Install the MDT console extensions for ConfigMgr 2007

    ☑ Install the MDT console extensions for ConfigMgr 2012

    ☑ Add the MDT task sequence actions to a ConfigMgr server

        Site server name: CM16.doctor.com

        Site code: PA1

( ) Remove the MDT extensions for Configuration Manager

    ☐ Remove the MDT console extensions for ConfigMgr 2007

    ☐ Remove the MDT console extensions for ConfigMgr 2012

    ☐ Remove the MDT task sequence actions from a ConfigMgr server

        Site server name: CM16.doctor.com

        Site code: PA1

Script integrating MDT with ConfigMgr server

This script copies MDT binaries to the ConfigMgr installation catalog, and thanks to this, the console contains additional task sequence tasks which are not available by default on ConfigMgr:

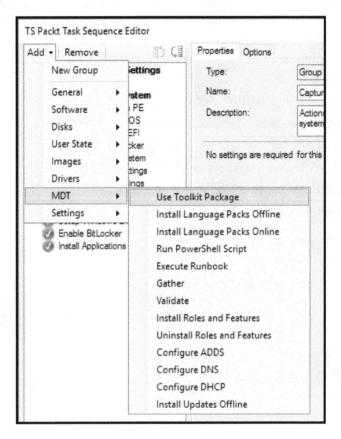

Additional MDT tasks in task sequence

User State Migration Tool

User State Migration Tool is a set of tools used to move user profiles between operating systems, and is a part of the Windows ADK package. It can be used by the administrator to move user profiles manually, or on a larger scale by ConfigMgr during operating system deployment.

ConfigMgr has a built-in mechanism for migrating user profiles during operating system installation:

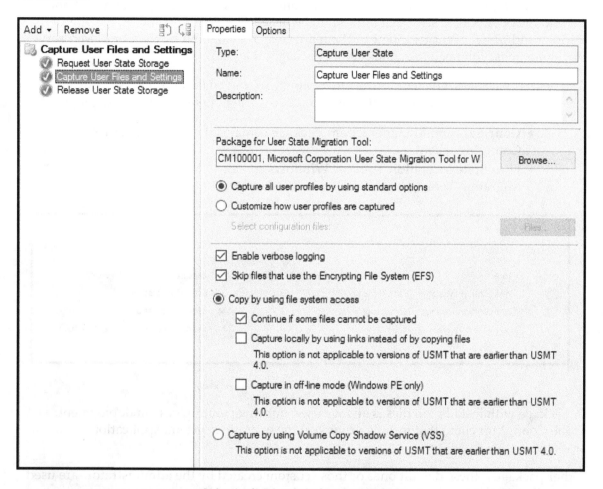

Configuration of built-in mechanism for user profile migration

It is not possible to migrate user profiles between the systems if these systems have different language versions.

Packages during operating system deployment

During operating system deployment, apart from using two operating systems--Windows PE and the operating system that is about to be installed--very often, the administrator uses various additional packages. Some of them are created by default by the ConfigMgr server, but sometimes, you need to create custom packages manually.

The default packages, created during OS deployment, can be found under `Assets and Compliance\Packages`. One of them will be used during operating system deployment:

- **Configuration Manager Client Package** contains the installation files of the ConfigMgr client
- **User State Migration Tool for Windows** contains files for the User State Migration Tool described earlier in this chapter:

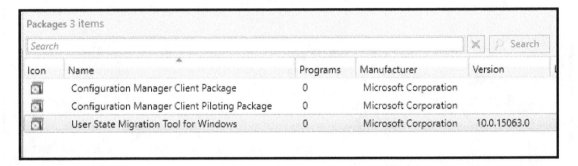

Default packages created during ConfigMgr server installation.

A package with installation files is always used during operating system deployment, as it is the ConfigMgr client that installs drivers on the operating system, applications, and updates.

Other packages--these default ones or those custom created by the administrator--are used depending on the requirement. A good example of such packages are those containing unattend files for operating system installation or User State Migration Tool files.

Unified Extensible Firmware Interface

ConfigMgr has the ability to install operating systems using BIOS and **Unified Extensible Firmware Interface** (**UEFI**). When creating a task sequence, two tasks are created--one for operating system deployment using BIOS and the second one using UEFI. When installing an operating system--depending on computer configuration--installation is done over BIOS or UEFI automatically. No other action is required, unless there is a need for changing the size or number of partitions:

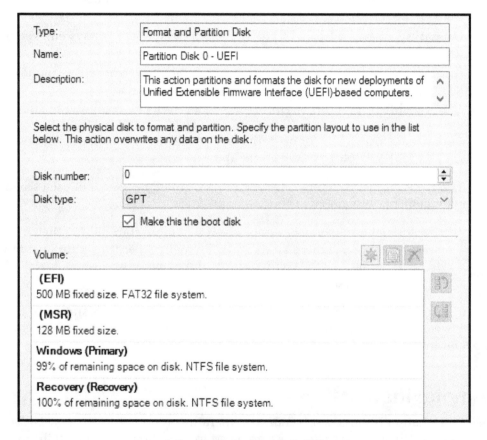

Configuration of the operating system using UEFI

It is possible to change the boot type from BIOS to UEFI after the system is installed, but such tasks need to be created manually in ConfigMgr.

Operating system deployment scenarios

Deployment of operating systems can be done using a few available scenarios. A deployment administrator must keep in mind which scenario will be used, and know how to prepare it.

In general, there are four scenarios of operating system deployment:

- **Bare-metal**: Operating system deployment on a new computer or a computer that needs to be reinstalled
- **Operating system refresh**: Deployment of a clean operating system, keeping user data
- **In-place upgrade**: Deployment of a new operating system replacing the old one, keeping user data
- **Side-by-side migration**: Migrating user data from one computer to another

Task sequences are not only used for operating system deployment. Since ConfigMgr 2012, they are used as a tool to deploy packages and applications.

Depending on the scenario, different roles of ConfigMgr will be used, but each scenario leverages management point and distribution point roles.

 Deployment of operating systems is much more complicated than it seems. Usually, in these kinds of deployments, there are additional things to be done, such as the configuration of the operating system, installation of applications, and updates.

If operating system deployment is done on virtual machines, then preparation of the installation is easier, as there is no need for preparing drivers. The topic of drivers will be taken up later in this chapter.

Bare-metal installation

Bare-metal installation is the *easiest* scenario of operating system deployment. The *easiest* as in, in this scenario, the administrator does not need to care about the data on the target computer.

To be able to leverage this scenario, the GUID of the computer or MAC address of the network card needs to be imported to the ConfigMgr operating system. If importing such information to the database is not possible, the **Enable unknown computer** option should be enabled in order to install an operating system over PXE.

Roles leveraged in such scenarios are as follows:

- Primary site, in order to import data about the computer and create deployment on a collection that contains this computer or a default collection, **All Unknown Computer**
- Management point shares policy, for the client with information about the operating system deployment
- Distribution point from where all the data needed for operating system deployment will be downloaded

A bare-metal scenario can be started using a network card or a USB drive, or by leveraging an already installed ConfigMgr client.

Operating system refresh

The operating system refresh scenario is very similar to the bare-metal scenario. The only difference is it is run by the ConfigMgr client installed on the computer. ConfigMgr server roles are exactly the same as for the bare-metal scenario.

In-place upgrade

In-place upgrade installs a new operating system for the user, keeping all his data and applications. Deploying an operating system using this scenario is quite sophisticated, as the administrator needs to take care not only of securing user data from being removed, but also installing all the missing applications on the new operating system.

It is always good to perform a backup copy of an operating system from a computer that will be processed, but this might significantly extend the time needed for deployment on a single computer. Deployment of that type is done by the ConfigMgr client, so there is no need to import any data to the ConfigMgr database.

Roles needed for such scenarios are:

- Management point shares policy, for the client with information about the operating system deployment
- Distribution point from where all the data needed for operating system deployment will be downloaded
- State migration point where all the users' profiles will be kept

> Users' migrated profiles can be saved over LAN on the state migration point, or locally. The second approach definitely shortens the time needed for the process on a single computer, as data is saved locally.

Side-by-side migration

The side-by-side migration scenario is more complicated, as it contains two phases. First, there is a need to back up all the users' profiles and next, on the new computer, install the operating system and restore user profiles. It is not possible to be done in one phase.

To tell ConfigMgr which profile from the old computer needs to be imported to the new machine, it is necessary to connect two MAC addresses in the ConfigMgr database. This can be done when importing information about the new computer to the ConfigMgr database. The new machine is then described as the **destination computer**, and the computer from which data was backed up is called the **source computer**.

> When backing up a user's profile from the source computer, data is copied over the network to the state migration point, compressed, and protected by a password, which is generated by the ConfigMgr server.

Roles leveraged in such a scenario are as follows:

- Primary site, in order to import data about the computer and create deployment on a collection that contains this computer or default collection, **All Unknown Computer**
- Management point shares policy, for the client with information about the operating system deployment
- Distribution point from where all the data needed for the operating system deployment will be downloaded
- State migration point where all the users' profiles will be kept

Task sequences

A task sequence is a sequence of tasks that are going to be performed on a computer. Tasks are performed from top to bottom.

> During creation or editing of a task sequence, ConfigMgr does not check if a particular task sequence is valid and makes sense. It only checks if particular steps have proper configuration. The administrator needs to know the proper order of tasks, as ConfigMgr is not capable of verifying it.

If the administrator at the end of the deployment creates a task to format local drives, ConfigMgr will perform the task, not checking if it makes sense.

When configuring a task sequence, it is worth remembering that it is possible to use variables built into the ConfigMgr server or variables created manually by the administrator. Leveraging variables and conditions available in TS allows us to create a mechanism that will deploy operating systems depending on the variables and current conditions.

A good example of a variable that is commonly used in a build is **OSDComputerName**. It is used to configure the computer name; when used in TS, each time it is used, it will give a different name to the computer.

Particular tasks or the whole groups of tasks can be performed or not by checking conditions. There are countless possibilities of using conditions; the most common one is reaching the WMI database asking for the computer model on which the deployment is performed. If there are five different computer models, it is possible to create five separate task sequences for each computer model. However, it is also possible to create one task sequence and based on the conditions, indicate which task groups should be performed depending on the computer model.

Task sequence creation

Task sequences can be created manually or using a wizard available on the ConfigMgr server console, which allows us to create a few basic task sequence types. If ConfigMgr is integrated with Microsoft Deployment Toolkit, the ConfigMgr console will contain an additional wizard that might be leveraged to create the same task sequences as when using Microsoft Deployment Toolkit.

Task sequences can be created on the console under `Software Library\Operating Systems\Task Sequences`. The administrator needs to choose the proper type of task sequence and later configure it. In the following example, **Install an existing image package** type has been chosen, so the fundamental operating system deployment type is leveraging the imported OS image:

1. The first step in the configuration is setting up a name for the task sequence and selecting the Windows PE image for the task sequence:

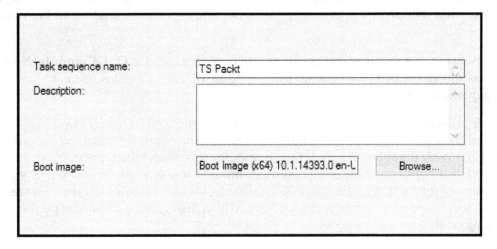

Setting up a task sequence name and Windows PE image

2. The second step is choosing the operating system that needs to be deployed. The **Image package** option is used to specify the used .wim file, and the **Image index** option is used to specify the OS image file. If the administrator wants to rearrange partitions and format disks, **Partition and format the target computer before installing the operating system** should be selected as well:

Specify the Windows operating system image and installation information.

Image package: Windows 10 Enterprise pl-PL   Browse...
Image index: 1 - Windows 10 Enterprise   ∨

☑ Partition and format the target computer before installing the operating system.

☑ Configure task sequence for use with BitLocker

Specify the licensing information for the Windows installation.

Product key:
Server licensing mode: Do not specify   ∨
Maximum server connections: 5 ⬍

⦿ Randomly generate the local administrator password and disable the account on all supported platforms (recommended)

◯ Enable the account and specify the local administrator password

    Password:
    Confirm password:

Selecting the .wim file used in deployment, as well as operating system image

3. The third step is adding a computer to a domain or work group. **Domain** allows us to specify to which domain the computer should be joined, **Domain OU** specifies the particular organizational unit where the computer account should be placed, and the **Account** option is used to indicate using which account the computer will be joined to a domain:

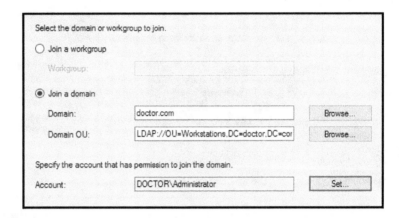

Adding computers to AD settings

If the computer's OU is specified as the target OU, then the computer will not be joined to a domain and deployment will end with failure.

4. The next step is optional, and is about adding switches to the ConfigMgr client installer, which are triggered after the operating system is deployed:

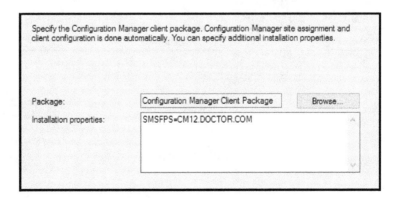

ConfigMgr client installed settings

The ConfigMgr client is not needed for a successful operating system deployment. However, if the administrator plans to install some applications, run scripts, or perform any other configuration on the operating system, the ConfigMgr client will be needed.

5. In this example, as it is about installing a fresh operating system, the boxes aren't selected. However, these are helpful in other deployment scenarios, like in-place upgrade or computer refresh:

Select the settings on the destination computer to migrate as part of this image deployment.

This action will capture the user specific settings.

☐ Capture user settings and files

USMT Package: Microsoft Corporation User State Migration To(Browse

◉ Save user settings and files on a State Migration Point

◯ Save user settings and files locally

☑ Capture locally by using links instead of by copying files

This option is not applicable to versions of USMT that are earlier than USMT 4.0

This action will capture the configuration of the network.

☐ Capture network settings

This action will capture the Windows specific settings.

☐ Capture Microsoft Windows settings

Computer to computer data migration settings

6. Step six is configuring update installation after the operating system is installed. For this step to work, the computer on which the operating system is installed needs to be placed in the collection for which update deployment is configured:

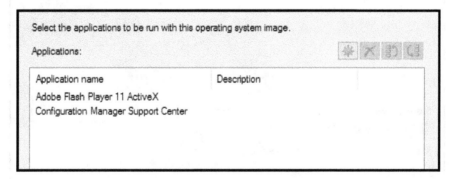

Install software updates based on the type of software update deployment:

○ Required for installation - Mandatory software updates only

○ Available for installation - All software updates

◉ Do not install any software updates

Update installation settings

7. In step seven, the administrator specifies which application should be installed on the operating system; apart from applications, packages can also be used in this step:

Select the applications to be run with this operating system image.

Applications:

Application name	Description
Adobe Flash Player 11 ActiveX	
Configuration Manager Support Center	

Application installation settings

8. The last step is saving the created task sequence:

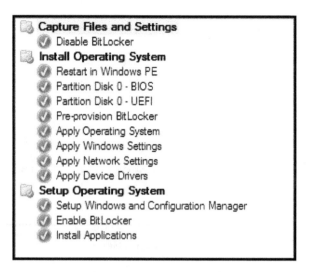

View of completed task sequence, creating using a wizard.

Of course, all created task sequences can be freely modified after they are created. It is also possible to create them manually, not using a wizard.

It has been mentioned before that a task sequence is not only the installation of the operating system; it is also its configuration after it is installed--such a scenario is a very common thing. Modification of the installed system can be done using, for instance, the **Run Command Line** task.

The following is an example of an easy task of adding certain AD groups to a local administrators group on the computer:

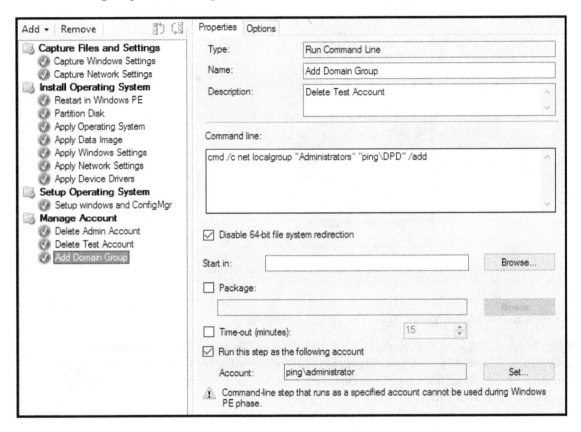

Example of Run Command Line settings

The example shows that to properly configure task sequences, the administrator needs to have wide knowledge about IT systems in general, not only about ConfigMgr.

An administrator who has a good knowledge about operating systems and their maintenance will create better task sequences than an administrator that has knowledge only about ConfigMgr.

Drivers

Installing drivers during operating system deployment can be the most time-consuming task. It might be considered as a standard that driver configuration for one operating system and one computer model might take up to one working day, sometimes even longer.

Driver installation on the ConfigMgr server can be performed in two different ways:

- By importing drivers to the ConfigMgr database using `.inf` files
- By installing the drivers using an application prepared by the vendor

 When installing operating systems, the only supported type of installation is silent type.

Note that when installing the drivers, what is worth checking is the proper order of installation. Each computer model might have a different supported driver installation order.

Installation of imported drivers

Importing drivers to the ConfigMgr database is not a hard task. The administrator needs to download drivers from the vendor site. On the server console under `Software Library\Operating Systems\Drivers`, the administrator needs to choose the **Import Driver** option by specifying the UNC path where the drivers have been saved.

The administrator will then see a list of detected drivers:

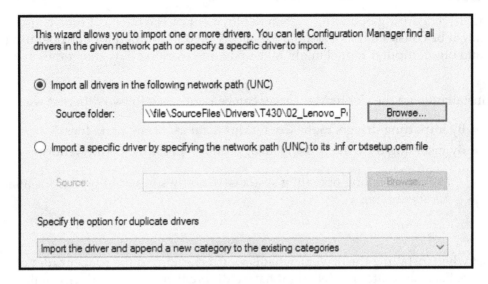

Specifying drivers source folder

When importing drivers, it is worth giving categories to them, as it makes later deployments easier. All of the imported drivers can be viewed on the console:

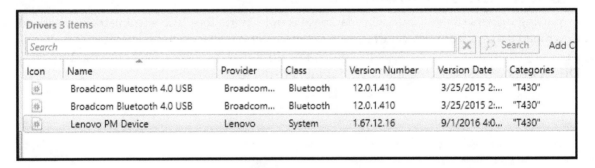

List of imported drivers from the ConfigMgr database

Drivers need to be imported on the distribution point in order to be installed during operating system deployment. This can be achieved using `Driver Packages`, under `Software Library\Operating Systems\Driver Packages`. After the relevant package is created, it can later be sent to a distribution point.

Unfortunately, during OS deployment, ConfigMgr does not check whether the drivers are available on the distribution point. If the drivers are not there, deployment will start and eventually fail, reporting an issue related to missing drivers.

The previously mentioned categories can be used to specify exactly which drivers shall be used by the installer. Normally, the installer checks what drivers are available in the database and installs those that suit it the most. However, that might extend the installation process, as the ConfigMgr database might contain thousands of drivers.

Leveraging categories allows us to narrow down the number of drivers that should be considered by the operating system installer. This can be performed in the **Apply Device Drivers** step, using **Limit driver matching to only consider in selected categories**:

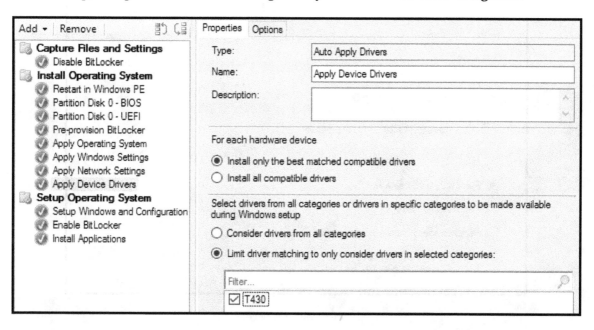

Configure install drivers for just the selected category

Driver installation using packages

Drivers can be installed as packages as well, using the installer. We need to prepare the package with a relevant application that installs drivers. The application needs to have the ability to run in silent mode. After the package is configured, two more options need to be set; in the program properties on the **Environment** tab, **Program can run** needs to be set to **Whether or not a user is logged on**:

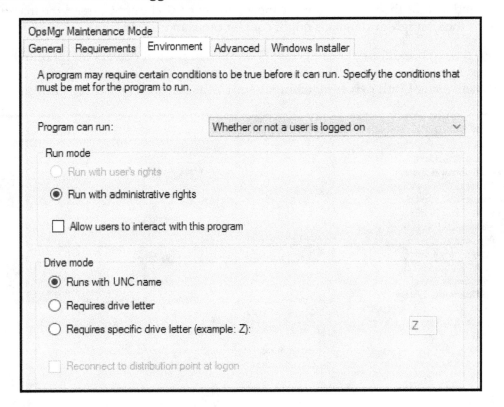

Program environment settings

The second option is on the **Advanced** tab; by enabling **Allow this program to be installed from the Install Package task sequences without being deployed**, the administrator specifies that that package can be used during operating system deployment:

Program's advanced settings

In task sequences, the administrator needs to choose **Install Package**, and, in **Select the software packages to install**, the package to be installed:

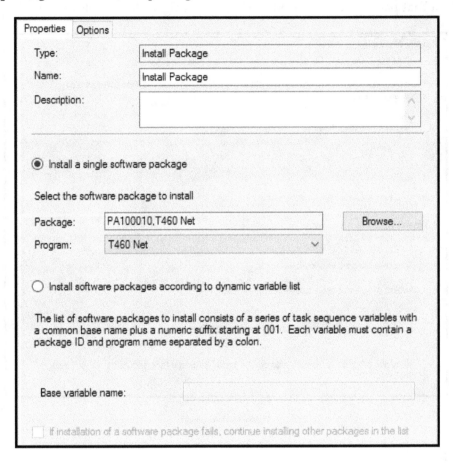

Task sequence configuration for package installation

Preparing drivers for branded computers is a little easier, as vendors often prepare drivers in the form of packages that are ready to import to ConfigMgr, or ready to install as .exe or .msi files.

Still, the most time-consuming task is testing drivers on a physical computer and checking whether all drivers have been installed properly and if all devices work correctly. Often it might not be enough to just check if a device is visible in device manager; it might need to be properly tested, for instance, by simply using it.

Deployment types

Deployment of operating systems is very similar to the deployment of applications and updates. There are, however, some differences which are a result of the specificity of each process. Application and update installations are always triggered by the ConfigMgr client; on the other hand, in the case of the operating system, there are three other possibilities-- starting the installation from bootable CD, USB drive, or a network card.

Same as the other deployments, the deployment types available are available deployment and required deployment.

 Administrators of ConfigMgr server have full access to computers added to the ConfigMgr server and all the data on them, because of ConfigMgr clients installed on these machines. All the data can easily be erased, even without having explicitly granted permissions on those machines.

Operating system deployment needs to be conducted with all due diligence, after ensuring that installation is performed in a controlled manner and strictly on the machines it is supposed to be. The administrator needs to be sure that the tasks sequence configuration is fully correct.

 Over the last few years, there were a lot of well-documented operating system deployments with incorrect configuration run by administrators. Some results of improper configuration were even the deleting of all the data from all the company computers after preparing a deployment on the **All Systems** collection.

ConfigMgr does no more nor less than what the administrator tells it to do, on the computers specified by the administrator, in the time span given by the administrator.

When creating the required operating system deployment, the administrator needs to--the same as for application or update deployment--specify a collection on which the deployment will be applied, since when it should work, and what the deadline is.

In the case of operating system installation, there is the additional option **Make available to the following**: which decides the way the deployment can be performed. The following options are available:

- **Only Configuration Manager Clients**: Only the ConfigMgr client installed on the operating system will be able to perform the deployment
- **Configuration Manager clients, media and PXE**: The deployment can be performed by the ConfigMgr client installed on the operating system, using the USB drive, or using the network card and PXE
- **Only media and PXE**: This deployment can be only performed using the USB drive or using the network card and PXE
- **Only media and PXE (hidden)**: This deployment can be performed the same as the previous one, with the difference that a special parameter needs to be provided that will allow us to start it:

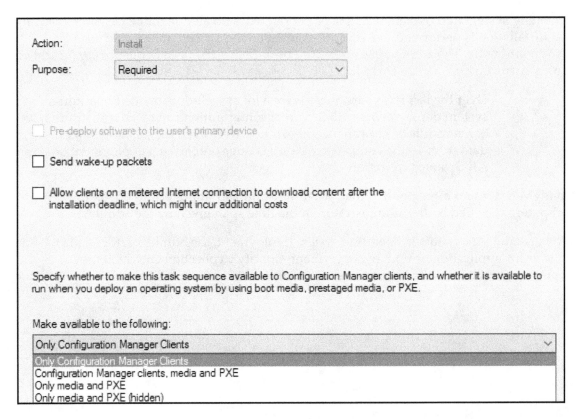

Setting up a way operating system deployment can be performed

The ability to reduce ways of starting task sequences significantly improves the security, as even if the administrator makes a mistake, it will affect fewer computers.

Windows 10 servicing

Windows 10 introduced a new way of operating system servicing. Since always, the administrator was responsible for installing updates that have been prepared for the operating system.

In order to properly maintain Windows 10, deployment of updates of two different types needs to be prepared:

- Standard updates, like for all the older systems
- Updates that upgrade the operating system to a new version, for instance, 1607 to 1703

Microsoft has split the handling of these two update types in the console. Standard updates are deployed along with all the other updates, but upgrades that change versions of the Windows 10 operating system are maintained on the ConfigMgr console under `Software Library\Windows 10 Servicing`.

Configuration and deployment have been described in `Chapter 8`, *Software Update Management*. The topic, for now, is the deployment of Windows 10 upgrades.

Servicing plan

As has been mentioned, upgrades to Windows 10 are located under `Software Library\Windows 10 Servicing` in the ConfigMgr console. Similar to other updates, these are also deployed using **Automatic Deployment Rules**.

Data in Windows 10 servicing will be available only after the WSUS server is synchronizing the **Upgrades** classification.

On the console, under `Software Library\Windows 10 Servicing\All Windows 10 Updates`, the administrator can see all available Windows upgrades and feature updates:

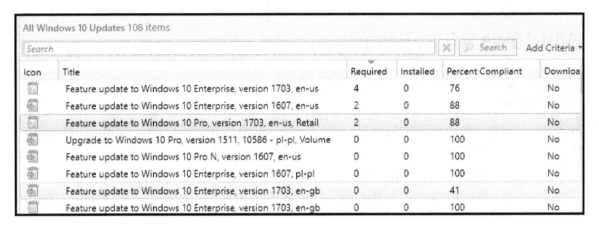

Icon	Title	Required	Installed	Percent Compliant	Downloa
	Feature update to Windows 10 Enterprise, version 1703, en-us	4	0	76	No
	Feature update to Windows 10 Enterprise, version 1607, en-us	2	0	88	No
	Feature update to Windows 10 Pro, version 1703, en-us, Retail	2	0	88	No
	Upgrade to Windows 10 Pro, version 1511, 10586 - pl-pl, Volume	0	0	100	No
	Feature update to Windows 10 Pro N, version 1607, en-us	0	0	100	No
	Feature update to Windows 10 Enterprise, version 1607, pl-pl	0	0	100	No
	Feature update to Windows 10 Enterprise, version 1703, en-gb	0	0	41	No
	Feature update to Windows 10 Enterprise, version 1703, en-gb	0	0	100	No

Information about available upgrades and feature updates for Windows 10

Information enclosed in there is exactly the same as for all the other updates. On the console, under `Software Library\Windows 10 Servicing`, the administrator can see information related to Windows 10 servicing:

- **Windows 10 Usage**: Shows data about Windows 10 versions used in the environment.
- **Windows 10 Rings**: Shows information by branch and readiness state. **Release Ready** is, in other words, Current Branch; **Business Ready** means Current Branch for Business; and **Long Term Servicing Branch** is just a Long Term Servicing Branch:

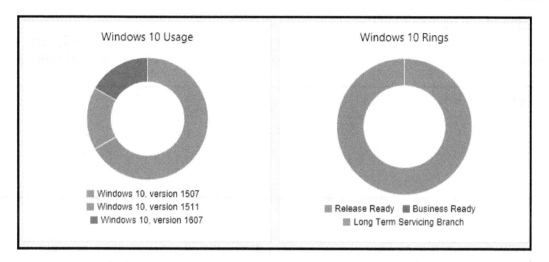

Information about Windows 10 discovered in the environment

- **Expired**: Shows the percentage of Windows 10 devices that are on a build of Windows 10 that is past its end of life. A build that is past its end of life is no longer receiving monthly cumulative updates, which include security updates.
- **Create Servicing Plan**: Allows us to create a Servicing Plan. A Servicing Plan is nothing different from normal **Automatic Deployment Rules**, with a few additional options which are not available for regular updates.
- **Expire Soon**: Shows the percentage of computers that will be at end of life in 4 months.
- **Alerts**: Informs if ConfigMgr console has any alerts related to Windows 10 servicing:

Servicing Plans can be created on the console under `Software Library\Windows 10 Servicing\Servicing Plans`. As has been mentioned earlier, they are created very similarly to the `Automatic Deployment Rules,` but there are some additional options:

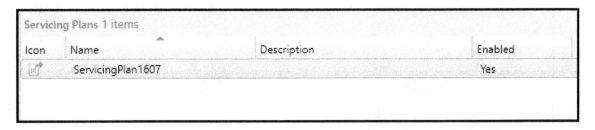

Servicing Plan

When creating a Servicing Plan, the administrator needs to decide whether there is a need for delaying the deployment of new Windows 10 versions, and if so, for how long. It is possible to postpone deployment to 120 days from the date it has been released by Microsoft:

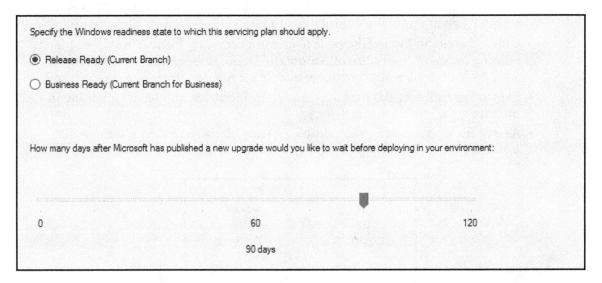

Postponing Windows 10 upgrade settings

You also need to choose updates related to the Servicing Plan. All the rest of the configuration is similar to **Automatic Deployment Rules**:

The upgrades that meet the specified criteria will be added to the associated deployment

Property filters:

- ☑ Language
- ☐ Required
- ☑ Title

Search criteria:

Language "English"

Title Windows 10 Enterprise,

Choosing updates related to Servicing Plan

Servicing Plans are always configured as a required deployment; it is not possible to create them as an available deployment.

Windows Update for Business policies

Starting from 1706, if managed operating systems are using Windows Update for Business directly, it is possible to create policies delaying **Windows 10 Feature Updates** or **Windows 10 Quality Updates**. Mentioned policies can be created on the console under `Software Library\Windows 10 Servicing\Windows Update for Business Policies`. Managed devices need to have an Internet connection in order to reach the Windows Update For Business service.

The **Branch readiness level** option is used to set up a branch for a computer, and **Deferral period (days)** is used to specify for how long the deployment needs to be postponed; the longest possible time is 180 days. Options **Pause Feature Updates starting** and **Pause Quality Updates starting** are used to stop receiving updates for Windows Update for Business. In case of a feature update, the longest available time is 35 days, the same as for quality updates. After that time, the computer automatically connects to the service, checking for the newest available updates:

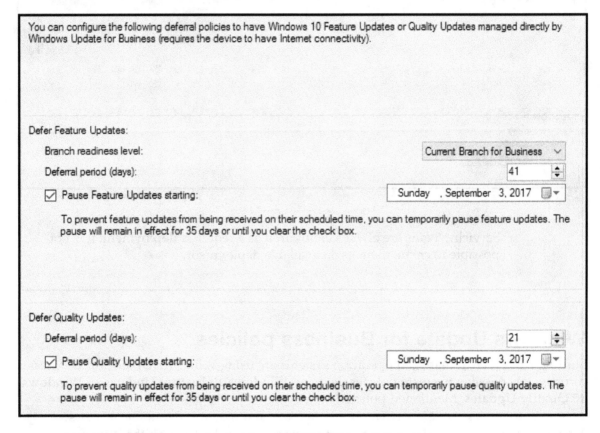

Policy for devices managed by Windows Update for Business

After the policy is created, you need to prepare deployments on proper collections.

Upgrade Readiness

Starting from 1610, it is possible to use the **Upgrade Readiness** service, which is a cloud service that enables you to assess and analyze device readiness with Windows 10. This data can be viewed on the ConfigMgr console under `Monitoring\Upgrade Readiness`:

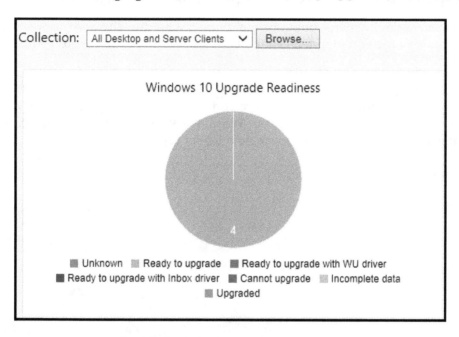

Upgrade Readiness data is available on the ConfigMgr server console

To be able to fully use this feature, you need to have an Azure subscription. Later, the administrator needs to create a Microsoft Operations Management Suite workspace and integrate ConfigMgr with Microsoft Operations Management Suite using **Upgrade Readiness Connector**.

Summary

This chapter covered the abilities of ConfigMgr for operating system deployment, which is definitely; not an easy task. It requires very good knowledge from the administrator of the operating system installation process, methods, and tools to configure operating systems.

Operating system deployment should be maintained with due diligence, as it is very easy to perform a deploy on an unintended group of computers, and unfortunately, this means losing data.

In the next chapter, we will cover topics related to gathering various data from the operating system, like for instance hardware and software inventory. It will be presented how to create queries and collect data from **Windows Management Instrumentation (WMI)** database, SQL and also how to create relevant reports.

11
Configuration Manager Assets

Previous chapters led you through the server installation and configuration process, as well as client installation and deploying of applications and updates.

All the operations that have been described in previous chapters are performed by the clients, and this happens because a computer where the ConfigMgr client resides has been assigned to a collection. All server deployments available on ConfigMgr are assigned to a collection, and the collection might contain computers, mobile devices, or user objects.

Collections are created based on data available in the **Windows Management Instrumentation** (**WMI**) database, and this is the topic that is going to be covered in this chapter. The chapter will explain how to gather data from the client computers and how to use this data for creating queries, collections, and reports. Not only WMI-related topics, but also some basic steps of how to use data from SQL databases for report creation, will be covered.

Specifically, we will discuss the following topics:

- Queries
- Reports
- Hardware inventory
- Software inventory
- Asset intelligence
- Collection queries
- Console queries
- Console reports

Data collection

Before explaining how to set up data gathering, it is important to explain an important issue related to available data sources in the ConfigMgr server. There are two kinds of data and two databases: a WMI and an SQL database. While creating reports, queries will reference different databases.

> To show the same data in the query as well as in the report, you need to perform two different queries, one to the WMI database and the second one to the SQL database. It is especially fiddly for new administrators, as you need to do the same work twice.

The ability to create queries and reports doesn't mean much if the administrator will not be able to get to the interesting data. Sometimes it is fairly easy, as the server collects a default set of data; however, there are moments when there is a need for manually adding some data to be collected.

> Topics related to gathering data are far beyond day-to-day server administration, as administrators need to know where the data is and how to get to it. It is also important to ensure that--if certain data has been found--it is consistent with reality, as there are situations where data is not consistent with the actual activities of a user or computer. This type of knowledge is completely unrelated to ConfigMgr.

Data sent by ConfigMgr clients is saved in the SQL database at the very end. After being sent from the clients, data is first saved in the WMI database, and as a next step in the SQL database.

To make use of data gathered in both databases, you need to have skills in database query writing. The basics are relatively easy to learn, but later, when you need to have much more granular and precise reports, you might need to have a separate person whose job it is to create such queries and reports and maintain them properly.

> Performing a hardware/software inventory scan with the ConfigMgr client can be monitored in the `inventoryagent.log` log file. All client log files are available under `C:\Windows\ccm\logs`.

Hardware inventory gathers configuration data about the hardware and operating system, including information about software installed; however, it is only about the ones that leave a trace in the operating system. If there is software deployed that is not installed, it will not be detected.

Software inventory gathers data about investigated files placed on the operating system drives. This data has nothing in common with installed software, something one would expect based on the feature name; however, thanks to this, it is possible to search for certain files and detect software that hasn't been installed and works, for instance, in portable mode.

Queries

Queries that create collections and are saved in the console are saved in the WMI database on the ConfigMgr server. Clients send gathered data to the WMI located in the management point, and then it sends them further to the site server.

On the internet, you can find many example queries that can successfully be used, but it is important to distinguish them from reports. For instance, something like the following is a query, not a report:

```
select Name, SMSAssignedSites, IPAddresses, IPSubnets,
OperatingSystemNameandVersion, ResourceDomainORWorkgroup,
LastLogonUserDomain, LastLogonUserName, SMSUniqueIdentifier, ResourceId,
ResourceType, NetbiosName from sms_r_system where Client = 0 or Client is
null
```

This query will show all computers without the ConfigMgr client installed. The easiest way to identify a query is that in each query, there is a table that starts with sms_; in this particular example, it was the sms_r_system table. This is how tables are named in the WMI database.

 It is a good practice to prepare additional queries for the console besides the ones created for collection in order to get relevant information faster. Such queries always return data faster than queries prepared for collection. Information from collections is not always available or might not refresh frequently enough.

An administrator that prepares queries and reports needs to know where the data is located in the database. While creating queries, the following terms are used:

- **Type object**: There are various types of objects in the WMI database; for instance, **System Resource** is the computer object type
- **Attribute class**: Each object type has an attribute class assigned to it; for instance, the System class contains information about the operating system, but not all of them are called what might be expected

- **Attribute**: Each attribute class has attributes assigned to it; for instance, **System Type** contains information about the particular operating system--whether it is an x86-based PC or x64:

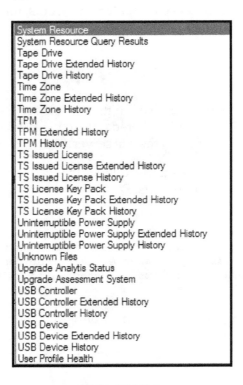

System Resource
System Resource Query Results
Tape Drive
Tape Drive Extended History
Tape Drive History
Time Zone
Time Zone Extended History
Time Zone History
TPM
TPM Extended History
TPM History
TS Issued License
TS Issued License Extended History
TS Issued License History
TS License Key Pack
TS License Key Pack Extended History
TS License Key Pack History
Uninterruptible Power Supply
Uninterruptible Power Supply Extended History
Uninterruptible Power Supply History
Unknown Files
Upgrade Analytis Status
Upgrade Assessment System
USB Controller
USB Controller Extended History
USB Controller History
USB Device
USB Device Extended History
USB Device History
User Profile Health

List of example attributes

There are a lot of attribute classes and attributes assigned to them. For a beginner administrator, it might be tricky to find all the information he or she needs, even if it is collected by the ConfigMgr server.

Searching for relevant information might be very problematic. For instance, information about the system where the ConfigMgr client is installed is saved in a few various places, like different attribute classes and other attributes, but not how it might be expected--in the System class.

List of example attributes of the System Resource class

 When creating queries, the **WMI Query Language** (**WQL**) is used, and the database that is queried is a WMI database.

Reports

Reports are also the queries to a database, but this time--unlike with WMI--the administrator is working on data from the SQL database. The SQL database contains data available in the WMI database as well as data related to the ConfigMgr server and the whole environment. Here is an example of a report showing the name of the operating system and the date of its installation:

```
SELECT v_R_System.Name0 AS [Machine Name],
v_GS_OPERATING_SYSTEM.InstallDate0 AS [OS Deployed On] FROM
v_GS_OPERATING_SYSTEM INNER JOIN v_R_System ON
v_GS_OPERATING_SYSTEM.ResourceID = v_R_System.ResourceID
```

As has been mentioned before, you need to know certain things to create queries and reports. When creating a report, the administrator needs to find relevant data in a certain table and join it with another table. Unfortunately, there isn't an available description of the ConfigMgr SQL tables, so administrators need to get familiar with the ConfigMgr SQL database. Unfortunately, this is neither an easy nor fast task.

 When creating reports, the administrator uses SQL to query the ConfigMgr SQL database.

Hardware inventory

The **Hardware Inventory** setting is enabled by default. The installer configures a standard dataset that the ConfigMgr client will be collecting from the WMI database and sending to the server.

By default, **Hardware Inventory** is done every 7 days; of course, it is worth considering shortening or extending that time. While changing the schedule, it is worth noting that the shorter the periods between scans are, the more data will be sent over the network, and the management point will have more data to gather from clients and send further to the server:

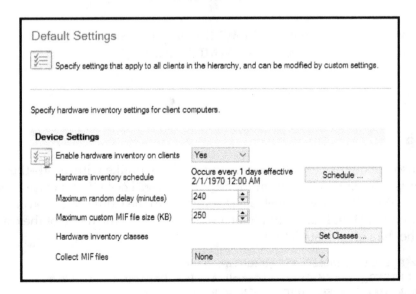

Hardware Inventory scanning settings

The second most important **Hardware Inventory** setting--apart from the scanning schedule--is configuring the data that will be gathered by the ConfigMgr client. The **Set Classes ...** option is used to configure what data should be collected just by selecting or unselecting classes or their attributes:

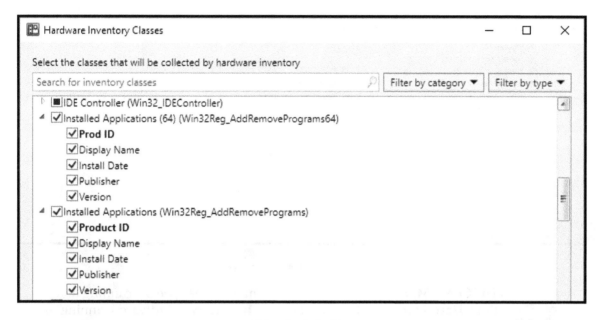

Configuration of gathered data

It is possible to create your own classes in the WMI database and save data in them. After the **Hardware Inventory** change, ConfigMgr clients will be able to read this data and send it to the server.

Data gathered by the ConfigMgr clients can be viewed in the console using **Resource Explorer**, by selecting a single computer and choosing **Start | Resource Explorer**. If the administrator would like to see results for a larger number of computers, the default or custom reports can be used for that purpose:

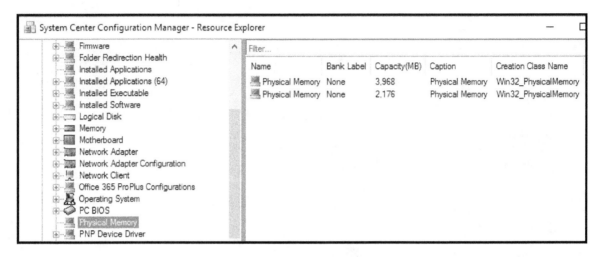

Resource Explorer with Hardware Inventory results

The ConfigMgr server client can perform only one type of scanning at a time: **Hardware Inventory** or **Software Inventory**. Hardware scanning runs quite swiftly; however, software scanning is rather slow, hence it is a good practice to set **Hardware Inventory** scanning to happen more frequently than **Software Inventory** scanning.

The first scan done by the ConfigMgr client is a full data scan; each following scan contains only a delta of data. This is a way to minimize the amount of data sent by the ConfigMgr client to the server.

Software inventory

The **Software Inventory** setting is enabled by default, the same as **Hardware Inventory**. The ConfigMgr client searches machine disks or catalogs looking for files following a pattern, which needs to be specified manually. This is the difference between hardware and software inventory. Of course, the same as for **Hardware Inventory**, you need to specify a scanning schedule. The **Inventory these files types** option is used to specify which files/file, and where, the ConfigMgr client will search:

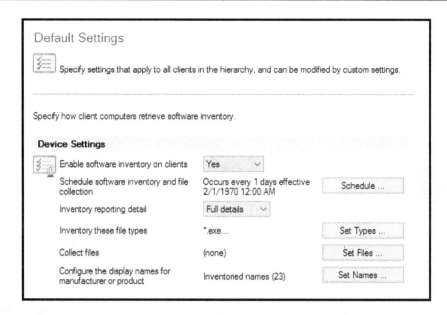

Software Inventory settings

Scanning can be configured to look for a single file or files with a certain file type; for instance, `.exe` is shown in the following screenshot. The **Location** option can be used to specify where these files will be searched, in all disks or only particular folders:

File types inventory settings

Software inventory results, the same as with hardware inventory, can be viewed using **Resource Explorer**, or--for a larger number of machines--reports:

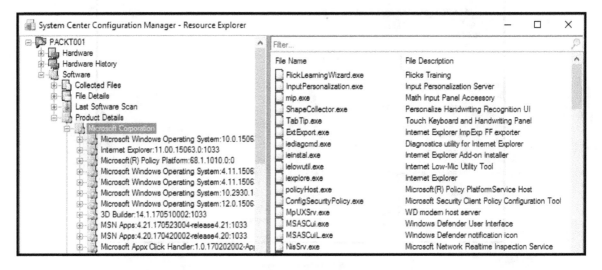

Results of searching .exe files

It is a common belief that searching for files on disks is not something that is desired and there is no real reason it should be enabled--this is far from correct. **Software Inventory** is a powerful tool, which can be used to:

- Search for files that shouldn't be on computers
- Search for legally forbidden materials, such as multimedia files
- Search for software that resides on the computer as portable versions
- Search for users that have the highest amount of multimedia files

Asset Intelligence

`Asset Intelligence`, in brief, is gathering additional information about installed software. Asset Intelligence classes are kept in the WMI database and are not enabled by default. This functionality can be turned on under `Assets and Compliance\Asset Intelligence` using the **Edit Inventory Classes** option, where the classes we need can be enabled. Each of these classes loads data to certain reports; these can be found under `Monitoring\Reporting\Reports\Asset Intelligence`.:

Asset Intelligence classes in the WMI database

After relevant classes are configured, to get expected results, the administrator needs to wait for the hardware inventory scanning to be done by clients. Data will be available in the reports and on the console under `Assets and Compliance\Asset Intelligence\Inventoried Software.`:

Asset Intelligence scanning results

In middle and enterprise environments, **Software Inventory** might contain a large number of items, as the server reports all of the installed software, such as .NET Framework. Even if the number of files is significant, it is relatively easy to spot unwanted software on the ConfigMgr console.

`Asset Intelligence` data can be viewed in default reports prepared by Microsoft:

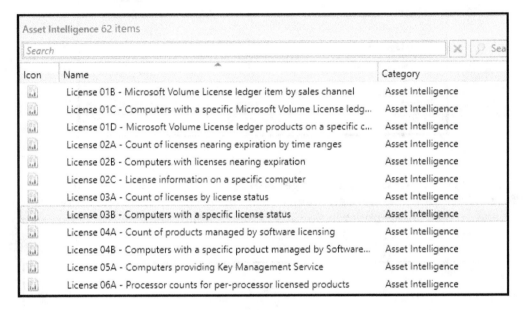

Default Asset Intelligence reports

Here is an example of one report, which shows the difference between inventoried software and numbers of licenses. It is an easy way to find OS license usage--whether more users have certain software installed than the actual number of licenses the company has:

			Microsoft System Center Configuration Manager

License 15A - General license reconciliation report
⊞ Description

Product Name	⬍	Version	⬍	Licensed Quantity	⬍	Inventory Count	⬍	Difference	⬍
1E AppClarity		3		5		0		5	
Ala		2		1		0		1	
Camtasia Studio 6		6		5		1		4	
Cisco Systems VPN Client 5.0		5		2		0		2	
Configuration Manager Client		5		15		15		0	
NetObjects Fusion 2013		13		1		0		1	
Snagit 11		11		5		0		5	
Snagit 12		12		5		2		3	

An example report showing information about missing licenses

`Asset Intelligence` gives information not only about the number of potentially missing licenses but also workstations with this software installed.

Collection queries

As has been mentioned, Inventory is used to create collections and reports. Collection queries can contain computer or user objects. A collection might contain:

- **Objects that meet conditions from the WMI query**: The number of collection members might be dynamic and change over time
- **Objects added manually to the collection**: The number of members will always be constant unless someone adds one
- **Objects added manually that meet certain WMI query conditions**: Such collections will also be constant unless someone adds objects that meet the requirements

It is not very important to know how to write **Hardware Inventory** queries. It is important to know if data that is used in the report is correct and if the results of the queries are relevant.

Let's assume that the administrator wants to prepare a collection containing all workstation type computers. This seems to be an easy task, but only at first glance, as all the workstation attributes are saved in the ConfigMgr database during **Hardware Inventory**. Only computers that have ConfigMgr clients and have done **Hardware Inventory** scanning will be in the collection. There won't be computers that haven't done **Hardware Inventory** scanning, as the workstation attribute is empty.

We, however, need a collection that will contain all workstations known to the ConfigMgr server. To achieve that goal, the administrator needs to use information from **Heartbeat Discovery**. According to the **Heartbeat Discovery** schedule, the ConfigMgr client sends data to the management point about basic system information--this data is sent separately from **Hardware Inventory**.

Device collection can be created under `Assets and Compliance\Device Collections`, while for users it can be under `Assets and Compliance\User Collections`. In both cases, first, the name and description of the collection need to be provided. The description is not a mandatory field but significantly eases future maintenance. Starting from ConfigMgr 2012, a mandatory option--**Limiting collection**--has been introduced, to narrow down the number of objects on which the query will work. If there is a need for a query to work on all objects, the **All Systems** collection should be chosen:

1. The first step is specifying the name of the collection and the parent collection that will be limiting the objects:

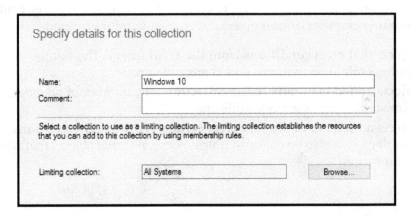

Initial set of collection

2. The second step is setting up a membership rule for this collection; there are three main rules. A **Query Rule** is a query reaching the WMI database and dynamically changing the number of objects in the collection. A **Direct Rule** is a rule for manually adding single objects until the objects are removed by the administrator. A **Device Category Rule** is a rule based on the category of a device. Apart from these main rules, there are also **Include Collections** and **Exclude Collections**, which are used to add to result objects from different collections or to exclude them from results. In the following example, **Query Rule** has been chosen:

Membership rules determine the resources that are included in the collection when it updates. You can use membership rules to add a specific object or a set of objects from a query. The collection membership can also include or exclude other collections. Membership rules can add only those objects that are members of the limiting collection.

Membership rules:

Rule Name	Type	Collection Id
There are no items to show in this view.		

| Add Rule ▼ | Edit | Delete |

Direct Rule

Query Rule

De̲vice Category Rule

In̲clude Collections

E̲xclude Collections

☑ Use incremental updates for this c

An incremental update periodicall   ds resources that qualify
to this collection. This option doe   te for this collection.

☑ Schedule a full update on this collection
Occurs every 7 days effective 8/20/2017 12:33 AM   Schedule...

Choosing a membership rule

3. The third step is providing a name for the query. A query can be created from scratch, or you can import an existing one from the console as a baseline and modify it:

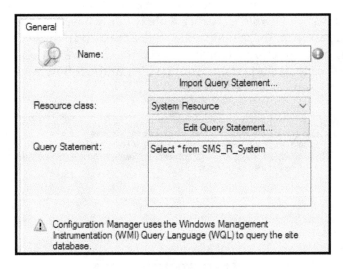

Query name configuration

4. The fourth step is the actual configuration of the query. To do this, click on the first icon on the right-hand side, and a query editor window will appear:

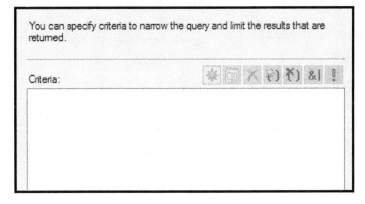

Editing query criteria

5. The fifth step is criteria configuration. First, the administrator needs to choose the **Criterion Type** option and choose which type will be used. In this example, the **Simple value** is chosen:

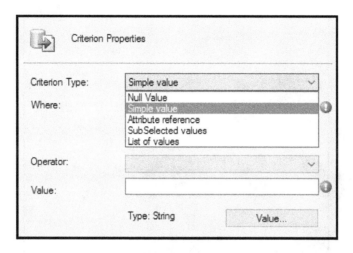

Choosing Criterion Type

6. The sixth step is choosing the attribute classes and the attribute that will be used to search for objects. In the following example, **System Resource** and **Operating System Name and Version** are chosen, as the goal is to create a collection with Windows 10 computers:

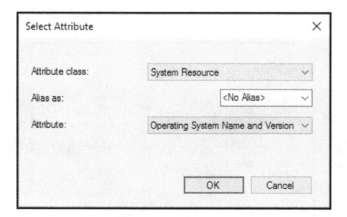

Settings of attribute classes and query attributes

7. The seventh step is the configuration of logical operators used in the query. As the goal is to look for all of the computers with a Windows 10 OS, the operator **is equal to** will be used:

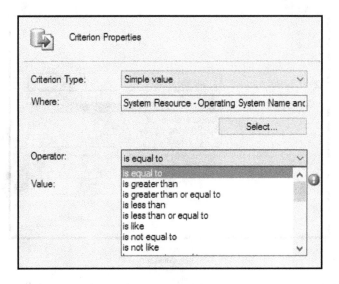

Logical operator configuration

8. The eighth step is providing a value that will be searched. It is possible to provide this value manually or use values suggested by the server. When using the **Value** option, ConfigMgr shows the first 100 values in the **Operating System Name and Version** field:

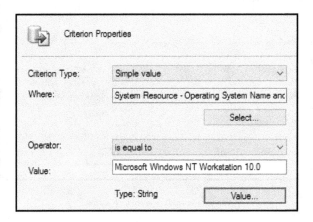

Configuration of search criteria

9. The ninth step is accepting the query configuration:

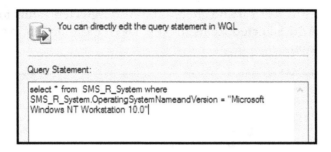

Ready query in the editor window

Membership rules assigned to the collection are in fact part of the collection definition. If the administrator deletes the collection from the console, all currently defined collection queries will also be deleted.

10. The tenth and final step is saving the collection configuration:

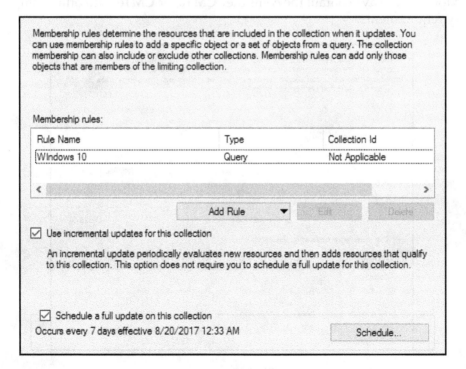

Collection configuration

At every moment, it is possible to change membership rules on the collection, for instance by adding a user or computer manually to that collection. To add a computer to a collection, the administrator needs to select it and choose the **Add Selected Items to Existing Device Collection** option, or **Add Selected Items to New Device Collection** to add the computer to a newly created collection:

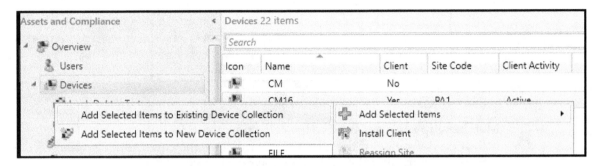

Adding computer to a collection

After adding the computer to the collection manually, the configuration looks as follows. The collection will always contain the computer **CM16**, or **CM16** with other computers that meet query requirements:

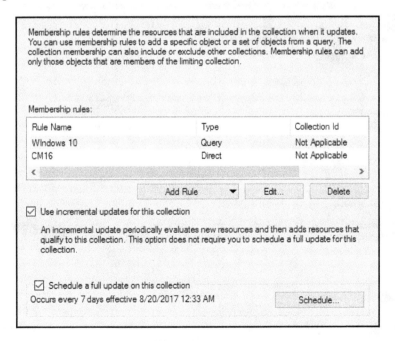

Collection membership rule settings

Creating a collection is a major and vital job for the administrator or operator, as actual actions performed on the clients depend on their membership in a collection. To create collections, it is good to know the WQL language to create queries and the WMI database.

Console queries

Queries can be created for two main purposes. Most often they are used to create collections--just as shown previously. Queries can be created and saved for later use on the console under `Monitoring\Queries`. After the server is installed, several queries are created by default:

Default queries created after ConfigMgr server installation

Very often, queries are saved and later used when working with ConfigMgr clients.

When using a query in the console, it works directly in the WMI database. However, if the same query is applied on the collection, it might take longer to see the actual effects. It might take a while because, for instance, ConfigMgr has many collections, and these might have the **Schedule a full update on this collection** option set up with a little-too-frequent refresh rate:

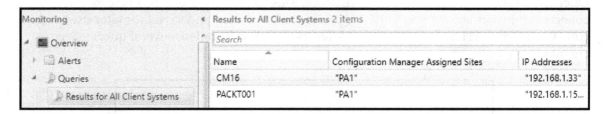

Query results on the console

Using queries on the console is a very practical and swift method of gathering information from a WMI database.

Console reports

ConfigMgr has always provided the ability to run reports for managed environments. Since ConfigMgr 2007, there have been a lot of important changes.

The most important change, introduced in ConfigMgr 2007 R3, was the ability of running reports using `Reporting Services`, and since ConfigMgr 2012, there is no other way to run them. Thanks to this, the ConfigMgr server does not have performance issues, and there is no limitation on the number of rows that can be viewed. Unfortunately, as a result of these changes, creating reports is not as easy as it used to be.

ConfigMgr has a report creator, but it only creates an *empty* file with a name and connection to the ConfigMgr database. Configuring the query and a method of returning results needs to be done in another tool. Created reports can be edited using Report Builder--this tool is an SQL Server component and can be installed on the ConfigMgr server or workstation.

Reports can be created under `Monitoring\Reporting\Reports`. After starting the creator, the administrator must provide a name for the report and a catalog in which it should be saved:

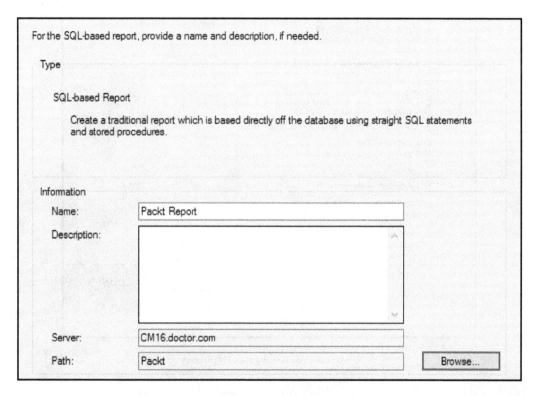

For the SQL-based report, provide a name and description, if needed.

Type

SQL-based Report

Create a traditional report which is based directly off the database using straight SQL statements and stored procedures.

Information

Name:	Packt Report
Description:	
Server:	CM16.doctor.com
Path:	Packt

Browse...

Report name and path settings

If the administrator wants to create a custom folder and save the reports there, this folder needs to be created using reporting services, as, on the ConfigMgr console, this is not possible:

Pointing to a folder in which the report will be saved

After the ConfigMgr console creator is done, the report is visible on the console. However, it will not show any data, as there is no query assigned to it and `Reporting Services` do not know how to display it:

Created report on the console

To edit a report, Report Builder should be used. After opening a report in it, you should see something like this:

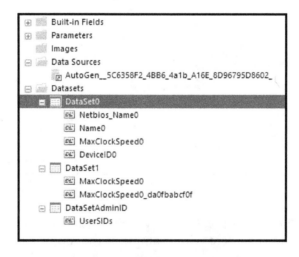

An example report configuration visible in Report Builder

In order to finish the report, there are at least two more things to be done. A dataset that the SQL database can query needs to be created, and you need a **Data source**, providing it the SQL Server name for connection purposes:

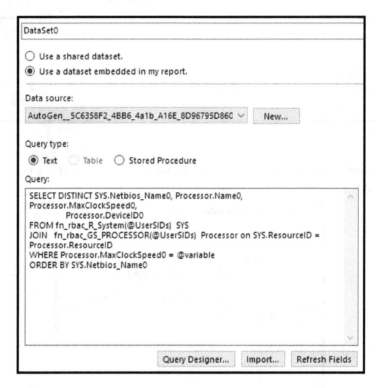

Dataset and data source settings

Configuring the query alone is not really enough. You also need to tell Report Builder how the report should be displayed. Here is an example of the report displayed as a simple table:

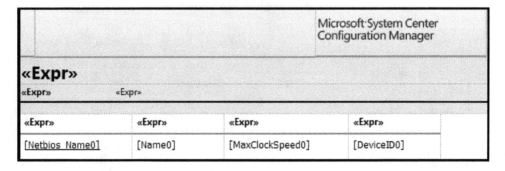

Configuration of a report as a simple table in Report Builder

After configuring how the report should be displayed, it is possible to check instantly how the report would look with data after it runs:

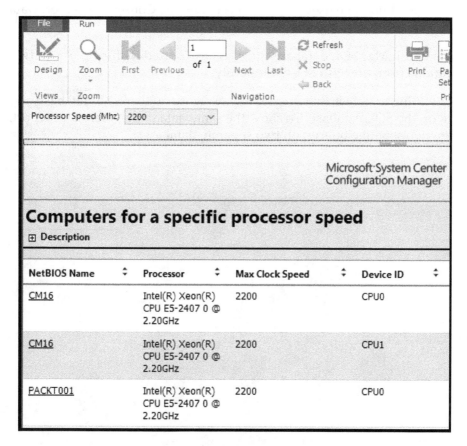

Report Builder allows you to check instantly how the report will look

After the report is configured, the administrator should save the changes. From this point, the report can be run from the ConfigMgr console.

 Creating reports in a ConfigMgr server is hard. First of all, it is important to know where data is located in the SQL database, how to connect to it, and how to write a good query. Secondly, you need to know how to use Report Builder to create a file that is run by Reporting Services and also how to properly configure how the report should be displayed.

Summary

This chapter covered possible uses of data collected by the ConfigMgr server. Data might be used for query creation, creating collections, and reports.

Data from the ConfigMgr SQL database can also be exported to third-party software or to other applications from the System Center family.

One important thing to note is that queries always work on the WMI database, while reports work on the SQL database. To show the same data in the query and report, you need to create two separate queries on two separate databases.

12
Role-Based Administration and Security

Previous chapters covered the most important ConfigMgr features. The ConfigMgr server should be properly secured against unwanted access, and if required, permissions should be granted only for particular users and groups; this process is covered in this chapter.

We will cover the following topics:

- Creating security roles
- Assigning AD security groups to different roles
- Assigning security roles to specific collections

Introducing role-based administration and security

A ConfigMgr server as an automatic system in the hands of an inexperienced administrator is a very dangerous tool, and, unfortunately, there have been cases where unskilled administrators have erased all the data on all computers managed by the server.

For this reason, when deploying the server, it is very important to properly secure the server and grant access only to those people who should have access; this needs to be well planned as well.

Securing the environment against unwanted access to data or the console might be done by:

- Turning on encryption of data that is exchanged between clients and the ConfigMgr server
- Turning on HTTPS instead of HTTP and securing the communication between clients and ConfigMgr server using **public key infrastructure** (**PKI**)
- Granting proper permissions to the console for users and groups only in a particular scope of objects with strictly defined permissions

Hardening the infrastructure

Hardening the environment by encrypting the data is an easy task from the console-configuration side. However, using certificates is not as easy, as it requires the deployment of PKI infrastructure and knowing how to prepare certificates, which will be used by the clients and ConfigMgr server for communication.

Encryption can be done by enabling signing and encryption for client-server communication as shown in the following screenshot:

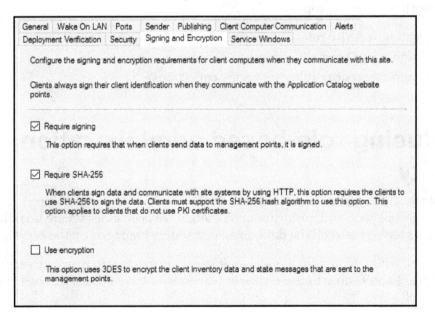

Enabling communication encryption for ConfigMgr server

The **Require signing** and **Require SHA-256** options are enabled by default. Additionally, it is possible to enable the **Use encryption** option to encrypt inventory data sent from the clients to the ConfigMgr server.

To elevate the level of security of the entire environment, it is possible to implement certificates and switch the whole environment to work on HTTP mode regardless of whether the client is working in the LAN or is on the internet. Configuring PKI for ConfigMgr server usage is out of the scope of this book:

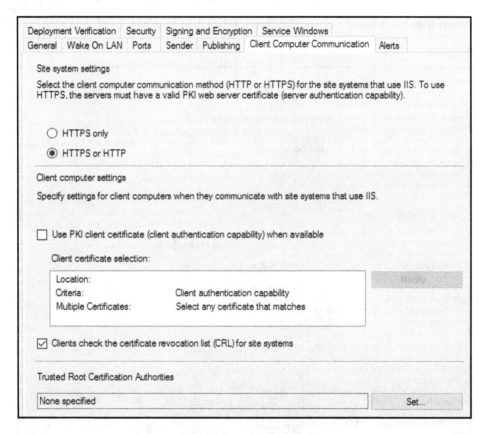

Decision whether to choose HTTP or HTTPS for ConfigMgr server

Working in HTTPS mode efficiently secures the environment, but, as mentioned, it is a configuration that requires the administrator to have knowledge not only about the ConfigMgr server but also about PKI.

Access to the console

Granting permissions to users is seemingly an easy and straightforward task. However, this is only a delusion, as often during deployment, there is a need to create your own sets of permissions to meet particular project requirements. The ConfigMgr console has some technical constraints, so it is not possible to create a single permission model meeting every project's requirements.

Going to `Administration\Security\Administrative Users` in the ConfigMgr console is useful when there is a need to quickly check who, and at what level, has access to the console:

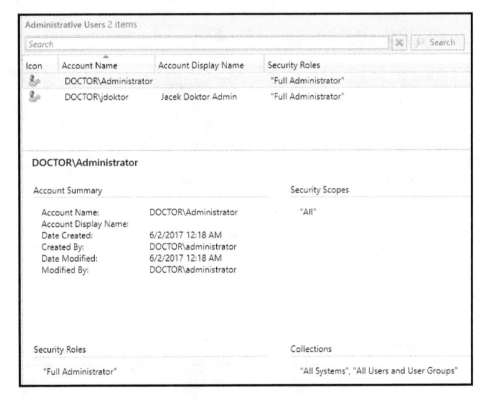

Users with their permissions on the ConfigMgr server

Additionally, there are a few default reports available under `Monitoring\Reporting\Reports\Administrative Security` that visualize data regarding console permissions, security scopes, and changes made by the ConfigMgr users on the server.

Important factors when granting permissions on ConfigMgr server are as follows:

- **Who**: Who needs to have access to the console, a single user or a group.
- **What**: What kind of permissions should be granted to the users, which means what tasks users have permission to do. It is possible to leverage default sets or create custom ones.
- **Which**: Which security scopes will be assigned to the users, which means what objects on the console will be visible to the users. It is possible to leverage default scopes or create custom ones.
- **Where**: Which collections will be visible on the console for particular users.

Granting permissions on the console is done using one wizard, where the administrator needs to define who access is granted to, and which objects in particular are within the security scope and on which collections. If the user isn't seeing objects in the console, it means that permissions were not granted for that particular object.

Security scopes

Security scopes are used to select which object should be shown to the users in the ConfigMgr console. By default, under `Administration\Security\Security Scopes`, there are two scopes created: **All** and **Default**. It is worth creating our own security scope and as the next step to add objects to it such as packages, applications, and software update groups:

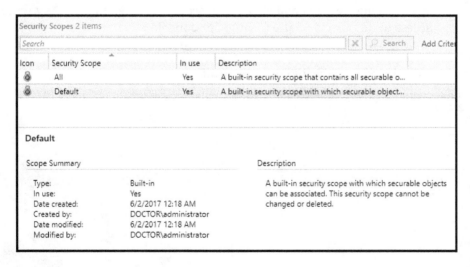

Listing of all available security scopes

Creating a security scope is easy. These can be created under
`Administration\Security\Security Scopes`; the first step is to define a name and
who will be assigned to it:

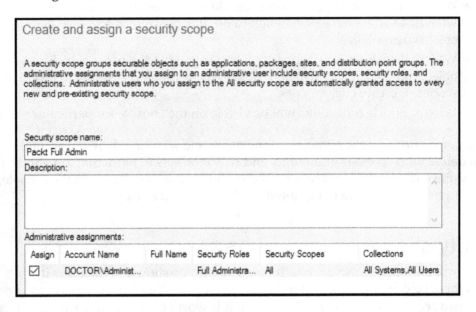

Create and assign a security scope

A security scope groups securable objects such as applications, packages, sites, and distribution point groups. The administrative assignments that you assign to an administrative user include security scopes, security roles, and collections. Administrative users who you assign to the All security scope are automatically granted access to every new and pre-existing security scope.

Security scope name:

Packt Full Admin

Description:

Administrative assignments:

Assign	Account Name	Full Name	Security Roles	Security Scopes	Collections
☑	DOCTOR\Administ...		Full Administra...	All	All Systems,All Users

Security scope settings

Administrators assigned to the security scope **All** have, by default, access to all old and newly created security scopes. Thanks to this, they will have access to all objects on the ConfigMgr console.

After creating this, the administrator can start adding objects to it. One object can belong to many scopes, and needs to be assigned to at least one. The console will not save the data unless there is at least one security scope assigned:

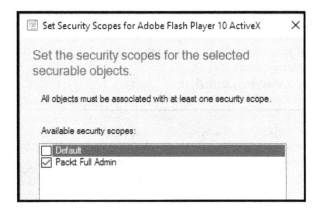

Assigning security scope to an object

A security scope can be assigned to the following objects:

- Boundary groups
- Applications, packages, and deployments
- Boot images
- Operating system images
- Task sequences
- Queries
- Sites
- Custom client settings
- Distribution points
- Distribution point groups
- Software update groups
- Software metering rules
- Compliance configuration items
- Compliance configuration baseline

Security roles

Security roles are sets of permissions that can be assigned to users or groups. By default, after server installation, under `Administration\Security\Security Roles`, there are 15 built-in roles, which cannot be modified:

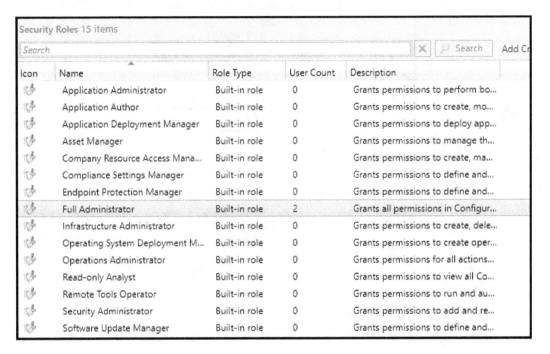

Icon	Name	Role Type	User Count	Description
	Application Administrator	Built-in role	0	Grants permissions to perform bo...
	Application Author	Built-in role	0	Grants permissions to create, mo...
	Application Deployment Manager	Built-in role	0	Grants permissions to deploy app...
	Asset Manager	Built-in role	0	Grants permissions to manage th...
	Company Resource Access Mana...	Built-in role	0	Grants permissions to create, ma...
	Compliance Settings Manager	Built-in role	0	Grants permissions to define and...
	Endpoint Protection Manager	Built-in role	0	Grants permissions to define and...
	Full Administrator	Built-in role	2	Grants all permissions in Configur...
	Infrastructure Administrator	Built-in role	0	Grants permissions to create, dele...
	Operating System Deployment M...	Built-in role	0	Grants permissions to create oper...
	Operations Administrator	Built-in role	0	Grants permissions for all actions...
	Read-only Analyst	Built-in role	0	Grants permissions to view all Co...
	Remote Tools Operator	Built-in role	0	Grants permissions to run and au...
	Security Administrator	Built-in role	0	Grants permissions to add and re...
	Software Update Manager	Built-in role	0	Grants permissions to define and...

Built-in security roles

In a simple environment, these built-in scopes would be sufficient. However, in real-life scenarios, there are situations where there is a need to grant permissions that are not covered by the built-in scopes. The default scopes cannot be modified, but can be used as a baseline for creating custom scopes by copying them and editing later:

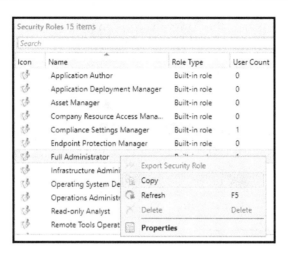

Copying of security roles

The next step is giving a name to the security role and granting proper permissions:

Granting permissions to a security role

It is always worth checking if the given permissions provide the expected access and if objects visible in the console are only those that should be visible to users.

Granting permissions to the ConfigMgr console

Granting permissions is easy. It is done using the **Add User or Group** wizard under `Administration\Security\Administrative Users`. The wizard will ask for the user or group that should be granted permissions; next, security scopes need to be assigned, and, last but not least, we need to define which objects should be visible in the console:

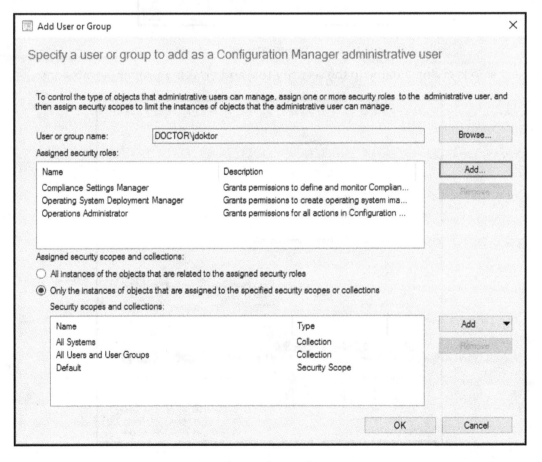

Granting permissions to the ConfigMgr console

After changing permissions for a user, the ConfigMgr console needs to be reopened for the new permissions to work.

It is always possible to change the permissions back after granting them or checking what the effective permissions for the user are:

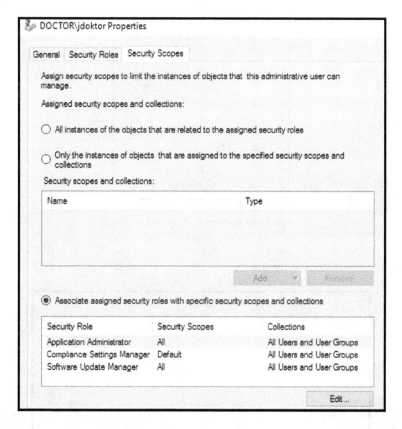

Assigning security scope to the user

It is a good practice to check whether granted permissions align with the project assumptions. This can be checked simply by running the console with certain permissions and verifying visible objects and tasks that can be done on them by the user.

After granting permissions as in the previous example, `Application Management`, `Software Updates`, `Windows 10 Servicing`, and `Office 365 Client Management` will be the only options visible to the user in the `Software Library`:

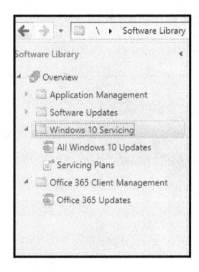

Objects on the console visible after granting permissions

However, under `Assets and Compliance\Device Collections`, there won't be any collections visible/accessible to the user:

Visible collections on the console after granting permissions

 If a non-administrative user creates objects on the console, the administrator, by default, is granted full permissions to these newly created objects.

Service accounts

When configuring the server and its single-server roles, an AD account with proper permissions needs to be used; all these accounts are visible under `Administration\Security\Accounts` on the console.

These default accounts cannot be deleted; the only option available is to set a new password for the account--in situations where one account is used in many places, having to change the password in only one place eases administration and maintenance significantly:

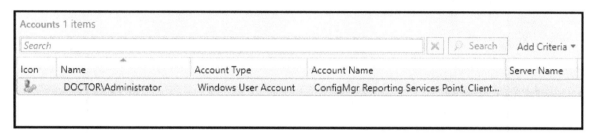

Listing of all the accounts used by the ConfigMgr server

The **Account Name** tab shows the places in the console where an account is used.

Remote Tools

Remote Tools is a ConfigMgr feature that gives you the ability to connect directly to a managed computer. Depending on the settings, a user can connect to an existing session on the remote computer with permissions to request control over the mouse and keyboard, or connect with permission only to view the screen.

Granting such permissions is rather easy. For this, the default security role **Remote Tools Operator** can be used.

These **Remote Tools** are as follows:

- **Remote Control**: This is used to remotely connect to the client operating system. It is possible to connect remotely to an existing session in order to provide help to the user, or log in to the computer with a separate remote session.
- **Remote Desktop**: This is used to connect to the remote computer using the standard, built-in **Remote Desktop Protocol (RDP)**.
- **Remote Assistance**: This is used to connect to the remote computer using the standard, built-in **Remote Assistance**.

Remote Control is the option used most often, as it has the widest scope of usage--it is possible to connect remotely to the user's session and take control of the mouse and keyboard to swiftly and efficiently resolve a problem.

Client Settings

Remote Control settings for the client are under `Administration\Client Settings` in the ConfigMgr console. By default, these are not enabled:

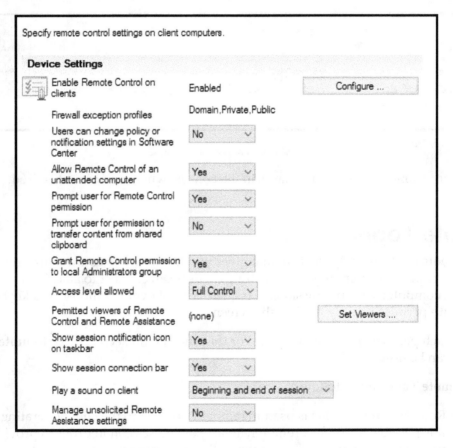

Remote Control settings

In order to enable the usage of **Remote Control** by users, the following settings need to be present on the console:

- **Enable Remote Control on clients**: Yes. Additionally, it needs to be specified on which firewall the profile settings will work.
- **Allow Remote Control of an unattended computer**: **Yes**. This option enables logging in to a computer that is locked or has no one logged in to it.
- **Prompt user for Remote Control permission**: **Yes**. This option forces asking the user whether he/she agrees to a remote connection to his/her session.
- **Grant Remote Control permission to local Administrators group**: Enabled by default. This grants local administrators group permissions to log in remotely using **Remote Tools**.
- **Access level allowed**: **No Access**, **View Only**, and **Full Control**. These options allow us to define the access level when connecting remotely to a user's sessions. By default, the option is set to **Full Control**.
- **Permitted viewers of Remote Control and Remote Assistance**: This option allows us to grant permissions to certain users to log in remotely to the computer.
- **Show session notification icon on taskbar**: This option allows us to show a notification to the user if someone connects using remote control. By default, it is enabled.
- **Show session connection bar**: This option allows us to show a connection bar to the user; by default, it is enabled.

There are two options for using **Remote Control**:

- On the console--select the computer and choose the **Remote Control** option
- Run **Remote Control Viewer** from the Start menu

Remote Control Viewer in Start menu

If run from the console, the remote tool automatically grabs the computer name and tries to connect; when run from the Start menu, you need to provide the name:

Configuration Manager Remote Control

After the computer name has been provided, a connection is initiated and the user can connect to the machine:

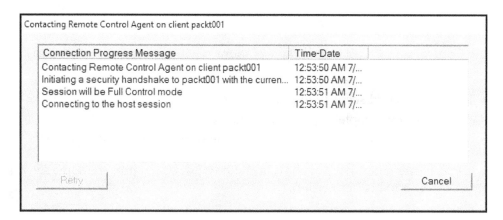

Initializing connection with the computer

Depending on the mode the computer is working in, after initializing the connection, the user might get a login screen or see an open session that a user is working on:

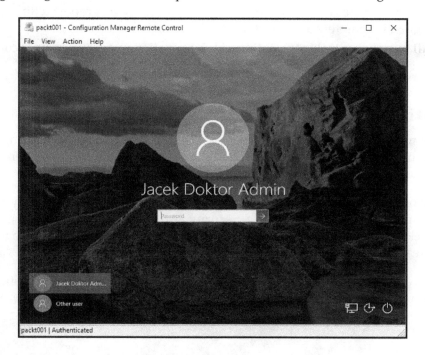

Result of connecting to a computer using Remote Control

Remote Control Viewer is installed as a part of the ConfigMgr server console.

Securing remote control

As **Remote Control** might lead to privacy violations when not configured properly, there are few factors worth considering:

- Using role-based security to grant access to remote control
- Having as few people as possible in the permitted viewers list
- Not disabling the **Prompt user for Remote Control permission** option

> The user should always have a choice whether to agree for someone to connect to his/her session.

In order to check who has used remote control, there are two default reports that can reveal information:

- **All computers remote controlled by a specific user**: A report telling who has logged in remotely and to which workstations
- **All remote control information**: All information regarding remote control usage

Summary

This chapter focused on securing the server against unwanted access, hardening communication between clients and the ConfigMgr server, and configuring remote access to managed computers.

The security of the environment is composed of a few factors, not just properly configuring and granting permissions on the console. Security also comprises preventing server failure, making a backup copy, and checking if the backup is correct and which can be used in the event of a breakdown.

To know more about role-based administration and security here is a very useful link with very interesting materials from which you can start digging for more: `https://docs.microsoft.com/en-us/sccm/core/understand/fundamentals-of-role-based-administration`.

Adding to these security topics, the next chapter will cover various useful maintenance tasks that are available in the ConfigMgr console and can be very important for the server to work.

13

Site Server Maintenance Tasks

The previous chapters covered all essential issues related to the design, installation, and administration of a ConfigMgr server. This last chapter will tell you about a very important topic related to the maintenance and monitoring of the site server. There are various important maintenance tasks for a ConfigMgr server; the most important ones covered by this book are as follows:

- Creating a backup copy and restoring the server after a failure
- Configuring maintenance tasks, especially ones related to cleaning the SQL database
- Monitoring the ConfigMgr server

Maintenance tasks can be configured for site servers as well as for the central administration site.

Maintenance tasks

Maintenance tasks are tasks performed automatically by the server. Some of them are configured and enabled during server installation, while others are disabled by default and might be enabled after the server is installed.

The most important task, which must *always* be configured, is the backup. There are a few ways to configure backup, but the one *recommended*, is leveraging the built-in mechanism to create a backup copy.

In general, there are always three steps that need to be done for each project:

1. Installing the ConfigMgr server and configuring it according to the project needs.
2. Immediately after the basic configuration is done, configuring the backup, along with the schedule of performing a backup copy.
3. Starting the backup job and *checking* if the backup copy can be used to restore the server after a failure.

This ensures that:

- The environment is properly secured against failure and unwanted administrative action
- The backup is done correctly and can be used to restore the server after a failure

Working in an environment that is properly secured is a lot easier, as the administrator is aware that, if something goes wrong, it is possible to restore the environment back to a running state.

> Situations, where the ConfigMgr server fails, are really rare; however, despite this, the basic task immediately after the server is installed and configured, is performing a server backup and testing recovery.

Server maintenance can be divided into the following tasks:

- Configuring and creating the backup copy
- Configuring the specified maintenance tasks
- Monitoring server operation and performance or its individual roles
- Monitoring the operation of the OS on which the ConfigMgr server environment exists

The topics we will cover are restoring in the event of a failure, maintenance configuration, and server monitoring.

> A good practice is to prepare a maintenance plan and perform tasks according to the schedule. This provides even better

ConfigMgr backup

Site server backup is the most important maintenance task available in the ConfigMgr server; it is not enabled by default after installation, so it is also good to configure it straight after the server is installed.

Apart from choosing the proper method of creating a backup copy, it is very important for administrators to know how the backup copy is being made. Generally, a server backup copy consists of two parts:

- SQL database and logs
- Server files and registry entries

The built-in mechanism stops the SMS_EXECUTIVE service prior to the backup job. As the mentioned service is stopped while performing the backup copy, it will not be possible to save any changes to the ConfigMgr server, the database, files, or the Windows Management Instrumentation database. Such a prepared backup copy can be used later to restore the server after a failure.

> Securing the site server against failure can be done in a few ways. However, it is recommended you use the built-in mechanism to create a backup copy.

Maintenance tasks are available under Administration\Site Configuration\Sites in the ConfigMgr console:

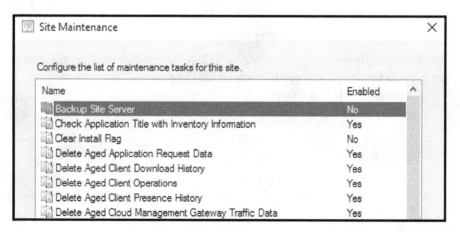

Backup Site Server is disabled by default

The **Backup Site Server** option allows us to configure proper server backup options; this configuration is very easy. The **Local drive on site server for site data and database** option is used to specify a local path in case the site server and database server are installed on the same machine. The **Network path (UNC name) for site data and database** option is used to specify a UNC path in the same case as before. The **Local drive on site server and SQL Server** option is used to specify a local path that exists on both the site server and SQL server. Files will be saved in both locations:

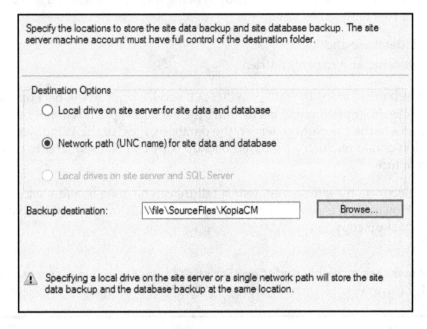

Specify the locations to store the site data backup and site database backup. The site server machine account must have full control of the destination folder.

Destination Options

○ Local drive on site server for site data and database

◉ Network path (UNC name) for site data and database

○ Local drives on site server and SQL Server

Backup destination: \\file\SourceFiles\KopiaCM   Browse...

⚠ Specifying a local drive on the site server or a single network path will store the site data backup and the database backup at the same location.

Settings of the backup copy location

 To properly secure the mentioned UNC path, it is worth implementing the UNC Hardened Access feature in GPO or at least minimize user permissions on the folder.

After setting up the backup copy location, it is important to set up a backup schedule. Additionally, it is possible to decide the hours during which the backup should be performed. The **Start after** option sets the earliest hour during which backup can start, and the **Latest start time** option is used to set the latest possible time:

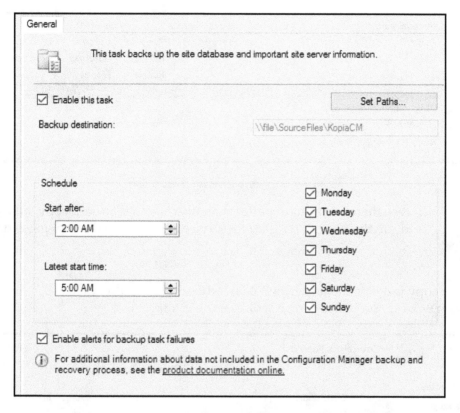

Backup copy schedule configuration

It is worth using the **Enable alerts for backup task failures** option. In case the backup copy task fails, a proper alert will be shown on the server console. Backup-related services are installed along with the server installation. The SMS_SITE_BACKUP service is used to manage a backup copy; it is disabled by default, and its status becomes **Running** only when a backup is being performed.

It is a good practice to set up your backup window outside business hours so that the backup task does not disrupt users' work.

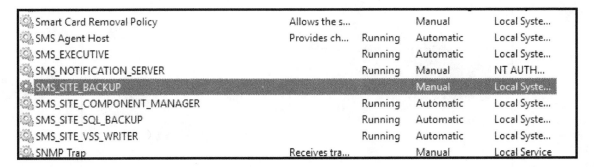

The SMS_SITE_BACKUP service used to manage backups

In case there is a need to perform an unscheduled backup copy, all it takes is to run the SMS_SITE_BACKUP service and wait till the copying is done.

The backup copy is created in a specific folder, whose name is always like <SiteCode>Backup; so, in our case, it will be PA1Backup:

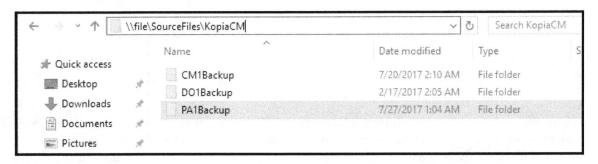

The folder where the backup copy is created

The status of the backup copy can be checked in the server logs, where the server saves the start time, backup information, and the end time.

Custom reports created in the reporting services are not part of the backup; these need to be exported manually. In the case of a failure and restoration, only the default reports will be restored.

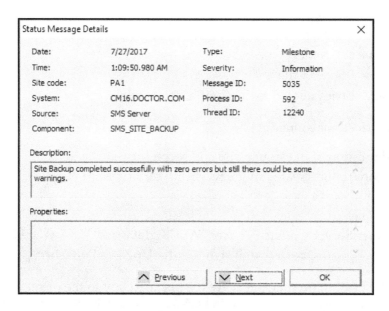

Log entry informing about a finished backup job

A built-in mechanism to perform a backup copy has been available since ConfigMgr 2007, although there are differences in the current branch version, which makes it much better. Now, apart from all the files needed to restore a server, a backup folder consists of a ConfigMgr installation CD, located in the CD.Latest subfolder. It is important, as the restore process is managed by the server installer, which is run from the installation CD:

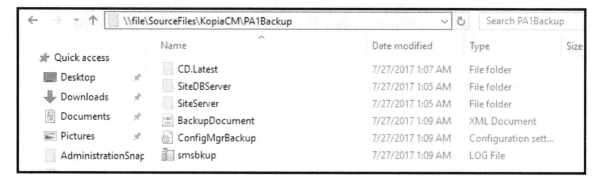

Content of a backup copy

The ConfigMgr server backup copy consists of:

- ConfigMgr server database and logs
- The `inboxes` folder
- The `logs` folder
- The `data` folder
- The `srvacct` folder
- The `install.map` file
- Registry entries related to the ConfigMgr server

The backup copy does *not* contain:

- Configuration of the system site and secondary site
- A custom report created in the reporting service point
- Content libraries
- Source files packages
- Windows Server Update Services (WSUS) database
- Custom updates created in System Center Updates Publisher

 The built-in mechanism saves the backup copy to the provided folder and overwrites it with the newest backup. This is why it is important to back these up with another software or simply prepare a mechanism that will copy the files to the other location each time after backup.

ConfigMgr server recovery

Creating a backup copy is just one part of securing the ConfigMgr server. The second part--and this might be even more important--is to check whether the backup copy can be used for restoring. This is a very important step, which makes the administrator sure that the backup they've taken is actually useful.

In environments with a central administration site, backup should start from that server, followed one-by-one by all the servers that comprise the ConfigMgr environment. Ideally, each backup job should be done at a different time.

A few components might get corrupted in the ConfigMgr server:

- The SQL database might stop working
- The site server might stop working, while the database remains untouched
- The site server and the database might both stop working
- The operating system on which the database and site server reside might stop working

In each case, the restore operation requires a different approach. In the case of an SQL database failure, we must restore using the **Recover the site database using the backup set at following location** option. In case the SQL database is fine and the site server is corrupted, restoring should be done using the **Recover this site server using an existing backup** option. In case the operating system is corrupted, the proper way of restoring is to freshly install the operating system, with the same name and configuration of disks, IIS, and SQL according to the documentation, and only after those steps have been performed should we restore the ConfigMgr server. In this case, both options should be selected as both the SQL database and site server are going to be restored.

Restoring can be done in two ways:

- Starting `setup.exe` from the ConfigMgr server installation CD, for instance when performing a database restore, or restoring both the database and site server. The best option is to use the CD located at `CD.Latest`.
- Starting Configuration Manager Setup creator in the menu, for instance, when restoring the site server and not the database.

In both scenarios, the restoration procedure is similar:

1. The first step is choosing the task to perform. In the following example, it is **Recover a site**:

Available Setup Options

Setup has detected an existing primary site on this computer and has enabled the following options.

Install a Configuration Manager primary site

   Use typical installation options for a stand-alone primary site

    - Install a Configuration Manager primary site

    - Use default installation path

    - Configure local SQL Server with default settings

    - Enable a local management point for Configuration Manager

    - Enable a local distribution point for Configuration Manager

Install a Configuration Manager central administration site

Upgrade this Configuration Manager site

◉ Recover a site

Perform site maintenance or reset this site

○ Uninstall this Configuration Manager site

Choosing recover site task

2. The second step is choosing what needs to be restored. In this example, the SQL database has failed. It is worth mentioning that if the administrator has made an SQL backup with a different tool than the built-in mechanism, it is possible to use it to restore the SQL database:

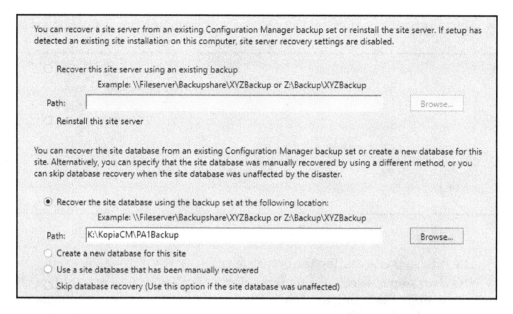

Choosing the restore mode

3. The third step is selecting whether the site server or central administration site is going to be restored. The available options depend on what has been discovered by the installer:

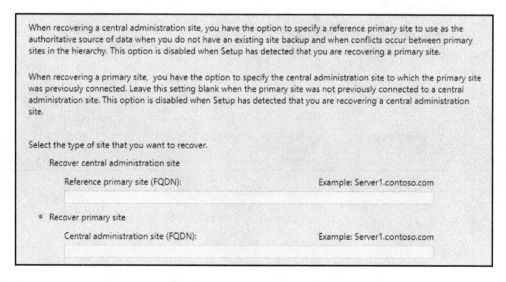

Choosing the type of ConfigMgr server to restore

4. The fourth step is providing a license key or installing the evaluation version:

⦿ Install the evaluation edition of this product
　When you install the Current Branch evaluation edition of this product, it is fully functional for 180 days.

○ Install the licensed edition of this product

　┌───┐
　│ ＿＿＿ - ＿＿＿ - ＿＿＿ - ＿＿＿ - ＿＿＿ │
　└───┘

　I acknowledge that I currently have an active Software Assurance license agreement with Microsoft. I understand that
　this version of Configuration Manager will have regular updates that can include new feature offerings.

Passing the license key

5. The fifth step is accepting the license terms.
6. The sixth step is selecting a folder with the installation files required for client installation or pointing to a folder to which this data will be downloaded:

Setup requires prerequisite files. Setup can automatically download the files to a location that you specify, or you can use files that have been downloaded previously.

○ Download required files

　　　　Example: \\ServerName\ShareName or C:\Downloads

Path:　┌──┐ ┌─────────┐
　　　　└──┘ │ Browse… │
　　　　　　　　　　　　　　　　　　　　　　　　　　　 └─────────┘

⦿ Use previously downloaded files

　　　　Example: \\ServerName\ShareName or C:\Downloads

Path:　┌──┐ ┌─────────┐
　　　　│ C:\Download   │ │ Browse… │
　　　　└──┘ └─────────┘

Providing a path to the ConfigMgr client binaries

7. The seventh step is accepting server settings. All options are grayed out, as these pieces of information have been retrieved from the backup copy:

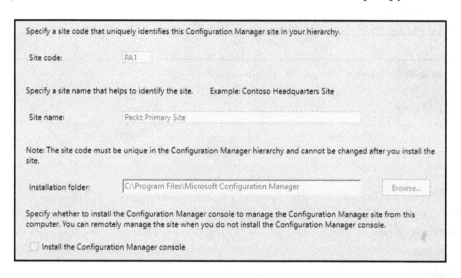

Data of restored ConfigMgr server

8. The eighth step is selecting an SQL server, on which the restored database and logs will be deployed:

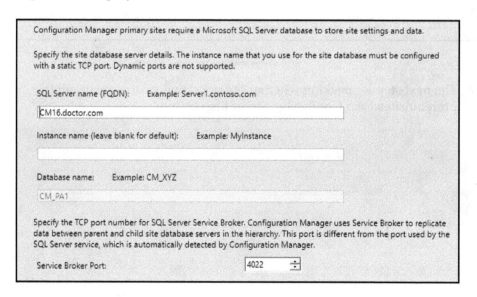

Providing the SQL server where the ConfigMgr backup copy will be restored

9. The ninth step is providing a folder to which the database and logs will be saved.
10. The tenth step is information about the diagnostic data send by Microsoft to its infrastructure.
11. The eleventh step is a summary of all the restored ConfigMgr servers:

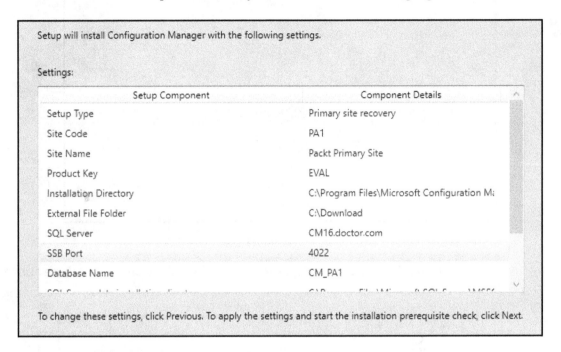

Setup will install Configuration Manager with the following settings.

Settings:

Setup Component	Component Details
Setup Type	Primary site recovery
Site Code	PA1
Site Name	Packt Primary Site
Product Key	EVAL
Installation Directory	C:\Program Files\Microsoft Configuration Mi
External File Folder	C:\Download
SQL Server	CM16.doctor.com
SSB Port	4022
Database Name	CM_PA1

To change these settings, click Previous. To apply the settings and start the installation prerequisite check, click Next.

Summary of restored ConfigMgr server

12. The next step is checking whether the operating system meets all the prerequisites for a ConfigMgr server installation:

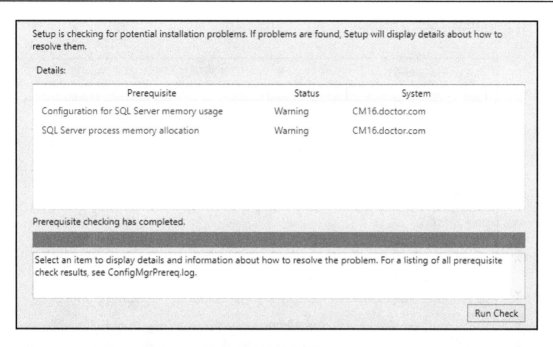

Checking prerequisites for ConfigMgr server

13. The next step is starting the server restoration process:

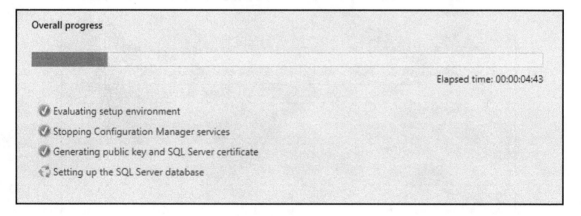

Starting the server restoration process

14. The next step is waiting for the restore process to end:

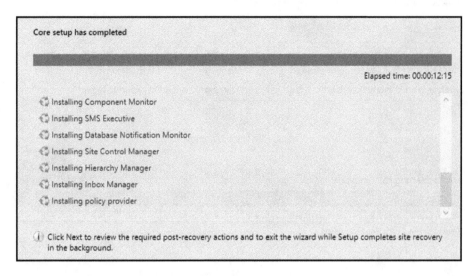

Finishing the restore procedure

15. The last step might contain two additional tasks--providing passwords to all the accounts used, and installing missing hotfixes:

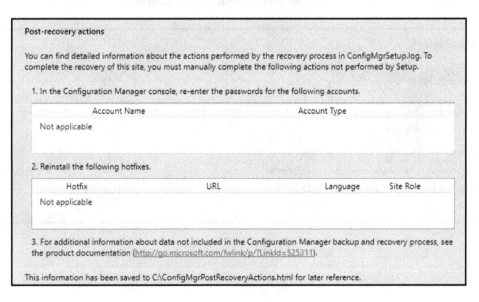

List of post-recovery tasks that need to be fulfilled

After the server has been restored, taking a look at the ConfigMgr console will tell you whether the restore process was conducted properly.

Other ConfigMgr server maintenance tasks

Maintenance tasks can be found in the ConfigMgr console under `Administration\Site Configuration\Sites`. Some of them are disabled and some enabled by default. Most of them correspond to database cleanup. There are various settings for erasing data from a ConfigMgr database; however, these configurations need to be made carefully:

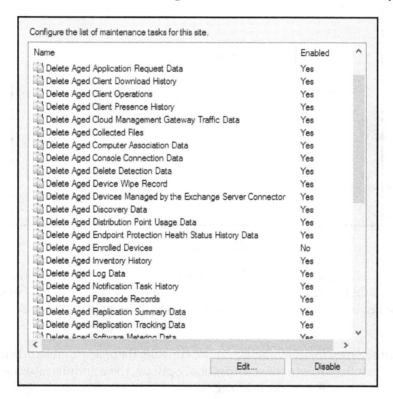

Available maintenance tasks

Deleting old inventory history from the site database is one of the available tasks, which deletes data from the inventory that are older than 90 days; let's assume that the hardware/software inventory is set to run every 7 days, and data deletion is set to 1 day. The server will not alert you about this misconfiguration, and it will keep on deleting items older than 1 day, which means that after 6 days, there will not be any data on the server until the next deletion cycle--6 days later:

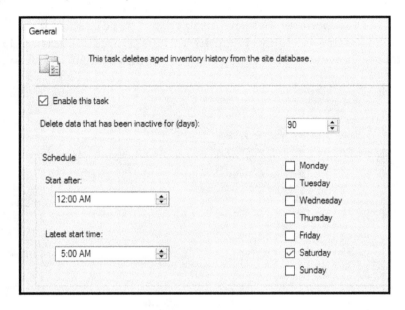

Inventory data cleanup settings

 The settings of some maintenance tasks rely on others, and these settings should be made carefully as the system has no possible way of checking whether the settings applied by the administrator make sense or not.

Apart from maintenance tasks available on the console, there are a few additional options available in the installer. To see these additional options, the administrator needs to choose **Perform site maintenance or reset this site**:

Available Setup Options

Setup has detected an existing primary site on this computer and has enabled the following options.

Install a Configuration Manager primary site
  ☐ Use typical installation options for a stand-alone primary site
    - Install a Configuration Manager primary site
    - Use default installation path
    - Configure local SQL Server with default settings
    - Enable a local management point for Configuration Manager
    - Enable a local distribution point for Configuration Manager
Install a Configuration Manager central administration site
Upgrade this Configuration Manager site
Recover a site
◉ Perform site maintenance or reset this site
◯ Uninstall this Configuration Manager site

Available options of ConfigMgr installer

After choosing this option, additional tasks related to site maintenance appear. The **Reset site with no configuration changes** option is used to reassign permissions to files and registry settings related to the ConfigMgr server. Additionally, all server roles will be reinstalled and reconfigured.

The **Modify SQL Server configuration** option is used when providing a new SQL server to ConfigMgr. As a result, it is possible to move the SQL database to a different location after the server is installed.

Modify SMS Provider configuration adds or removes the SMS Provider role for the specified server; it is important as this server role is responsible for connections to the ConfigMgr console and has no console of its own--this is the only place where this role can be configured.

The **Modify language configuration** option is used to change the language configuration of the server. **Upgrade the evaluation edition to a licensed edition. Enter the 25 character product key** is used to provide a license key and switch from the evaluation version to full:

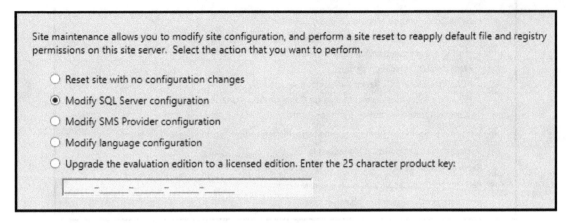

Site maintenance allows you to modify site configuration, and perform a site reset to reapply default file and registry permissions on this site server. Select the action that you want to perform.

- ○ Reset site with no configuration changes
- ◉ Modify SQL Server configuration
- ○ Modify SMS Provider configuration
- ○ Modify language configuration
- ○ Upgrade the evaluation edition to a licensed edition. Enter the 25 character product key:

Site maintenance options

Sometimes, you need to move the database from one SQL Server to another. After the move, a new SQL database needs to be specified:

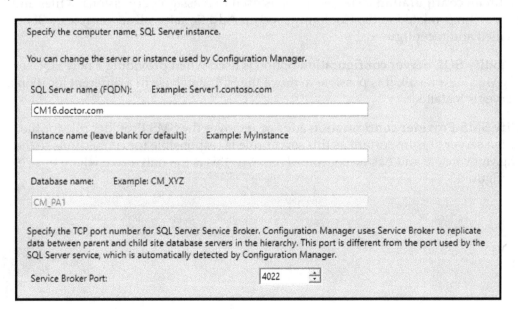

Specify the computer name, SQL Server instance.

You can change the server or instance used by Configuration Manager.

SQL Server name (FQDN):   Example: Server1.contoso.com

CM16.doctor.com

Instance name (leave blank for default):   Example: MyInstance

Database name: Example: CM_XYZ

CM_PA1

Specify the TCP port number for SQL Server Service Broker. Configuration Manager uses Service Broker to replicate data between parent and child site database servers in the hierarchy. This port is different from the port used by the SQL Server service, which is automatically detected by Configuration Manager.

Service Broker Port: 4022

Changing the ConfigMgr SQL database

The SMS Provider role simplifies connecting to the ConfigMgr console. It is configured by default during server installation. It is the only role that is not visible on the server console and cannot be configured:

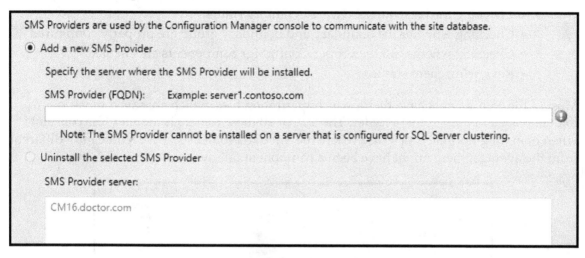

SMS Providers are used by the Configuration Manager console to communicate with the site database.

◉ Add a new SMS Provider

    Specify the server where the SMS Provider will be installed.

    SMS Provider (FQDN):   Example: server1.contoso.com

      Note: The SMS Provider cannot be installed on a server that is configured for SQL Server clustering.

○ Uninstall the selected SMS Provider

    SMS Provider server:

    CM16.doctor.com

Changing settings for the SMS Provider role

As has already been mentioned, all the maintenance tasks need to be configured carefully knowing exactly what can be expected with particular settings, as misconfiguration might lead to data loss or un-fixable errors.

Environment monitoring

Monitoring the ConfigMgr server is a maintenance task that needs to be performed daily by the administrator. There are many factors that impact a ConfigMgr environment, and sometimes ConfigMgr administrators do not have access to all the elements, which can make troubleshooting a difficult task.

Fortunately, ConfigMgr is a system that fails really rarely, although it should always be properly monitored. This task contains the following elements:

- Monitoring the `inboxes` folder in order to check backlog
- Using **State Message Queries** to check what a server or its users do
- Using **Site Status** and **Component Status** to check if all the servers and components of a ConfigMgr environment work correctly
- Checking synchronization status with WSUS
- Checking the configuration state of distribution points and management points

- Searching logs for the root cause of failures and any server malfunction
- Reviewing reports on the console to see whether all the ConfigMgr clients connect to a management point and download policies with proper settings
- Checking the hardware/software inventory status
- Checking whether the boundary and boundary group are properly configured
- Checking whether all the proper ConfigMgr components are enabled
- Reviewing client statuses

Most of the components have their own configuration files, which are saved in various folders placed in the `inboxes` folder. The size of all these folders is more or less constant when operating normally; in a case where the `inboxes` folder's size is significantly different from the average, there might have been a component failure:

Name	Date modified	Type
adsrv.box	6/2/2017 12:46 AM	File folder
aikbmgr.box	6/2/2017 12:49 AM	File folder
amtproxymgr.box	6/2/2017 12:47 AM	File folder
auth	6/2/2017 12:46 AM	File folder
bgb.box	8/19/2017 8:49 PM	File folder
businessappprocess.box	6/2/2017 12:48 AM	File folder
ccr.box	6/30/2017 1:02 AM	File folder
ccrretry.box	6/2/2017 12:46 AM	File folder
certmgr.box	8/19/2017 8:04 PM	File folder
clifiles.src	6/25/2017 11:31 PM	File folder
CLOUDMGR.box	6/2/2017 12:51 AM	File folder
cmupdate.box	6/25/2017 11:11 PM	File folder
colfile.box	6/2/2017 12:46 AM	File folder
coll_out.box	6/2/2017 12:46 AM	File folder
COLLEVAL.box	8/19/2017 7:54 PM	File folder
CompSumm.Box	8/19/2017 7:54 PM	File folder
dataldr.box	6/2/2017 12:46 AM	File folder

Folders inside inboxes

Status Message Queries, which is available on the console, is a very powerful tool when it comes to checking ConfigMgr status. After installation, there are some default queries available that are quite enough at the beginning. It is also possible to create custom queries:

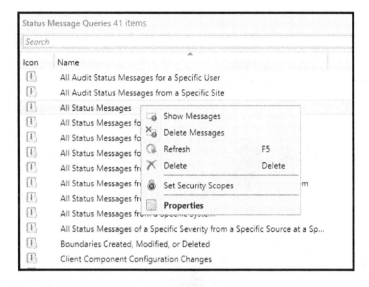

Default Status Message Queries

The result can be viewed directly on the console, thanks to which the administrator can check what tasks are done by which server. These pieces of information are great to begin troubleshooting since--if they know which error to look for--the administrator has a nice view of the logs:

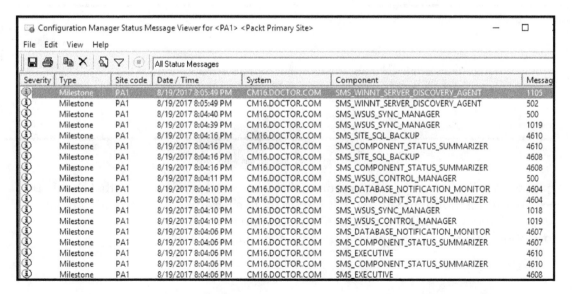

The result of Status Message Queries

Starting with ConfigMgr 2007, there were two tabs available to check the status of particular ConfigMgr environment components. Site server **Status** presents the status of particular server roles, while **Component** status shows the state of all the components:

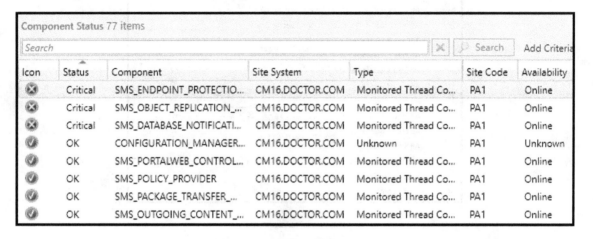

Component status shows the ConfigMgr environment components' status

If the ConfigMgr server is used to deploy updates, it is also important to check whether synchronization between WSUS and ConfigMgr works correctly:

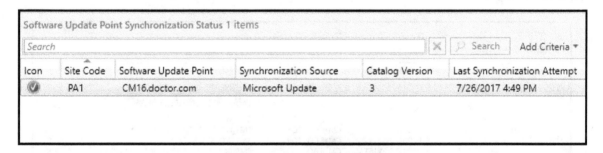

Status of ConfigMgr synchronization with WSUS server

Deploying applications, updates, and operating systems depends on files that should be placed on the distribution point, so it is important to check that the distribution point operates correctly. **Distribution Point Configuration Status** provides fundamental information about errors that are reported by distribution points:

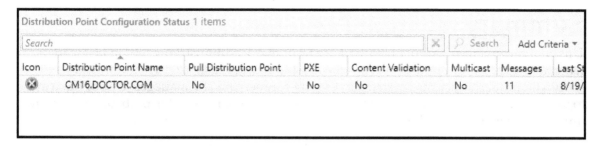

Icon	Distribution Point Name	Pull Distribution Point	PXE	Content Validation	Multicast	Messages	Last St
✖	CM16.DOCTOR.COM	No	No	No	No	11	8/19/

Distribution Point Configuration Status shows information about the status of all distribution points

Server logs are the great knowledge repository of server activity, or what it should do, but doesn't, because of a failure. There are many logs in ConfigMgr, and each and every one provides information about different pieces of the environment:

Name	Date modified	Type	Size
ADService	8/19/2017 7:55 PM	LOG File	23 k
adsgdis	7/27/2017 12:00 AM	LO_ File	2,561 k
adsgdis	8/19/2017 8:00 PM	LOG File	864 k
adsysdis	8/9/2017 5:00 PM	LO_ File	2,561 k
adsysdis	8/19/2017 8:00 PM	LOG File	364 k
adusrdis	6/25/2017 6:00 PM	LO_ File	2,561 k
adusrdis	8/19/2017 8:00 PM	LOG File	2,121 k
aikbmgr	8/19/2017 8:22 PM	LOG File	1,139 k
amtproxymgr	8/19/2017 8:50 PM	LOG File	2,413 k
awebsctl	8/19/2017 8:04 PM	LOG File	1,182 k
awebsvcMSI	8/19/2017 7:52 PM	LOG File	221 k
bgbisapiMSI	8/19/2017 7:58 PM	LOG File	443 k
bgbmgr	8/14/2017 6:02 PM	LO_ File	2,561 k
bgbmgr	8/19/2017 8:50 PM	LOG File	848 k
BgbServer	7/18/2017 5:24 AM	LO_ File	2,561 k

Some of the ConfigMgr logs

You should not be worried about the number or size of the logs; thanks to them, ConfigMgr is a top Microsoft product in terms of documentation and useful information that can be found in logs when troubleshooting.

Summary

This chapter covered essential maintenance tasks every administrator should be aware of when it comes to a ConfigMgr server. The most important task for each administrator should be properly securing systems in the environment he/she manages. One of the ways to secure the server is to secure data with proper backup and--what is probably even more important--ensuring that this copy is reliable and can be used to restore a server.

A ConfigMgr server could be very useful and can provide a lot of benefits to the company, but, in the wrong hands, it might do a lot of harm, so protecting and securing the server is also important.

To know more about site server maintenance tasks here is a very useful link with very interesting materials from which you can start digging for more: `https://docs.microsoft.com/en-us/sccm/core/servers/manage/maintenance-tasks`.

Index

www.ingramcontent.com/pod-product-compliance
Lightning Source LLC
Chambersburg PA
CBHW080612060326
40690CB00021B/4672